PRAISE FOR *B*

"A stunning accomplishment! . . . Lisa Jones captures the wild beauty of the Wind River Reservation, the pathos and joy of the Arapahos who live there, and the remarkable life of a modern-day medicine man. All of this while on a healing journey into the broken places of her own heart."

— Margaret Coel, author of *Blood Memory*

"A great endeavor; a beautiful and powerful tale. I would treat myself to *Broken*, relishing the language, and like a woman with the best dark chocolate red chile fudge, I would savor its pages."

— Winona LaDuke, Anishinaabe activist and author of *All Our Relations: Native Struggles for Land and Life* and *Recovering the Sacred: the Power of Naming and Claiming*

"A beautifully written, heart-wrenching journey into the depths of the soul. A tale of mystery, courage, and love between men, women, and horses."

— Jim Fergus, author of *One Thousand White Women* and *The Wild Girl*

"A true spiritual adventure. Moving, powerful, humbling, beautifully rendered. Arapaho elder Stanford Addison is the most wonderful of heroes—and Jones is exactly the guide to bring him to us."

— Alexandra Fuller, author of *The Legend of Colton H. Bryant* and *Don't Let's Go to the Dogs Tonight*

"Intrepid only begins to describe Lisa Jones, who goes to admirable and adventuresome lengths to take the measure of a singular American spirit."

— Ted Conover, author of *The Routes of Man* and *Newjack*

"The author has a knack for describing events, people, and scenery so well that the reader can almost taste the weak, sugary coffee and feel the oppressive heat of the ceremonial sweat lodge."

— *Library Journal* (starred review)

"It is the rare non-Native writer who can gain access to the hearts of Native people to share their stories; rarer still is the non-Native writer who tells those stories with both a clear eye and a compassionate heart. Lisa Jones has not only succeeded on both counts, she has offered us a story of a man, a people, and the bond between human and animal that will touch the heart of any reader. . . . What a fine book."

— Kent Nerburn, author of *Neither Wolf nor Dog*
and *The Wolf at Twilight*

"*Broken* is about life loving us all equally and connecting us to spiritual responsibility. If you don't read *Broken*, you are missing out!"

— Tiokasin Ghosthorse, host of
First Voices Indigenous Radio, WBAI, New York

"I love this book . . . a harrowing and ecstatic journey of mind, body and soul—so beautifully told that the reader is not just transfixed but transformed."

— Abigail Thomas, author of *A Three Dog Life*

"Jones locates herself beautifully in a story that is hers and not hers. This is her first book. We look forward to the next."

— *Los Angeles Times*

"*Broken* makes me proud to be who I am, a Northern Arapaho from the Wind River Reservation."

— Sterling Charles Blindman, Northern Arapaho, tenth grade,
Wyoming Indian High School

Broken

A Love Story

A Woman's Journey Toward Redemption on the
Wind River Indian Reservation

LISA JONES

HAY HOUSE
Australia • Canada • Hong Kong • India
South Africa • United Kingdom • United States

First published in the United States by Scribner, a division of Simon & Schuster, Inc,
1230 Avenue of the Americas. New York, NY 10020

First published and distributed in the United Kingdom by:
Hay House UK Ltd, Astley House, 33 Notting Hill Gate, London, W11 3JQ
Tel: (44) 02 3675 2450; Fax: (44) 20 3675 2451. www.hayhouse.co.uk

Published and distributed in Australia by:
Hay House Australia Ltd, 18/36 Ralph St, Alexandria NSW 2015.
Tel.: (61) 2 9669 4299; Fax: (61) 2 9669 4144. www.hayhouse.com.au

Published and distributed in the Republic of South Africa by:
Hay House SA (Pty), Ltd, PO Box 990, Witkoppen 2068. Tel./Fax: (27) 11 467 8904.
www.hayhouse.co.za

Published and distributed in India by:
Hay House Publishers India, Muskaan Complex, Plot No.3, B-2, Vasant Kunj, New
Delhi – 110 070. Tel.: (91) 11 4176 1620; Fax: (91) 11 4176 1630. www.hayhouse.co.in

This book is true. To respect privacy I have changed a few people's names and
omitted or modified certain details of Arapaho spiritual life. I also presented
the story of Stanford's life earlier in the book than he actually told it to me,
so the reader would have the benefit of knowing it as soon as possible.

The passage quoted from Mike Grudowski's "100-Proof Americana,"
Outside magazine, August 2005, appears courtesy of *Outside* magazine.
Copyright © 2005, Mariah Media Inc.

DESIGNED BY KYOKO WATANABE

ISBN 978-1-8485-0332-8

To Stella Addison

(1930–2008)

who brought so much life into this world

And to my husband

with all my heart

Broken

PREFACE

The day I met Stanford Addison, I sat with him outside his corral watching the horse inside it try to escape. First she got down on her belly like a cat and tried to crawl under the pole fence. Then she snaked her head between the upper poles and pressed her chest against them in an unsuccessful attempt to push the whole thing over. Then she ran around and around, squealing her disapproval of her new surroundings. Until the day before, she had spent her entire three years of life on the open range.

After a few laps, she stopped in front of Stanford. He sat in the wheelchair he had occupied for twenty-three years, letting the mare's skidding hooves throw up a small hurricane of dust onto his long black braid, his half-toned, half-atrophied arms, and his slack legs. He squinted up through the fence. The mare tossed her head and whinnied, rolling her eyes piteously. I didn't know much about horses, but it struck me as strange that she would make a point of stopping right there in front of Stanford. She tossed and whinnied in what started to look to me like an appeal. Stanford watched until she was finished. Then he said in a low voice, "I can't save you."

This was a common occurrence at the corral—horses explaining things to Stanford. In the months and years that followed, he never discussed this phenomenon with me. He would finish up at the corral, roll his electric wheelchair into the house, and turn on the Food Network, now and then interrupting the program to ask me questions about pesto and sushi. Or we'd sit at his battered kitchen table, sipping on mugs of Folgers, and this paralyzed, six-toothed, one-lunged Plains Indian would take a drag of his KOOL Filter King, sigh, and say something like "I guess the thing I miss most since the accident is ski jumping."

A joke. Stanford made me laugh a lot, which was a nice break from the confusion that often enveloped me during the five years I was a frequent visitor there. I wasn't trying to write an authoritative book about Native Americans or Native life. I was there to write a book about Stanford's evolution from what he had been, a bad-boy outlaw, into the renowned spiritual healer he had become. But I didn't get the information I needed in the quick question-and-answer sessions that had been the staple of my work as a journalist. I learned to wait and watch. And a lot of what I ended up watching was what was going on inside of me. Only when I was nearly finished with this book did I realize what it was about—the journey I took following Stanford's gentleness back toward its source, a journey so joyful, painful, and different from anything I'd experienced that there was no way to prepare for it.

Which brings me back to the mare, breathing hard and kicking up dirt and trying to make sense of where she had found herself. That was exactly what I did for much of the time I spent at Stanford's. I, too, skidded to a halt and silently pleaded with him to save me, or at least to explain what was happening. But he couldn't. Or wouldn't.

The thing is, not only horses get broken around here. Everything does, starting with the ground itself. Millions of years ago, a new mountain range broke through the Ancestral Rocky Mountains, leaving the original range's broken remains leaning against the flanks of the Wind River Range and the other mountain chains that comprise the modern-day Rockies. In 1878, at the end of the Indian wars, the Northern Arapaho people arrived at the upthrust of the Wind River Range in their own state of brokenness, defeated and hungry.

And then there was Stanford. His accident had smashed his spine and left him on a slab in the morgue. He had revived only to spend the rest of his life in a wheelchair. Along with his physical paralysis had come some powerful healing gifts. At first both his disability and these gifts seemed a terrible burden, but he haltingly came to understand that he had emerged from a small life into a big one. He had broken, broken through, broken out. His body was changed forever, but so was his heart. This happened in different ways to a lot of people around Stanford. I had no idea, that first time I visited him and watched his curious dialogue with the mare, that the same thing would happen to me.

PART 1

on the corral and the horses. Mostly young Arabians, they were
rounded up just yesterday. They swooped and turned in the corral, as
restive and beautiful as caged birds.

Stanford bumped off toward them and pulled up in a square of shade.
The Colorado contingent followed him and started pulling up lawn
chairs nearby. I followed. Stanford usually had local Arapaho kids
work the horses in his corral, but this was an organized clinic for out-
siders; it would last four days. I'd been told that participants took
turns entering the corral with a horse rounded up fresh off the range,
and—this was the part that boggled my mind—often within a few
hours, ride it around the corral. Two of our number were bona fide
horsewomen. The rest had come mostly to watch and to be around
Stanford.

"I'm not here to ride," I blurted to Stanford. "I had a bad time with
a pony when I was little."

"Okay," he said.

We were joined by half a dozen Arapaho kids—boys in baggy
gangsta jeans and girls in basketball shorts and white T-shirts. I
thought Stanford would shoo them away, expecting he'd need everyone to be quiet while he worked. But he didn't. The kids fanned out
and perched like a flock of sparrows on corral poles, watching the
action. Stanford joked with them, fielded phone calls on a cordless
phone, and directed the goings-on in the corral. His presence was large
and still and accessible, and I was suddenly, fabulously, at ease.

Paula McCaslin, a solid woman with clear blue eyes and short
black hair, stood outside the ring watching the light gray three-year-
old mare inside. The mare had led her Arapaho pursuers on a thirty-
mile chase the day before, and her night in captivity hadn't changed
her attitude much. She lunged with the flexibility and passion of a car-
nivore for the window of air that would lead her back to her known
world, away from the two-leggeds with their strong smell and scary
eyes, which, like the eyes of all predators, were located on the fronts
of their faces. God only knew what would happen now that her main
defense—the ability to run fast in a straight line—had been dimin-

ished into running in little circles within a confounding wooden structure, the faces she was trying to escape reappearing every few seconds.

Quiet and still, Paula stood next to Stanford outside the corral rails, watching the mare's antics. Paula was a forty-year-old government cartographer who had grown up with horses in suburban Denver. After attending one of Stanford's demonstrations in Boulder she had tried his technique by herself and broken her arm. This morning she had eaten her breakfast alone in her parked car, staring straight ahead while the rest of us chatted and brewed coffee.

It was time to start. Paula scootched through the corral rails, joining the mare inside.

"Make her run," said Stanford.

"Yah!" Paula hollered. "Yah!"

The mare startled and broke into a trot. After many laps she stopped, looking at Paula with her ears pricked forward.

"That's the kind of look you want," said Stanford. "When she's ready to communicate, she's going to drop her head." Sure enough, the mare's head went down. But when Paula approached, the mare turned away.

"Okay, make her run," said Stanford. As the horse swung into a trot, he said, "I'm making it so the horse can only rest when she's paying attention to Paula." He was satisfied with the mare's progress. "She's seeing that Paula's not in there to hurt her or threaten her," he said. "And she's a smart horse, too; she's in there thinking."

I looked at the mare's still brown eyes. I could see what he meant. Within an hour, Paula was stroking her. It seemed as if the horse were shedding wildness like a tight shoe she'd always wanted to take off.

Paula put a halter on the mare and secured it with a rope to an overhead pulley apparatus. The rope holding the mare had no slack; she could stand comfortably only when she was directly below it. Stanford had us all leave the corral so she wouldn't associate people with this elemental lesson: *The only way to endure confinement is to accept it.* Stanford called it "finding your center." After an hour of tossing her head and trotting in place with her head in all kinds of awkward positions, the mare calmed down and stood still, as serene and eager as a show horse.

That lovely girl, I thought. That angel.

Paula "tarped" the mare, tossing a strip of blue tarp tied to a pole across her hindquarters, back, neck, and head. It would get the mare used to human-made movement and noise. Then, slowly, Paula took a saddle blanket, throwing it gently over the mare's back and taking it off several times from both sides before saddling and bridling her. Within three hours of entering the corral, Paula mounted the mare, who stood still and blinked, looking surprised at her rapid change in fortune.

I couldn't believe my eyes. I was amazed by how quickly the mare had started to trust Paula, and how clearly she *wanted* to do so. Paula hadn't been aggressive with the mare, and her gentleness had been repaid in kind. Every license plate in this state depicts the silhouette of a horse with its head down, legs flying, and rider leaning back toward the horse's heaven-bound butt in an effort to stay mounted. This is the Cowboy State, but what I'd just witnessed had been no rodeo. It had unfolded like a love scene or a ballet. The mare had not seemed to take any solace in the fact that she weighed more than five times what Paula did, or that she was far faster and stronger. She knew a predator when she saw one and simply wanted to know what to do to survive.

My own equestrian history bore no resemblance to what I had just seen. When I was about five, my older sister and I decided that ponies were the center of the universe. We became ponies, jumping over stumps in the forest, whinnying and stamping all through the backyard, down the driveway, and along the road. Later, we humbly bowed our heads to receive the invisible Olympic medals we awarded each other: gold for my sister, silver for me. At bedtime we read about horses. We thought the best book ever written was *Jill Enjoys Her Ponies.*

All this happiness came to an abrupt halt when I was seven and our parents bought us a living, breathing pony. Bobby was four years old, with a dirty white coat, the build of a soccer ball, and the soul of Charles Manson. He had a particular affinity for a holly tree into whose low-hanging, spiky-leaved foliage he deposited us with enough regularity that I still dream about it. When I was nine, we sold him back to the man we'd bought him from. Since then I had ridden half a dozen times—always on the oldest, gauntest, safest horse I could find. To me, horses were conniving and dangerous. But they were also the most beautiful creatures on earth.

But here at Stanford's corral, one gray mare, at least, wanted peace. Excited by the possibility that I'd been all wrong about horses, I put my notebook in the dust under my folding chair, counted to three, and asked Stanford if I could break a horse, too.

"Sure," he said.

I walked into the holding corral, Stanford rolling alongside me in his chair. I'd been told that he was a spiritual healer who held sweat lodges twice a week, so I half expected some piercing shamanistic insight on which horse I should choose.

"Which one do you want?" was all he asked.

I pointed to a black stallion who was inseparable from a brown and white pinto. They moved together, running straight at the corral fence and then swooping to one side when it proved once again that it wasn't going to move out of their way. I picked the black stallion because he was beautiful, with fine limbs and a perfect white star on his forehead. I also picked him because he was, as wild stallions go, small.

Some Arapaho boys ran into the holding corral, separating him from his pinto pal and scaring him through the gate into the round corral. I slid through the poles of the fence, not quite able to take a full breath. My horse-breaking career had begun.

I cracked the nylon lead rope to make him run around the little round corral, and he sauntered over to the fence, put his head through the poles, and whinnied to his pinto friend, who practically shrieked back. The stallion could read my past perfectly. His disrespect for me was total. I didn't have the nerve to do what I'd seen the Arapaho kids do—simply walk up to the horse's butt and push it until it started moving.

Stanford was quiet until the horse presented me with his gleaming hindquarters for approximately the twenty-seventh time. "You're being too accommodating with him," he said.

"Of course I'm being too accommodating!" I barked back, embarrassed. "He's a wild stallion!"

"Still, you're being too accommodating," Stanford said, dragging on a cigarette from one of the two packs of KOOL Filter Kings he would smoke that day.

"I'm an American woman!" I blurted. "We're taught to be this way!"

My half-joke failed miserably. Stanford sat silent. I tried again to get the horse trotting and failed. I looked to Stanford for help, but he was on the phone, his back to me.

Hey, buddy, I thought miserably. I could freaking die out here.

Boulderites with water bottles, Indians with cigarettes—maybe fifteen people in all—watched from outside the corral. The horse walked, stopped, and occasionally broke into a desultory trot. I waved my arms at him, yelped, and wished the ground would open and swallow me whole. The Boulderites looked sympathetic. The Arapahos laughed. The little boys on the corral fence shouted, "Just git *on* him!"

"He's training you to run," said Stanford, who had ended his phone call.

I wished Stanford, or the horse, or I, would drop dead. "I'm scared," I rasped back, fear and anger catching in my throat.

Stanford sat, imperturbable. At last he spoke. "You'll do okay," he said.

At the side of the corral sat a rangy, silver-haired woman named Jeannie Ash. She had moved from rural Nevada to Boulder after a car accident ended her thirty-year career training horses. After watching me flail for about an hour, she stood up with an air of grave finality.

"Yeah, let Jeannie give it a try," Stanford said.

Jeannie wiped her hands on her jeans, climbed through the fence, drew herself to her full five-feet-eleven height, and slapped the ground with the lead rope as if she were Zeus and the rope her lightning bolt. All of us, including the stallion, jumped a little bit. I hurried to the side of the corral and hoisted myself onto the pole fence. Jeannie whacked the horse over the butt with the rope, and he stepped into a fine, sustained trot. Within a few minutes he was looking at Jeannie, ears pricked forward with anticipation while she stroked his nose.

"Your turn," said Stan.

Damn.

I climbed into the corral. The stallion seemed to regard me with considerably less enthusiasm than he had Jeannie, but he let me stroke the gleaming, bony length of his face. Miraculously, I managed to put the halter on without dropping it. We adjourned for the night. I fell into an exhausted sleep.

The next day I woke up with the conviction that if persistence was all I had going for me, then dammit, I was going to persist. And I remembered something from white-water kayaking, a sport I'd practiced and loved for years: To begin a scary task is to be close to finishing it. In fact, beginning takes more courage than anything else, because once you make contact with the forces of nature, your most practical and clear-eyed self emerges.

In the corral, the stallion let me stroke him, lean against him, and even jump up and lie over his bare back, my arms on one side and my legs on the other.

Stanford's directions took on the repetitive nature of a chant. "Do it again," he said every time the stallion flinched or spun. "Get back on," he said every time I slithered off.

The sun climbed in the sky. The heat ticked through the dust. Someone mentioned that the temperature was 97. After I'd hoisted myself onto the stallion's back time after time, my arms felt like noodles. My worries and internal arguments bled away. I felt disembodied, calm, unencumbered by free will.

Slowly, I put a saddle blanket and a saddle on the horse.

"Mount him," said Stanford.

At my zombie's pace, I did, settling in the saddle. I inhaled. I exhaled. Then the stallion flicked his ears back, and the next thing I knew, I was standing in the dirt, the horse was in the dirt on his back kicking around below me like an overturned turtle, and I was pointing to his writhing form and announcing, "I'm not afraid of you anymore."

"You looked like the Bionic Woman!" Stanford yelled excitedly. "That was cool!"

I registered that his tone of voice had changed from the gentle monotone he had used since we began, and as the stallion scrambled to his feet, I walked over to Stanford and Jeannie. They told me what had happened: The horse had reared up and I'd kicked myself out of the saddle, floated next to his head, grabbed him by the neck, and thrown him on his back.

I bent over laughing. I wasn't exactly the horse-throwing type, I assured them. But I couldn't remember what had happened. All I knew was I mounted the horse, then I was standing up, the horse was on his back in the dust, and Stanford was shouting.

I leaned on the fence, waiting for them to tell me they were kidding and let me in on what really happened. They didn't.

"Get back on him," said Stanford.

I did.

He suggested I lie down on the stallion's back with my head on his rump, and I did it, even though when I'd seen it done earlier in the day, I swore I'd never do it in a million years. A few minutes later, I rode the stallion around the ring. We progressed as slowly as if we were crossing a pond of glue.

After I let the stallion go in the holding corral, I walked over to the teepee and sank to its floor, feeling the strength drain from my body. About an hour later, I heard the whir of Stanford's wheelchair outside the teepee.

"Your horse needs to be petted around and reassured some," he said.

The horse. My horse. Feeling sheepish, I labored to my feet and went to the corral. The stallion's head hung. His eyes stared dully. He looked exactly the way I felt. Only then did I realize how exhausted he was, how terrified he'd been. He hadn't been trying to hurt me; he just hadn't known what I was doing, so he'd tried every trick he had to get me to leave him alone. But I'd been too afraid, and then too detached, to recognize that he had any emotional life at all. Now my heart fairly cramped with love. I brushed him and hugged him and petted him.

Jeannie joined me, and together we stroked the little black stallion back to life. I joked that the horse reminded me of other studs I'd encountered in life—when the going got rough, I got scared and didn't realize until later that they were scared, too. Oh, the men I wished I'd had a chance to brush back to life!

Jeannie laughed. She said she'd never seen anything like what she saw in the corral that day.

What happened? I asked her.

"These horses will bring up every fear that you ever had about everything," she said. "And Stanford can look at the fear, he can look at the courage that sits there behind the fear."

I could easily recall my fears: I was scared of ridicule and pity; I was scared of being disrespected by horses and little boys on fences; I was scared of being pounded to death by eggbeater hooves; I was scared of having my kneecap blasted sideways in a collision with a corral pole. I was scared of being a weak, out-of-shape, no-longer-young woman. I wanted everyone to think of me as strong and brave—the stallion, the onlookers, Stanford.

But as for the courage that sat behind all that fear, that had eluded me. I'd gone into some zombie fugue state and missed the fact that I had knocked the horse down in the dirt. All I could remember was that Stanford never once ran out of patience or pushed or criticized. Later, he told me he'd spent a good amount of time praying for the horse and me. His gentleness was so foreign to my system that it took me a while to figure out what it was. And he wasn't gentle only with me and the stallion. He was gentle with the dogs, the children, and the other spectators.

The thing Stanford said that weekend that stuck in my mind most was something he called out to his four-year-old grandnephew A.J. The little boy was trotting around among horses whose knees nearly came up to his butt. Most uncles would either not see A.J. weaving among the giant creatures, or start yelling at the sight.

"Hey, A.J., be careful," Stanford called gently. "Those horses are huge, and you're real tiny."

He gentled us. All of us. He gentled us along.

CHAPTER 2

A TRIBE WOULD BE BETTER

"Wanna go for a drive?" asked Stanford's sister Arilda. She had to pick up her cousin in the nearby village of Ethete.

My whole body ached from my experience with the stallion the day before. The temperature at the corral was about 100 degrees. A drive in an air-conditioned car sounded like a fine idea. Arilda had been around for much of the clinic, and I liked the gentle, easy way she teased her little brother Stanford, the big horse trainer.

We pulled away from the corral, air conditioner blasting. She turned on Bob Dylan, lit a Marlboro, and steered off the road down a precipitous drop and onto an adjacent pair of parallel tracks. I thought it was a joke to rattle her white visitor, but it was really to protect her car from the relentless washboard of the dirt road.

Outside the window, the occasional house or dog or piece of idle machinery glided past.

"So," she said, "what are you here for?"

"To write an article."

"What kind of article are you going to write about my brother?"

A sliver of apprehension passed through my abdomen.

"An article about his horse training technique," I said, my voice sounding more defensive than I wanted it to be. "And a little bit about his life. That's about it."

That satisfied her. She was protective of her little brother, but her protectiveness wasn't driven by anger or racial resentment. She was friendly. Relief washed through me as we turned west toward Ethete. What a nice sister, I thought.

After we picked up her cousin, they talked, and I watched the cottonwoods and modular homes and fields of horses and jagged mountains roll by. The reservation covers a swath of Wyoming 151 times larger than Manhattan and over half the size of Connecticut. It's home to about 8,000 Northern Arapahos and 4,000 Eastern Shoshones. From its weather to its history to its economy to its police blotter, the place is defined by struggle. Even its flattest, lowest portions lie nearly five thousand feet above sea level. Away from the mountains and the river for which the reservation is named, there are hardly any trees. Sun-blasted in the summer and freezing in the winter, paint blisters off wooden houses here. Shutters blow off trailer homes. Plastic bags cartwheel from family dumps to barbed-wire fences, taking the shapes of animals jumping or old men working.

The glaciated Wind River Range slumped along the western horizon like a broken granite wall. The wind whomped and scuffed its way across the plains in Wyoming's best attempt at silence. This place bore a strong resemblance to the landscape around Denver, Colorado, which happened to have been the last home the Arapaho chose for themselves. By the 1700s, bands of Arapaho had moved from Minnesota and Canada onto the High Plains, concentrating along the Front Range of the Rocky Mountains in an area that now bristles with the glass skyscrapers of Denver, the university buildings of Boulder, and the tourist-choked streets of Estes Park.

When the whites arrived and dotted the plains with settlements and forts, some Arapaho traded buffalo hides in present-day Wyoming, others in Colorado. These two groups became the precursors of the Northern Arapaho of Wyoming and the Oklahoma-based Southern Arapaho, yet in the mid-1800s they were very much still one tribe, hunting and ranging all over eastern Colorado and Wyoming into western Kansas and Nebraska. They often met for ceremonies or to camp with their close allies, the Cheyenne. Stanford is, in fact, descended from White Antelope, a prominent Cheyenne peace chief.

The Arapaho and Cheyenne—each of which numbered about three thousand—mostly kept the peace with the settlers. Their chiefs signed a treaty that defined and reduced the territory where their people were entitled to roam. Relationships worsened after the discovery of gold near present-day Denver in 1858, which turned the trickle of white people entering into a flood of 150,000 the following spring. Frontier settlements buzzed with aggression and expansion, and the tribes were frustrated by the whites' insatiable need for land, then angered by Native lives lost in skirmishes. In June 1864 a band of Arapahos were blamed for murdering a ranch manager, his wife, and their two daughters. The bodies were put on display in Denver, where the spectacle galvanized those who wanted to expand aggressively into Indian Territory. They coalesced around Colorado territorial governor John Evans and Colonel John Chivington, a former minister and Civil War hero whose disregard for Native women and children was aired when he said his policy was "to kill and scalp all Indians, little and big . . . Nits make lice."

Neither the Arapaho nor the Cheyenne, or even the more numerous Sioux, could defeat the newcomers or get them to go away. There were just too many of them. "[The tribes] were forced to want peace," said Eugene J. Ridgely Jr., a self-taught Northern Arapaho historian who developed the Northern Arapaho Studies program at the Wind River Tribal College in Ethete. "They would have died fighting to get their land back if they thought they could win," said Ridgely. "But they couldn't." He added that Chief Left Hand went as far as showing the whites where the gold was so they could take it and leave.

In September 1864 a group of peace-seeking Cheyenne and Arapaho chiefs traveled to Denver with Major Edward Wynkoop, commander of Fort Lyon in southeastern Colorado and a friend to the Indians. The governor did not welcome the chiefs or the upstart commander.

"What shall I do with the Third Colorado Regiment if I make peace?" he thundered. "They have been raised to kill Indians, and they must kill Indians." His aggression had its roots in political reality: Dee Brown wrote in *Bury My Heart at Wounded Knee,* "Washington officials had given him [Evans] permission to raise the new regiment because he had sworn it was necessary for protection against hostile Indians, and if he now made peace the Washington politicians would accuse him of misrepresentation."

Evans refused to meet with the chiefs, but Wynkoop announced that he and the Indians would happily wait in Denver until Evans joined the discussion, effectively flushing the governor from his mansion. A Cheyenne chief, Black Kettle, assured Evans and the other assembled officials, "All we ask is that we may have peace with the whites." The governor's noncommittal response heartened the chiefs, who left the meeting optimistic that a peace treaty was in the works.

But the governor had other plans. First Wynkoop was relieved of his command and replaced by Major Scott J. Anthony, who told the tribes that they would be safe if they moved to Sand Creek, about eighty miles southeast of Denver. Anthony reported to his superior, "I have been trying to let the Indians that I have talked with think that I have no desire for trouble with them . . . thus keeping matters quiet for the present, and until troops enough are sent out to enforce any demand we may choose to make."

The suspicions of one Southern Arapaho chief, Little Raven, were sufficiently aroused that he ignored Anthony and led his band elsewhere. He was joined by Medicine Man, a Northern Arapaho chief. According to Ridgely, another Northern Arapaho, Sharp Nose, had an eerie feeling about the encampment at Sand Creek, so he and some warriors rode down from the north and induced some of their kinsmen to pull up stakes and leave.

But hundreds of Cheyenne and Southern Arapaho camped at Sand Creek, tired but confident that hostilities with the whites had finally ended. They were so sure, in fact, that on the night of November 28, most of the men had gone off to hunt buffalo. About six hundred Indians, two thirds of them women and children, were wakened at sunrise by more than seven hundred troops advancing on their settlement.

Seeing the approaching soldiers, Black Kettle hoisted the American flag he'd received in Washington, D.C., from men who had told him it would always keep him safe.

"I heard him call to the people not to be afraid, that the soldiers would not hurt them; then the troops opened fire from two sides of the camp," an onlooker wrote. "When Left Hand saw the troops, he stood with his arms folded, saying he would not fight the white men because they were his friends. He was shot down." He died of his wounds a few days later.

White Antelope shouted, "Don't panic! There is no danger! The soldiers will not hurt you." As the soldiers opened fire, he understood that he had been deceived, crossed his arms over his chest, and spent the short time before he died singing his death song: "All my relations, remember, only the rocks and sky stay forever."

All told, 163 Indians and 9 of Chivington's men were killed at Sand Creek. Three soldiers made a game out of shooting a toddler whose route across the sand evaded the bullets of the first two men. The third dropped the child in his tracks. Women's genitalia were hacked off and used to decorate the soldiers' hats and saddles.

The soldiers went home.

"Our march back to Denver was leisurely and uneventful," wrote one of them, Irving Howbert, in his 1914 book *The Indians of the Pike's Peak Region.* "We dispersed to our homes, convinced that we had done a good work and that it needed only a little further punishment of the savages permanently to settle the Indian troubles so far as this Territory was concerned."

Even in those expansion-mad times, the Sand Creek Massacre became a national disgrace. A year later, the Committee on Military Conduct castigated Chivington, who had "deliberately planned and executed a foul and dastardly massacre" against Indians who "had been actuated by the most friendly feelings towards the whites, and had done all in their power to restrain those less friendly disposed. . . .

"Having full knowledge of their friendly character, having himself been instrumental to some extent in placing them in their position of fancied security, he took advantage of their in-apprehension and defenceless [*sic*] condition to gratify the worst passions that ever cursed the heart of man."

Even Major Anthony, who had been instrumental in setting up the attack, was heartsick. He wrote to his brother that he was concerned that other officers, his family, and his friends would not think him human when they learned that he had been engaged in the Sand Creek battle.

The Cheyenne and Arapaho were finished seeking peace.

"On January 7, 1865, the war that Governor Evans had long been predicting finally erupted on the plains," wrote Margaret Coel in her historical biography *Chief Left Hand.* "One thousand warriors— Cheyennes, Brulé Sioux, and Northern Arapahos—struck the settlement of Julesburg on the South Platte near the Colorado-Nebraska line, killing 15 of 16 soldiers and looting stores and warehouses. Three weeks later, war parties went on a five-day rampage up and down the South Platte, capturing wagon trains and destroying telegraph lines, before they attacked Julesburg for the second time."

Warriors streamed across the plains, striking settlements from Wyoming to Texas, and Kansas to Montana.

The cost in money and human life was huge. "Within the first six months the government had spent $40 million to launch an army of 8,000 troops in an attempt to subdue the Plains Indians. By the war's end countless millions more had been spent on armies, military posts, equipment and supplies. Thousands of lives were lost, mostly those of the noncombatants, the women and children, the old and infirm, who were caught in a guerrilla-style conflict," wrote Coel.

Sand Creek had made settling the frontier much bloodier than it might have been. General Nelson A. Miles, one of the officers who took part in the subsequent battles, said, "but for that horrible butchery it is a fair presumption that all subsequent wars with the Cheyennes and Arapahos and their kindred tribes might possibly have been averted."

As for the Northern Arapaho, reduced to less than a thousand battle-scarred, hungry refugees by 1878, they made what they were assured would be a temporary move onto the Wind River Indian Reservation in Wyoming. It was already occupied by the Eastern Shoshone, a tribe they usually fought with. The Shoshone were at home here. They had started hunting in the foothills of the Wind River Range in the 1600s. When this favored hunting ground was designated a reservation in 1868, the Shoshones took its cooler, wetter, more mountainous portion. The Northern Arapaho took the land near the Little Wind River, a parched, undulating plain of sage and rabbitbrush that stretched eastward.

*   *   *

Arilda's car crossed the Little Wind River just a mile from Stanford's house. I couldn't even imagine what life had been like for the Arapahos after Sand Creek. I don't know the first thing about fighting or killing or going hungry. I have been sheltered from violence and struggle since the day I was born; I am a creature of privilege. While the Addison kids were riding their horses across the high desert on the reservation, I was riding my pony along the edges of our family's grass tennis court. The only shred of the Plains Indians' experience I could share was this: I know what it's like to have to leave your home.

My family left Scotland when I was nine years old. Even though my mom was from Stockholm and I had been born at Stanford University during a sabbatical year my psychiatrist father spent teaching there, I felt completely Scottish. The quilted green fields, forests, lakes, and rivers of the Scottish Borders belonged to me and my sisters. The old beech and oak forests, full of moss and holes dug out of the earth by mysterious creatures, were perfect for playing and making up stories.

But we had to move to Colorado so that my father, who was in his fifties when he married my mother, could keep working past Scotland's mandatory retirement age of sixty-five. He had three little girls to support and a wife thirty years his junior. He couldn't retire, which was fine with him. Work consumed and inspired him; family life did not. The move to America drove a wedge between my parents—my mother was not excited about raising her children in a country she considered threatening and aggressive compared to Europe. But she went. Not long after we crossed the Atlantic, there was a new set to her jaw. There was a tearful scene involving the bombshell twenty-six-year-old nanny who'd come with us from Scotland. Then there was a large bag of Cheetos into which I kept plunging my hand for more thrillingly fluorescent, salty, uniquely American snacks as the news came: Mom and Dad weren't happy together. Dad was moving to the little prefabricated cabin he'd had delivered to a little parcel of land he had bought in the mountains. Our nanny was going with him. We would stay with our mom in suburban Denver.

We were in America without a father. My mother had spent her married life playing tennis with the local aristocrat Lord Haig and his wife, and being fitted for dresses that made her lanky Nordic frame the talk of southern Scotland, and taking us on windy hikes to wide, shallow streams where she'd dispense goggles and we'd crouch and plunge our faces into the cold, looking for agates in the gin-clear water. But here in this sprawling city at the foot of the Rocky Mountains, there was no time for my mom to be the privileged nature girl she'd been in Scotland. Dad contributed only the scantest support to our upbringing, and Mom's jaw began to tighten even more. By the time I was a teenager, Dad and our former nanny had split up and Mom was leaving my sisters and me at home for three days at a time to sell encyclopedias to farmers in eastern Colorado and western Nebraska. When she realized it was foolhardy to leave her daughters home alone, she started working on commission in a suburban furniture store in Aurora, eventually switching to a highbrow design center in the city.

She quickly married again, and then again. Her second husband was a bespectacled psychiatrist who snapped at us if we spoke during the national anthem before televised baseball games. My older sister, Greta—whose highbrow sensibilities were emerging in the form of playing first flute for the high school band at football games—narrowed her subtly made-up eyes at our new stepfather and pronounced him "deeply unattractive." This consigned him to a new category in my twelve-year-old mind that he would not escape before leaving the following year. My mother's third husband came along when I was fourteen. He was a poet, a social worker, a charmer, and an alcoholic. I loved him. My mother threw him out two years later.

What had taken American culture five hundred years to do, my family had accomplished in seven: cross the Atlantic in search of prosperity, trade nativeness for colonialism, and dissolve itself.

As soon as we were old enough to drive, Greta and I turned to the Rockies. Unmoving and solid, they received us as we backpacked or skied with a group of friends up blue-shadowed valleys and through sunny, tilted meadows. We did this every weekend we weren't working to earn our spending money. The mountains delivered us the kind of introduction to cause and effect that a father might deliver: If you get sweaty when you cross-country ski up a mountain, change your underclothes quickly before they clam up and suck the warmth out of you like a suit of dead fish. Wear a hat at night because you lose most of your heat through your head. Even when it's cold, at altitude the sun can burn you scarlet.

"We don't have a dad," we'd say to each other. "But we have the Rockies."

I wanted conformity and belonging so badly that I became a high school cheerleader. This horrified my bohemian parents—who had kept in touch—and didn't really help me on the normalcy front: I was one of three white girls in an otherwise all-black squad. Our family had never fit in. During my idyllic childhood years in Scotland, my father was an iconoclastic intellectual in the sheep-herding outback. When we left that and moved into a modernistic pointy house on a lake in suburban Denver, all my friends at school had fathers who were truck drivers and drank beer out of cans. Later, when Dad was gone and Mom was scrambling to support us, we lived in the corner of a neighborhood where the adults were lawyers and investment bankers.

I went to the mountains—those pacifiers, those equalizers—as often as I could. The need to belong hummed in my blood. An ocean away from the only place I'd ever known as home, what I really wanted was a tribe.

AN INCOMPLETE ADDISON FAMILY TREE*

Mervin Addison (1925–1981)   Stella Addison (1930–2008)

THEIR CHILDREN (B. 1951–1971)

Glenn Bill Arilda Stanford Frenchie Jay-R George David Gwen

. . . SOME OF THEIR GRANDCHILDREN (B. 1973–1994)

Adrian	Suzi	Garnet	Beau
Sass (Andrew)	Richard	Robert	Daniel
Cody (Andre)	Alicia		
Aaron	Janelle		

. . . AND SOME OF THEIR GREAT-GRANDCHILDREN (B. 1995–2003)

Adrian's kids: Laticia, Suzanna, A.J.
Cody's kids: Quamé, Triston

*This represents only a fraction of the family and includes only the Addisons who are named in this book.

CHAPTER 3

STELLA ANTELOPE

Stanford's mother was born in 1930. Her name was Stella Antelope. She lived in a log house on the reservation with her mother, her younger sister and brother, now and then her father, and a couple of dozen other relatives. Stella's mother suffered from tuberculosis. When Stella was six, her mother called her to her bedside, told her to take good care of her brother and sister, rolled over, and died.

The children stayed in the house, but nobody really took care of them.

"After Mom died, my dad kinda left—wandered in New Mexico and Oklahoma and Montana," she said. "I fended for me, my brother, and my sister. Back then, these old Indians, if someone died in the family, people helped themselves to your stuff and you'd have to replace it. People took all her stuff, cookware and stoves.

"We were being abused. If I didn't babysit or wash dishes for my relatives they'd whip me. I wanted to get out. Sometimes there'd only be, like, two pieces of bread. I'd save one for brother and one for sister. You know me—I could go without."

I knew her well enough to know that. She was tough in just about every way. When her drug-dealing teenager Stanford was in the middle of selling some pot in Riverton, for example, he was interrupted by a tap on his shoulder. He turned to see a fist in rapid trajectory toward his nose. The fist belonged to his mother. After the blow, Stella dragged him into the car.

Stella shook with laughter when she told me that story.

"I was all embarrassed," Stanford told me later, smiling. "I just lay in the backseat 'til we got out of town."

I knew that when a rogue stallion named Two Warriors killed a colt, Stella ran into the field to chase him off. He turned on her and she sprinted to the shelter of a parked car with seconds to spare.

I had seen that she was softer on her grandchildren and grand-nephews than she had been on her own kids. When one of her grandsons finished serving a six-month jail term for beating the crap out of a state trooper—"I figured I'd at least make one point for the Indians," the twenty-three-year-old told me—she had a barbecue party for him as if he'd just graduated from college.

But on the day we sat on a couple of plastic chairs under a shade tree outside the house Stella shared with a son, a daughter, and sundry grandchildren, I realized I did not know her well enough to tell if her difficult childhood caused her despair. She was animated when she told her stories, and she laughed a lot, but the map of wrinkles on her face revealed only the mental strain of recovering the details of her early life: She and her younger brother and sister had spent years sleeping on coats given to them by an older relative, and eating meat their grandpa brought after he killed one of his sheep. When she was seven, she started a two-year stint at a nearby boarding school where they beat kids for speaking Arapaho.

"As I grew up, I lost my voice and I couldn't talk," she said. "My aunt told my boy cousins to kill a meadowlark. She told them, 'Tell it you're taking its life for a good reason,' and she cooked it in a pan with grease and flour. I ate it. Two or three weeks later, a man came, an Indian doctor, to see how I was doing.

"I spoke. I said something nasty to him, I told him, 'You stink!' They started calling me meadowlark after that—*cooxuceneihii.*

"Us kids used to do a lot of night riding," she continued. "We were in groups. A bunch of kids out there, riding. We'd have a rodeo with sheep. We'd ride the sheep like bucking broncos. Once when we were out, we were real hungry. We kidnapped a turkey off a white lady's fence. We cooked it all night on wood we found. We didn't even give it time to gobble!" She wrapped her hands around her stomach, laughing. "We'd ride down the river on slabs of ice." As she grew older, she learned to defend herself. "If I knew someone was going to use a whip on me, I'd grab it and use it on her."

When Stella finished seventh grade, she got into a hair-pulling fight with one of her aunts. After this, the social workers wanted to send her to boarding school in South Dakota.

"Send me anywhere you want," she told her father, who was around at the time. "I want away from here. If I leave now, I'm never coming back." Her father defied the social workers and let her stay.

"That's when I started the cowgirling," she said. "I got real bow-legged. There were cattle camps all over. They'd float those logs from Dubois to Riverton, and they'd make railroad ties out of them. It was a tie camp. It was a camp of Indians near town. Some were working, others were gambling and drinking. Everywhere you looked there was an Indian staggering around. It was like a party. The old Indians have pretty much drunk themselves to death.

"That's where I met this Mervin Addison. He was real good-looking, and the girls were all thrilled over him."

Was Stella thrilled, too?

"Naw. He just made me shy. I used to get real shy over him. I never really wanted to kiss him or anything. I might've jumped outta my shoes if he did. He had two wives before me. I thought maybe he was just playing around with me. When he came around and married me, I didn't want to. I was fighting him off. I used to say, 'Maybe there's another girl down there that's ready for you.' Then we were together. We got married at the justice of the peace. I was eighteen."

"But then he broke my heart. He was with me, then another woman, then me. I tell my grandkids now, 'Oh, my heart was broken to pieces.'

"The next thing you know, I was pregnant. Me, I had nine children. Stanford was number four. I'd nurse the kids 'til they were two. I was like a cow. I'd have Stanford on one side and his cousin on the other. If him and Stanford couldn't hear my voice, they'd cry. In the winter I went to cut wood with the kids. I hauled water. The kids helped with all that stuff. They hardly ever got sick. Their main medicine was castor oil. I made 'em drink it. We ate deer and sage hens. We'd kill 'em with a twenty-two.

"Mervin was a good provider. This was his land. We had a little adobe house. He hired out as a ranch hand and hunted for food. After he shot his deer, he'd dismount, and the horse would come home. I'd see the horse and go and get Mervin. We'd come home and make deer jerky and chokecherry jam.

"Mervin was happy, mostly, but he had a temper, too. When he'd go drinking, he'd be that way, he'd be mean. I'd try not to fight in front of the kids, but sometimes he wanted to. I never left. I was tempted to when he was drunk and mean. But I stayed 'cause of the kids. When he'd fight, I'd fight back."

Stanford would sometimes pull his father off his mother. If someone else intervened instead, Stanford would walk outside the house and lie on the ground. The horses would gather around, their liquid brown eyes fixed on him. He'd roll away across the dirt. They'd put their noses down and follow him until he stopped rolling.

CHAPTER 4

STANFORD MEETS THE SPIRITS

It was 1974, and by August the grass on the reservation had gone brown. But next to the river, the cottonwoods were as green as limes. When the breeze came up, their leaves clattered softly, flashing in the sun like pocket mirrors.

Stanford was fifteen. He rode a green-broke horse beside the Little Wind River. Then he turned away from the river and headed into the sagebrush. His horse tensed up, fussing and bucking slightly. Stanford wanted to put some miles on the horse to tire him out, gentle him down. Everyone in his family rode. His father broke all their horses. His sister Frenchie and the younger kids sometimes sneaked out on horseback before dawn to get away from all the housework. They'd eat corn and berries from the fields and knock one another off their ponies with long sticks, pretending they were the jousting medieval knights they'd seen in old movies.

Years before, when he was seven, Stanford rode alone up the Little Wind River, above the swimming hole, and crossed over near his aunt Florence's house. On the far bank a man sat, challenging some boys playing near him to fire his twelve-gauge shotgun. No one would take him up on it; everyone knew shotguns kicked you in the shoulder like a mean pony. Stanford dismounted. He took the gun, fired both barrels at once, and handed it back. He mounted his horse, received the man's compliments, and rode off. When he knew he was out of sight, he stopped and spent a few minutes writhing in pain. His shoulder hurt like hell.

These days Stanford and his brothers liked to drop from the rafters of abandoned buildings onto the backs of horses that had never been trained and see if they could stay on until the bucking stopped. Arilda rode a horse to school in her miniskirt, tying the animal to a tree before she went inside. Stanford was earning good money breaking horses the white ranchers and their sons couldn't handle.

Riding through the sage, he was contented and calm. He was miles into the hills when something ahead startled him. There was a person on foot, an unexpected sight so far from civilization. But he or she—Stanford wasn't sure which—beckoned him over, plain as day. He rode over the next rise, wondering if there was some kind of emergency, but when he got to where the person had been standing, he found nothing but a spindly willow frame used in fasting ceremonies. There was nowhere for a person to hide—no gully, no trees, no buildings, just a shrubby slope. Stanford felt unsettled, as if he were being watched. The horse swiveled its ears around expectantly as if it did, too. Stanford dismounted, left a cigarette at the structure as an offering, and rode home. But he couldn't shake that feeling of being watched.

This was his first brush with the world of spirits. They would appear to him again. More accurately, they would intrude upon him, because intruding was the only way they could enter the life of a teenager who was completely determined to ignore them. Stanford Addison's mind was almost wholly focused on riding horses, having sex, drinking, dealing dope, driving fast, and raising hell. When a high school teacher called him a "dumb Indian," he wrestled the man to the ground and tried to strangle him. He broke in to a café and robbed it. He shot white ranchers' cattle just for fun. He reserved his most wanton behavior for women, whom he used "sexually, financially, the works." As a teenager spending some time in Albuquerque, Stanford seduced a Navajo girl—"a three-beer girl," he called her, meaning it took three beers in his belly for her to start looking good. He lured her away from a party and an aspiring young Navajo medicine man who loved her. Later, the Navajo boy came after Stanford. He ripped out a handful of Stanford's hair and told him he would regret what he'd done. Stanford paid no attention. His favorite saying was "Eat shit and howl at the moon."

"I was evil," he told me. "Totally selfish."

So when he saw the apparition out there in the sage, he didn't really think about what it was or what it might be trying to show him. He would ignore the spirits for years. But they would wait.

A couple of years later, a friend of Stanford's was fishing on the Little Wind River with a group of friends and brothers when Stanford walked by.

"Stanford looked like he was about seven feet tall," he said. "His long hair was flowing. He really looked good in the wind. I remember that so vividly. The beautiful background with the river. We called, but he never turned around. He didn't recognize our truck. He just kept walking. In a way, he reminded us of a mystical spirit creature that inhabited that stretch of river. We have spiritual things that inhabit between worlds, between this life and the next life. He disappeared into the brush."

When Stanford was twenty, he had a dream: He was with some horses, and then he felt excruciating pain and couldn't move. An old man appeared and told him he needed to get "smudged," or cleaned, with the smoke of burning sage—a method known for getting rid of bad spirits and negative influences.

Then he woke up. "My neck was in a world of hurt," Stanford said.

He didn't get smudged. Although he had recently begun to wonder if he should cut down on fighting and drinking and messing around with women, his friends would come over, "and I didn't want to disappoint them," he said with a sheepish smile.

Four nights after his dream, it was Halloween—a big party night. Stanford had lined up five dates at five different parties. He wasn't planning to have sex with all of the girls. Maybe just four of them.

It was eight o'clock. There was a bit of moon, but the night sky was black and spiky with stars. Stanford and his three friends set off for a party where a girl was waiting to give Stanford a leather jacket she'd bought him. He looked good in his Levi's and platform shoes and silky polyester shirt, and he knew it. He and his friends got into a truck that Stanford's best friend, James Wanstall, had just bought from his brother Dennis—a 1970 short-bed gold Chevy. Richie Lone Dog drove, with James and Stanford in the middle and Tony Eagle Staff next to the door. They popped their first Budweisers and sped down the road.

"That truck was a real rez ride," Stanford recalled. "The hood didn't close. I think the headlights were actually duct-taped on. The lights were no good."

The truck was barreling along just shy of the tiny town of Ethete when the faltering headlights caught the shapes of horses wandering across the road. This was a common sight on the reservation, where few people had the money or inclination to fix fences, but this close, it was terrifying. Tony jumped out of the moving truck, breaking his ribs when he hit the road. The Chevy hit a horse, and the impact turned the truck sideways. It rolled three times. Stanford fell partway out, and then the truck hit the horse again and the door crashed closed on the bell-bottom of his jeans, trapping him on the outside of the cartwheeling Chevy. He slammed against the pavement, unconscious.

When the truck stopped rolling, Stanford lay pinned underneath the cab. A loaded .30–30 rifle in the cab of the truck had discharged during the accident, shooting him through the thigh. His ribs were so badly shattered that he was bleeding from his mouth and would lose a lung. James—who, along with Richie, emerged from the truck unscathed—ran to the nearest house for help.

The police arrived and began to jack up the truck. "I told them to fucking wait for the ambulance!" James told me later, his usually whisper-quiet voice rising with panic and anger.

They didn't wait. They jacked it up. And the truck slipped off the jack, cutting Stanford's spinal cord at the neck. He would never walk again.

Stanford didn't see, hear, or feel any of this. He was watching his dead grandpa beckon. He remembered that the old man had been angry with him the last time they spoke. That had been a few weeks before, when his grandpa was still alive. Stanford never figured out the source of the old man's anger—he'd just fixed his grandpa's car where it had broken down on the side of the highway. It was no small thing; Stanford had crawled under it on a dangerous stretch of road where white people were always speeding to get from the white town of Lander to the white town of Kinnear. Shortly after, before the two could make up, the old man had died.

Stanford was sure of one thing: He wasn't going anywhere *that* guy wanted to take him.

His next vision took him home to his family, but he was in some kind of bubble. No one could see or hear him. He'd heard his father and uncles talk about this. It was the impoverished existence of a "poor soul"—a spirit who hadn't moved on once the physical body had died. A poor soul could watch everyone live their lives, watch his former girlfriends get new boyfriends, but he would be motionless, invisible, and inaudible.

Then Stanford was in a hospital room, thrashing to get his head away from an apparatus called a halo, to which they'd screwed his skull to prevent further injury. A woman he'd never met stood next to him. She had long, shiny black hair and wore a white buckskin dress with blue beads. She asked him if he was tired of all the pain. He was. She started swimming up toward the ceiling, pulling him behind her. Below him, his heart monitor flatlined. Arilda ran out of the room, and a few seconds later, his mother ran in and put her arms around him, holding him, crying. A doctor materialized, who greased Stanford's chest and applied a pair of electric defibrillator paddles to shock his heart back to life. Three times Stanford jolted into the paddles. Three times he collapsed, unmoving, on the bed. His heartbeat on the monitor was flat.

Everything went quiet except for the murmurs of his mother begging the Creator to spare her son, please, no matter what. Seeing his mother crouched over him like that, repeating her terrified prayer again and again, was too much. Stanford went back into his inert body with its bolted-down head. It felt like he was being poured from a bowl into a heated skillet. The pain hit and he began to scream.

CHAPTER 5

MY HOME

AUGUST 2002

The horse clinic I attended at Stanford's lasted for four days. When it was over, I drove back to the house I shared in western Colorado with my boyfriend, Peter. I finished my *Smithsonian* article on Stanford, and returned to writing about the environment and food for other magazines. But my thoughts kept swinging back to Stanford and the black stallion. Nine months passed before I called him and asked whether he'd mind if I wrote his life story. He said he liked the idea and mentioned that in a month he and three other men were driving to help out some friends embroiled in a tribal conflict in Iowa, a state so disassociated in my mind from any kind of friction that I'd filed it under Canada. The trip would take three weeks. Did I want to come?

Heck yeah I wanted to come. But I wanted to visit Stanford for a weekend before we left. It had been a long time since I'd seen him, and I wanted to renew our acquaintance before getting into the confined quarters of a Winnebago and the even more confining conditions of a tribal conflict severe enough to require the help of a spiritual healer.

The drive to Stanford's took a whole day. Six hours into it, I stopped for gas in Rawlins, a threadbare, windy town on the interstate. (WARNING! said the sign right next to the cashier's booth. THE WIND WILL TAKE YOUR CHANGE!) I grabbed my stack of ones soon enough, but the wind went a long way toward slapping my resolve right out of me.

I battled my way through the windy parking lot and found a phone booth to call Peter. He was on his way to spend ten days in silence at a Buddhist meditation retreat in California. While he listened to the sound of his own breathing, I'd be riding in a Winnebago with an Arapaho man I barely knew and three others I'd never met, heading into the middle of a tribal war with only a cup of gas-station coffee to sustain me.

I wished I were with Peter. He was my love, my best friend, the needle in my heart. We'd done plenty of meditation retreats together; in fact, we had become friends at a meditation center three years before, in Massachusetts. I had been spending a year working there as a cook and secretary, and he would travel down from Vermont and his job as a biologist to meditate for weeks at a time. He came every chance he got; he was one of the meditation center's most frequent visitors. One day we took a hike through the woods together. The sun glinted off his copper-colored hair, and he told stories about a summer he'd spent tracking bears back to their dens. I tried to hide how much I liked to look at him—my friend and I had joked for months about how handsome he was, calling him Teen Idol. Hiking along, the two of us were exchanging a lot of smiles and shoulder brushes.

"Isn't it amazing that right here in this very spot, there used to be huge prehistoric beavers?" he said suddenly. "Eight-hundred-pounders the size of grizzly bears! Wouldn't it be cool to see one right here?" He stopped walking. "I just love beavers."

Oh no. Was this some kind of latter-day frat-boy come-on? Or was he joking? I hoped so.

I looked at him. But he wasn't looking at me; he was gazing intently at the pond before us, obviously imagining a prehistoric eight-hundred-pound beaver.

I burst into relieved laughter. He turned to me, curious about what I thought was so funny.

"It really would be great," I said, managing a smile, which he returned enthusiastically. "Think of the size of their teeth! *Beaverus dentata*?"

"I *know*," he replied. "They must have been really long."

I knelt to inspect a flower, finish my giggling in silence, and register: This guy is not an operator; he is an innocent.

Back home in Colorado, the phone started ringing with calls from Vermont. We quickly got into the habit of talking until the phone battery made the bipping noise that meant the call had exceeded two hours. He was intelligent and sensitive, with a frequent laugh that hit two pitches and reminded me of a duck quacking. I loved ducks.

Five months after my return to Colorado, I picked Peter up at the Grand Junction airport with two kayaks strapped to the top of my car. A few hours later, we were sitting on a red beach along the Colorado River, our boats pulled up beside us, throwing rocks into the air and trying to hit them with handfuls of mud before they splashed back into the water. We were covered with mud, doubled over with laughter, alone in a red rock canyon. We knew where all this was leading. But we felt so full of ease that we weren't in any particular hurry. We were laughing, talking, warming to the reality of being equally matched souls. And when we did crawl into the same bed a few nights later, I thought, At last. I've found the one. Late, but my God I've found him.

But after the initial inventory of all the things you share with your beloved comes the inventory of what you don't. That began half a year into the relationship, after a month together in Peter's studio apartment in Vermont. Working side by side—he on the wildlife biology courses he taught at the University of Vermont, me on articles I sold to magazines—we washed up on the far shore of infatuation; shipwrecked, really, on the hard fact that I wanted to get married and perhaps have a baby and he did not. Sure, he wanted to be with me. But he also wanted to meditate. A lot.

We didn't break up. We waited each other out. I thought he'd see the error of his ways. Ours was a compatibility so rare it would be a sin against God not to arrange our lives around it. Or maybe I was waiting myself out. We were both thirty-nine, and my maternal instincts had emerged only the year before we got together and were perhaps, I figured, rooted in hormones alone. I loved my free, adventurous life, and I'd refused several offers of marriage. I battled Peter and I battled myself. Was I selling out my dream to stay with him? Or would I be crazy to leave someone with whom it worked so well just because of some rogue hormones?

We couldn't afford to keep flying from Vermont to Colorado to see each other. Peter knew New England's biology, not Colorado's, while my job as a journalist was portable. We spent a year and a half in Vermont before I had to get back to the sun and space of the West. Peter came with me. We moved to my house in its dusty, tiny town. He murmured appreciatively at the bright sun and high mountains, put on some sunglasses, and started a new job as a carpenter. He loved his new, simple life. He meditated two hours a day and started offering free meditation classes at the Catholic church. He missed academia not one bit.

But the marriage issue did not go away. Our confusion was shot through with the question of just where spirituality belonged in our lives. I used spiritual life for short periods of rejuvenation. For Peter, however, it was the center of life, the real deal, the source of his sanity and well-being. He loved meditating. He did it every day. It showed him the ephemeral and temporary nature of all things, especially his negative thoughts and opinions. He didn't understand how people could consider it a dour, dry practice. It made him joyful, and the happier he was, he reasoned, the more he would have to offer the world. He showed me pictures of the undeniably sweet smiles on the faces of men who had spent their entire lives meditating in caves, and he spoke admiringly of acquaintances who had taken vows and entered monasteries in Asia. I was in it for a little bit of sanity; Peter was going for flat-out enlightenment.

He was even expanding his focus from Theravada Buddhism—the tradition taught at the meditation center where we had met—to include the more charismatic Tibetan Buddhism. Theravada was a spare form of Buddhism; stripped to meditation practice and simple Buddhist teachings. Tibetan Buddhism was all golden thrones and reincarnated rinpoches and great leaps of understanding given from your teacher to you in what was called a transmission. This was all vaguely threatening to me. The linchpin of the practice was devotion to a single teacher, or root guru. Gurus scared me. I felt like a buttoned-up Presbyterian watching her husband take a shine to Southern Baptist faith healing.

*   *   *

I got to the pay phone and punched in Peter's cell phone number. He was in a bus terminal in San Rafael, California, trying to organize a taxi ride for several people traveling to a Tibetan retreat. Come to think of it, his spiritual explorations didn't scare me nearly as much as my own.

"I'm freaking out!" I shouted into the pay phone, a finger stuck in my free ear to keep out the whomp of the Wyoming wind. "What the hell am I doing?"

He couldn't tell me. He could hardly hear me. We had a disjointed conversation for a couple of minutes, and then he had to hang up.

"Shit," I said, and put the phone back in its cradle, fought my way through the wind back to my car, and pointed it north.

I pulled up to Stanford's weather-beaten modular home at about seven. The trio of white teepees that had been there during the horse clinic was gone; they were only for white visitors and horse training clients. Inside Stanford's house, a cluster of relatives staying there greeted me and told me he was in his room. I found him lying face-down on his waterbed with a flannel sheet over him. He had been lying down since January, when the pressure sores on his butt flared up, making wheelchair life impossible. I didn't know where to stand or sit or be, so I perched on a far corner of his bed. But he was so friendly and at ease that I was soon sitting on a pillow on the floor right next to him so we could see eye-to-eye. His urine bag hung about six inches from my elbow. He chain-smoked KOOLs, and we talked until eleven about our upcoming trip, which would include a stay with the Meskwaki tribe of Tama, Iowa.

The Meskwakis' territory covered only about twenty square miles, but the tribe was rich because it ran a casino accessible to Des Moines and other cities along Interstate 80. The tribe was in the midst of a political crisis, Stanford told me. Threats of violence were flying. He knew this from his Meskwaki friends, who often drove out to his sweat lodge. Stanford was traveling to Iowa to run sweat lodges that would bring the Meskwakis some spiritual protection and calm.

I sat on the floor underneath the TV showing one of Stanford's favorite cooking shows.

"Out in Iowa, when things get real conflicted, they sometimes use the tree spirits to get at each other," he said, glancing at the TV to ascertain how a pair of beautiful blond sisters made crepes. "They can be dangerous."

It was late. I wrote what he'd said in my notebook and went to bed in his daughter Laticia's room. Laticia, who went by Tisha, was six years old and had gone to spend the night at a friend's. She wasn't really Stanford's daughter, she was his nephew's daughter, but his nephew had died a couple of years before in a car crash, and four of his children had been taken in by uncles and aunts and their grandma. Tisha's bedroom had closet doors with holes for doorknobs, a bare mattress, and a distinct odor of dog poop ("Tiny had her puppies there last week," Tisha told me before she left). The floor consisted of particleboard in a shade of brown that made me keep my socks on for the entire visit. I lay down on the sheetless mattress to go to sleep. Then I got up again and walked back to Stanford's room. Tree spirits? What was this, *The Lord of the Rings*? As incredulous as I was, I also knew that Stanford was not crazy. And we hadn't just been idly talking; I was going to this place, Iowa with tree spirits, with him.

"Stan?" I asked awkwardly. "Are you going to protect me from these tree spirits?"

"Yeah. I'll give you a protection when we get there."

That was as much reassurance as I was going to get.

"Well," I said. "Okay."

The next afternoon, people started arriving for the sweat lodge. Stanford asked me to assist him there, to handle his medicine bag and four eagle wings, keep him supplied with cigarettes, and hold a dipper of water to his mouth so he could drink before each of the four sweltering "rounds."

The lodge frame was constructed of shiny red willow limbs. It was round and about twenty feet across. Several layers of tarps and quilts stretched over the frame. It looked like a giant cloth-covered turtle. The lodge was supposed to. In Plains Indian cosmology, the turtle represents family or a woman's womb. It was a place for sharing and rebirth. We would spend several hours in and around this structure, suffering in the heat so that the Creator would better hear our prayers. Stanford told me that Arapaho spiritual practices are painful and difficult because that's how Arapaho life is.

"People don't see the good in suffering," he said.

The sweat lodge fosters humility before the Creator. The hotter you get, the harder you are supposed to pray. Sweating is a means of purification, achieved with the aid of prayer, singing, and close human companionship, with the goal that you pray hard enough to bring healing to the people who need it.

Meditation, too, is an act of purification, but it is practiced in cool, quiet solitude. Even if you do it in a meditation hall with other people, you don't talk to them and you often spend the whole time with your eyes closed. This provides the time and quiet to witness the impermanent and ephemeral nature of thoughts, emotion, physical pain, and life itself.

The practices are aimed in different directions: In a sweat lodge, you reach out with prayer and songs that take the message of suffering to the Creator. On the meditation cushion, you travel inward to your own core to make peace. Meditation goes in. Prayer goes out. But they both aim for the same place of union between you and the Divine.

I entered the lodge and sat cross-legged next to Stanford, who, due to his broken neck and pressure sores on his buttocks, lay on his stomach on some couch cushions covered with a towel. A few teenage boys filled the pit in the middle of the lodge with river rocks that glowed white-hot from several hours' heating in the big bonfire just outside. At Stanford's instruction, I had brought in his bag of medicines. I unrolled a wool rug about the size of a legal pad. It contained a Ziploc sandwich bag of sweet sage, some little leather pouches bound tight to a leather thong, and a whistle made from the bone of an eagle's wing. Then I tucked four eagle wings up in the framework of the lodge.

The lodge filled with Arapahos, perhaps a dozen women and a lesser number of men. They all wore baggy basketball shorts and carried towels. The women wore oversize T-shirts. The men were bare-chested.

Stanford introduced me to them as they came in. They were polite and friendly, but I felt hideously self-conscious. I was the only non-Native person there. I was nervous, toy-poodle nervous, a blond curly-haired imposter at Stanford's right side. Their glances prickled my skin.

Soon the rock pile was high enough that I was getting hot, and the doors were still wide open. But there was no rushing. Everyone sat on the floor, smoking cigarettes and joking and gossiping. They seemed to have known one another all their lives. Then Stanford gave the word and the doors were closed, the flashlight extinguished, and I gratefully relinquished my foreignness, whiteness, and discomfort to the encompassing dark. Stanford instructed a man to pour some water onto the hot rocks, and the heat bit into my face and arms and burned my lungs.

I pressed my nose to the ground and used my Buddhist training, which encourages you to note the feeling or sensation you are experiencing without exaggerating or attaching a story line to it.

Fear, I thought, my heart lunging, my nose and mouth moving along the base of the lodge where it met the ground, seeking coolness like a trout in a summer stream. This is just fear, I thought. Also, heat.

Stanford said a prayer, then invited people to share their concerns. The stories poured slowly into the shared blackness. One man said he had vengeance in his heart.

Sure, I thought in commiseration, join the club.

He said his son had been murdered by some white boys in the wintertime. They'd taken his boy's shoes and clothes and dumped him in the middle of the high desert, leaving him to freeze to death. The investigation would go nowhere, the man was sure of it. He wasn't going to do anything irrational, but still, he said, he felt vengeance.

A wire of horror pushed into my heart, followed by a kind of hugeness. I felt glowing, luminescent, radioactive. A menace. My heart boomed in my ears. By the time I could listen again, a tribal official was speaking about the tribe losing land and how they'd have to unite to keep it.

Stanford led us in Arapaho songs and prayer. Then he made choking, convulsing sounds. The heat pressed against me. I took tiny breaths, the air hot metal in my throat and lungs. It was humbling. If a meditation retreat is like serving a sentence in solitary confinement, a sweat lodge is like visiting the surface of the sun.

Then Stanford yelled, "Open it!" The man sitting next to the door opened the door. The first of four rounds was over. It was downtime, comfortable time, the time after the pain and prayer when you can get up and stand by the fire, or go inside and use the bathroom, or stay in the lodge and chat. Everyone lay there and told jokes. Everyone but me. I was so shocked and saddened about the boy left to freeze that I couldn't even begin to chuckle at their relaxed humor. I was careful and quiet, hypervigilant of my duties: putting Stanford's cigarettes in his mouth, adjusting his towel. The second round passed. After that, the men brought in more hot rocks, just in case we were getting too comfortable. The third round came and went, and then the fourth. Near the end, I handed out the eagle wings I'd tucked into the willow structure above me to people who wanted to beat the air onto their skin and get even hotter. By the end, the singing was loud and joyful. Stanford said that the spirits take from him during the first three rounds but give it all back to him in the fourth.

This sweat lodge was difficult for me, and over the next few years they wouldn't get easier. But I always loved them, even when I emerged with a clanging headache that wouldn't go away until the next afternoon. I felt cleaned out afterward, in body and spirit. Stanford sometimes said he wouldn't be alive without them. Spiritually, I couldn't even imagine the benefits he received. I could only hear him retch early in the sweat and dispense little jokes during the breaks ("Time to get going again," he might say when it was time to start the second round, "Hand me my goggles and my cape"). Toward the end, he always sang with confidence and joy.

From a physical perspective, I reasoned that getting so hot could only be helpful for a paralyzed person with circulation problems: The heart races, the blood sprints, banging at the walls of your system, looking for a way out. Bringing new blood to old wounds.

*   *   *

It was nearly midnight when the sweat lodge ended. At the feast, I downed three bowls of meat chili. I hadn't eaten all day because of my excitement and nervousness about the sweat lodge. I'd bought dinner for everyone—six huge cans of Dinty Moore. Nicole, an eighteen-year-old with two small children fathered by Stanford's nephew Cody, had heated the chili while we were sweating. It was good. I felt surprisingly comfortable, eating with this roomful of silent Arapahos. Quamé, Nicole and Cody's beautiful, rambunctious two-year-old, kept coming to me and finally fell asleep in my arms. Children. The universal antidote. He was heavy and big-boned; I loved his glossy, solid, unstoppable healthiness.

I went to bed feeling clean from the sweat and pleased with myself for making it through, for being adequately absorbent for the task at hand. But I was wrong. It had been too much, too soon. I crashed through my dreams and woke up the next morning not knowing where I was. There was new snow on the ground and fresh unease in my heart. Tiny the dog had left two petite turds outside the bedroom door. I got a paper towel and threw Tiny's leavings into the wet, cold yard. The light was flat and promised more snow. It closed over me like a kidnapper's blanket.

I cleaned up what was left of the previous night's dinner, made a big pot of weak coffee the way Stanford liked it, and waited for him, or anyone, to get up. I wanted to go home. The prospect of being snowed in here, unable to leave, made me feel panicky. So did the fact that some of the people at the sweat lodge clearly saw Stanford as god-like. I'd felt his power myself when I was in the corral with the stallion. I'd certainly lost my own self-determination as I progressed with the horse; the calm I'd felt that afternoon had not felt like my own.

It had all been very interesting, and now I wanted the movie to be over and I wanted to be sitting in my own kitchen with its thrift-store floral patterned tablecloth, its fair-trade espresso beans, and maybe a nice big apple. But I was here, with the huge enamel pots that had held last night's chili dripping in the dish rack, and only Folgers to drink. I went to the coffeepot and poured some tea-colored brew, doctored it with nondairy creamer, and gulped. It tasted heavenly. By the time Stanford woke up, I'd had three cups. When I heard his voice, I started and nearly sprinted into his room. What he said didn't exactly calm me down.

"People will talk, you know," he said. "They'll think you're my white girlfriend."

I was working on a reply when we were interrupted by a sweet-faced guy named Damian who'd been living for the last two days on Stanford's couch. (*Staying* there, I mean. Northern Arapahos never ask where you live. They say, "Where do you stay?") Damian walked into Stanford's room, saw me, and made a U-turn back out the door, looking at the floor rather than at me.

No! I screamed inside. *I'm not his girlfriend! Don't leave! I'll leave!*

I scuttled back out to the kitchen, drank more coffee, darted back into Stanford's room to say goodbye, got in my car and drove.

If there is a landscape on this earth that supports the rooting and flowering of eerie thoughts, it's the 150-mile drive between Stanford's house and Rawlins. The scale of the rock basins seems off; boulders that look like crumbs from across the valley are really the size of horse trailers. The slamming wind tears the clouds into ragged strips and lays them across the sky. My aloneness pressed in on me.

I reviewed: I was going to spend a lot of time with this man. I was taken with his combination of gentleness and power. But if the powers I felt coming from him so palpably were real, they could play some nasty tricks on a woman. If he wanted that woman. Stanford was unguarded with me, extraordinarily so. But he was unguarded with everyone, right?

Two hours of snow-swept rock desert past Riverton, I rolled into Rawlins, pulled in to McDonald's, picked up the sticky pay phone in the lobby, and dialed Stanford's number. I plunged right in. I said I wanted to be clear that our relationship was strictly business. I was committed to, and in love with, someone else. He couldn't agree more, he said. He'd been hung out to dry too many times. He wasn't looking for a woman; he wanted the book to help us both, and yes indeed the relationship was strictly business.

The man's sincerity was as real as the scent of french fries. If I'd had to lay bets at that moment on whether Stanford was honest and good or someone who would mess with my head, I'd have emptied my pocketbook in his favor. But the drive home was long. Fear approached like a dark star. Fear, I thought, I see you. It slipped into me anyway. The mesas and rock outcrops begged for Indian ponies and their keening, feathered riders to stream right onto the highway. I thought, Stuck. Hypnotized. Stashed in an Airstream trailer somewhere on the reservation. Slave to a quadriplegic with magical powers.

By the time I saw Peter, fresh from his quiet and spacious meditation retreat, I was sitting on our porch steps wearing my usual jeans and T-shirt. But inside I was miles and years away, snatched from my covered wagon, my calico skirt billowing behind me, slung across a paint pony, and spirited away.

CHAPTER 6

THE SOUL DRAGS THE REST BEHIND

What did I want, anyway? That would depend on which part of me you asked. My soul was pointed like an iron filing straight toward Stanford Addison, toward the annihilating beauty of the Wind River Indian Reservation and the shift in my heart I had experienced on that now-distant day in the horse training ring.

My body, on the other hand, wanted familiar surroundings and safety and filtered water and organic food and to live, live, live—forever, if possible. It carried the fear of religious and racial wars and colonial bloodlettings, even though those wars were more than a century behind us. Even though my family had set foot on this continent for the first time in 1969, even though none of my direct ancestors had raised a hand against a Native American. They had busied themselves tearing up Africa, not America. Even so. The cells of the white person contain plasma and mitochondria and the fear that We'll Get Ours.

My personality, running interference, looked for signs of comfort and safety or simply someone to assure me that the adventure I was stepping into was not by any means a dangerous one. Things were going to turn out just fine.

And who would be a better person to tell me these things than Peter?

He was currently in the bathtub, which he showed no signs of leaving. He was not happy about my fear of Stanford's powers or my plan to leave with this magic man for three weeks in Iowa two days hence.

Nor was he thrilled about my tightly wound state or the increased level of emotional support I suddenly required.

A conversation started that would take months—no, years—to complete. Peter did not want drama. He wanted to be my partner, not some form of ground support for a crazy adventure of my own devising. Above all, he sought a simple life.

Simple was fine with me, but it was not, at this moment, a big priority. Some part of me was caught by Stanford and Wyoming. For me, the temperature of Buddhism was cool. Stanford's world was hot. I wanted heat.

I knew already that I would follow this adventure through, dragging my personality and body and cultural conditioning and relationship with Peter along for the ride.

CHAPTER 7

NOT IN IOWA ANYMORE

MAY 2003

The first leg of the trip to Iowa was my trip back to Stanford's, a route that would become familiar over the next five years. It started with a kiss from Peter, standing on the porch wearing his toolbelt. Our cat, Sandy, following me from the house, his one overlong claw tapping on the pathway until he reached my car and sat down, his white paws in a neat, quasi-military posture of goodbye. My heart lurching with love for both the man and the cat with whom I shared my home, as well as with excitement about what awaited me in Wyoming, where a magnificent and capricious God seemed to touch down more often than in my known world of Colorado.

I started the car and soon rolled past orchards and a string of elk at the edge of a field, red willows at the edge of the North Fork of the Gunnison River. Next came coal mines and aspen forests in bright springtime green. Then I came to the best view in Colorado, from McClure Pass, the mountains still gleaming with snow, and straight down a boulder-strewn stretch of road to the clear, deep turquoise, rushing Crystal River. In Carbondale I stopped one, two, three times at traffic lights surrounded by the SUVs driven by those who owned homes in nearby Aspen and the low-riders driven by those who cleaned those homes. A burst of speed west down Interstate 70 with the Colorado River sliding slowly along beside me, lined with willows, subdivisions, and the occasional rickety ancient-looking blue heron. A town called Silt. A town called Rifle.

I exited the highway and turned north past the pawnshop and the

Garfield County fairgrounds and the series of four road signs that said:

> *Folks wouldn't feel—*
> *in so much danger—*
> *if we still had—*
> *the ole Lone Ranger.*

A few months later, the last sign would disappear, leaving a more koan-like message:

> *Folks wouldn't feel*
> *in so much danger*
> *if we still had*

Western Colorado feels pretty empty to most people, but compared to Wyoming, it is as settled and folded and verdant as Massachusetts. When winter storms hit the West, Colorado lies still and takes it, getting all Christmas-cardy and perfect and muffled and silent. But Wyoming weather doesn't know about being still. It roars and rages and punishes.

"No one recommends Wyoming for its climate," wrote James Galvin, who lives on the Wyoming-Colorado border, in his novel *Fencing the Sky.* "They recommend its lack of human consequence."

Driving along on that May afternoon, I thought about how different the two states were; Colorado was scenic in the alpine sense, while Wyoming was all about rocks, the occasional rusted-out rigs left by oil and gas companies, and antelope.

Not far into Wyoming, in the middle of a wide valley, I was stopped by a flag lady. It was going to be a while before the pilot car would ferry the northbound cars through the construction, so I stopped, got out some cheese and crackers, sat on the hood, and asked her if she'd seen any wildlife. She said not really, except for the wild horses. My heart trilled like a kestrel in the air above its prey. Just the wild horses.

In windy Rawlins, the three-quarters-there mark for my drive, I went into the supermarket, where I started a years-long tradition of buying exactly the wrong things to eat—sliced turkey with enough salt to preserve me into the next Ice Age or Diet Coke that tasted like a tin can. This time I bought macadamia nuts that turned out to be be rancid.

After two more hours of rock, space, and tiny busted energy towns (one with a building that said MEN'S DORMITORY) I came to Riverton, Wyoming, with its numerous modular-home sales lots, then out of town and onto the reservation proper, where trailers and prefabricated houses were surrounded by dead or dying cars, lines of flapping laundry, and gorgeous horses. Appaloosas, paints, and, as I got close to Stanford's, Arabs. An artist named Alfred Jacob Miller had found some Arapahos on the Platte River back in the late 1830s and was impressed by their horses, which "partook somewhat of the Arabian breed . . . War ponies were second in splendor only to the painted warriors who fearlessly and expertly handled them."

The light was already long and golden. The Wind River Range loomed to the west, moody dark clouds and streaming evening sun playing on its white peaks.

We were to leave Stanford's for Iowa the evening I arrived. By the time I pulled up at his house, it was seven o'clock. I'd driven up in a T-shirt, but as soon as I stepped into the Wyoming wind, I needed a down jacket. A stocky man in his sixties wearing shorts and a windbreaker and holding a smoldering stick of sage stumped up to me, shook my hand, and introduced himself as Mark Small, Northern Cheyenne. Then he climbed into a large Winnebago parked in the dirt to smudge it with smoke. He called back out the door that I should load up my stuff, then started singing in Cheyenne. Each of my traveling companions had packed a small nylon bag, as if we were a high school basketball team going to an away game. I was stuffing my extra-large duffel bag, a tent, a daypack, and a laptop computer into a storage compartment when Mark saw me. He raised an eyebrow. "We *are* coming back, you know," he said.

Mark got in the driver's seat with an expression of relish, looking not unlike Mr. Toad from *The Wind in the Willows*. Stanford's quiet, solid twenty-one-year-old nephew Cody—the son of Stanford's sister Arilda—ran up the steps, said "Hey" to me, and took the shotgun seat. Stanford was carried in and laid down on the bed in the rear sleeping area. I took the chair in the living area. On a small couch across from me sat Stanford's thirteen-year-old nephew Robert. He had a spike hairdo and a deep commitment to avoiding eye contact. I thought some icebreaker would present itself. None did. I looked at him. He looked out the window.

We took off, drove a couple hundred yards, and pulled up at the house belonging to Stanford's mother, Stella. Relatives poured out of the house. Arilda's youngest son, Aaron, a plump high school student, said, "Out in the third world, those kids will run right alongside your Winnebago, like this." He waved his arms back and forth and bobbled up and down, just like a skinny child running along in Haiti or Senegal. I laughed out loud. Arilda and Stella came out. Stella wobbled up the Winnebago's steps with her cane. She tested the armchair and the little couch and nodded her approval.

Finally, the family drained back out of the Winnebago, and we started driving. Mark and Cody tried and quickly rejected my Ry Cooder tape, then cranked KTRZ and Christina Aguilera.

Green fields and shiny horses rolled by in the evening light, and the distant, snowy Wind River Mountains stayed still. So far, so good. The energy felt friendly, respectful, nonthreatening. All my doomsday fantasies had been for nothing. I went back to perch on Stanford's bed. Eighteen miles from his house, we turned onto Riverton's main strip.

"We probably used up a tank of gas already," joked Mark.

In Riverton, we were joined by Mike, a Meskwaki driving a comfortable, new-looking Chevy Suburban. We hummed and vibrated into the Wyoming night, pulling over in Casper to get Mark a thirty-six-ounce mug of coffee. ("Try to keep it to one cup, huh?" I teased him.) After that, Cody and Robert went back to talk to Stanford, leaving Mark and me alone in the front of the Winnebago. Mark told me he had been brought up on a ranch on the reservation in Montana. His father drank, and sometimes he beat Mark's mother so badly that she was unrecognizable to her son in the morning. Mark went to boarding school, which he figured saved his life because his home was so violent.

After college at the University of Kansas and a stint at law school in New Mexico, Mark worked for the Indian Health Service in

Alaska, then brought the first Alcoholics Anonymous group to Indian Country—the Northern Cheyenne reservation in 1963. Then came years spent in Alaska and Washington, D.C., where he repatriated "floors and floors" of once-buried human bones from the Smithsonian Institution back to the tribes. He worked all the time. Things started falling apart at home. Mark plunged into a deep depression. By the mid-1990s, he couldn't work. He could barely speak. He split from his wife. He lived in the basement at his brother's place back home in Montana and watched the concept of suicide take on a favorable glimmer.

"They put bad medicine on me back east in 1995," said Mark. It wasn't the bones, he said, or even the medicine bundles: It was the jealousy some Native Americans directed at him due to his professional success. "I was sick from 1995 until March 2003. The white diagnosis was I was bipolar."

Early in 2003, someone suggested he meet Stanford. Mark was so debilitated that he couldn't even walk into his first sweat lodge at Stan's. He crawled.

"I called him a medicine bag," Stanford told me later, laughing. "He had that much bad medicine on him. Man, it was exhausting. All the years of hurt and pain and confusion. And then it was like a constant moan, just hurting. By the fourth round, he wasn't moaning."

Mark sat through four lodges, and then four more. He stopped needing his medication, and he bought the Winnebago for Stanford.

"He couldn't travel," said Mark. "He couldn't sit up. Now I live in this, too. I live here."

When Stanford showed Mark how he worked with Arapaho kids by teaching them to train horses, Mark said, "You don't know the millions of dollars of taxpayer money I've wasted trying to get somewhere with kids! And failed!

"If Stanford could get ten Indian kids to heal, to have one mind and one heart, they could change Indian Country. I've searched Indian Country for thirty years, and this guy is the real thing. I think a powerful part of his medicine is when you look at him, you see someone with no ego."

No ego? Really?

"Well, he does have his stories."

And there's nothing like a road trip for stories. Stanford, reclining and smoking in his bed in the back of the Winnebago, told me that during his weeks in the Lander hospital following the accident, he received visits from a quiet gray-haired woman who would signal her entry into his room only by the squeak of the wheels on her cart of books. He asked a nurse about the woman, and the nurse looked blank. He described his visitor: She was white, her hair was pulled back from her face, she wore a dark green knitted sweater and a white flowered dress. Sure, a woman like that used to bring books to patients, the nurse told him, but she died seven years ago.

Then a man started coming by and asking Stanford if he wanted to get out for a bit. Stanford said yes, thinking the man would take him out of the hospital for a drive. They didn't drive, but somehow they arrived at the Lander Bar, where a guy Stanford knew was trying to impress everyone by taking a bite out of a bar glass. The next day James, who had been in the truck accident with Stanford, came to his hospital room to catch him up on the latest news. Stanford cut him off, describing exactly what had happened at the bar. He even knew the guy had been admitted to a different part of the hospital for a badly cut mouth. James was confused, but not nearly as confused as a cousin of Stanford's who came to visit a few days later, after resisting her father's pressure to see her paralyzed cousin. As soon as she arrived, Stanford told her it was okay if she hadn't wanted to visit: He, too, would be scared to see someone as hurt as he was. She ran from the room, sobbing.

He saw her point. Psychic powers were the last thing he wanted. Stanford's family had absorbed a good deal of Catholicism, but they still observed traditional spiritual practices, so he knew the crushing weight of responsibility carried by medicine men—the endless self-sacrifice, the thanklessness of the people who received help, the jealousy of people who didn't, the terrible temptation to use powers for your own ends, which, if given in to, would come back to haunt you and your family. Plus, he was only in his early twenties. Medicine men were usually older.

But he wasn't young anymore. Not really.

"Uncle Hiram—he was an old guy—said what made me older than him is I went through life four times. I died four times in the Lander hospital. The last time I woke up on a slab in the morgue. A guy was over me with a knife, ready to drain my blood. I yelled at him and he ran off. I don't know who was scareder, me or him!"

Stanford felt like a stranger to himself. Not only was he suddenly being ferried around Fremont County by the spirits to see things he didn't want to see, but his once powerful, once flexible, once tireless body was being subjected to unspeakable humiliations. People often think paralyzed people can't feel anything below their spinal injury, but Stanford was an incomplete quadriplegic. Three vertebrae in his neck had been crushed, the spinal cord severed three quarters of the way through. The remaining quarter still transmitted messages to his body, but they were garbled and confused. It didn't hurt if someone stepped on his foot, but if his legs touched each other, it felt like an electric shock, and the brush of a sheet over his foot was intolerable. A catheter was inserted into his penis, which was fully sensate and sexually functional, although that, at the time, seemed like a cruel joke. His most basic bodily functions required the aid and intrusion of strangers. His left lung had been so torn up when his ribs splintered underneath the crashing weight of the pickup truck that it had been removed, and his remaining lung had filled up with enough fluid that the doctors had to empty it with a long tube they threaded through his nose.

The self-styled outlaw and bronc buster who made all those girls eager with just a glance had become an unresponsive length of flesh with white people hovering over him, poking and prodding, watching his lean, strong limbs approach the first stages of atrophy and trying to prevent him from dying once and for all.

His mother made a phone call, and a priest came in to administer last rites. Stanford asked the priest if he believed in what he was doing.

The priest shrugged.

"I said, 'Well, if you don't believe in what you're doing, why are you here?'

"My mom told me to knock it off. And he gave me my last rites. I did it for her, to give her that comfort."

* * *

The Winnebago slowed to a halt. We were in Clear Lake, Iowa. Unlike the small towns of Wyoming or Colorado, the houses here were big and strong and square and looked like they'd been here forever. Gone were the trailers and modular homes of the reservation and the tumbledown mining cottages of Paonia, where, true to the norm in my neighborhood, my house had asphalt siding and a foundation that went only halfway around the exterior. The hastily constructed homes in small working towns in the Rockies gave the place a stolen, pillaged look. Clear Lake, Iowa, might as well have been in Luxembourg. But of course it wasn't. This place had been stolen, too.

We finished breakfast, picked up some gas money the Meskwakis had sent by Western Union, gassed up the vehicles, and hit the road again. I was happy; I wanted to hear more stories.

After a few weeks in Lander, Stanford was transferred to a bigger hospital in Seattle. His spirit visitors—the elderly man and the old lady with the green flowered dress—occasionally showed up there. So did his dead relatives. But when Stanford asked why all those other people were in the room, the nurses started treating him in the careful, probing way reserved for patients who were losing their grip—patients destined for another part of the hospital altogether.

"What's your name?" the nurses would ask. "When were you born?"

So Stanford stopped telling the nurses about what he was seeing, and he told the spirits that he wanted to walk, he didn't want to die, "and then I guess they gave me a break for a while, 'cause they saw I wanted to live."

Two years after the accident, Stanford came home to his parents' house. One night he was attending one of his father's peyote ceremonies when a cocky guy Stanford didn't know came in.

"I didn't like his attitude," Stanford said. "He started to sing. I was thinking to myself, Mess up on your song! I just thought it 'cause he was showing off. And as soon as I thought that, he lost his song. And I was thinking, Geez, did I do that or what?

"He collected himself and started singing the song again, and so I did the same thing, and sure enough, he lost his song again, and after that he kept looking at me, acknowledging me.

"I didn't want to do that. So I quit, and he finished the song."

Stanford took a final drag of his cigarette and handed his cigarette holder to me. I took it from him, extracted the butt, stubbed it out in a half-full ashtray, and laid the holder on the table next to his bed.

"I can do that, mess people up, when I want to," he said. "But I don't. Because everything you do comes back to you. That's why I try to be real careful and calm. That's why I don't like drugs or alcohol. 'Cause, man, it's no game."

A Lakota medicine man came to perform a ceremony to get him to walk again. But the spirits the medicine man called couldn't find his spirit anywhere. This didn't surprise Stanford. He'd recently seen it down by the river, wandering on its own.

"I didn't want to be around anymore, anyway," Stanford said. His father had just died. Mervin was only in his fifties, but he had been sick with diabetes for years before succumbing to prostate cancer. His death compounded the despair Stanford had battled since his accident. "I was real despondent," Stanford said. "I wanted to lay down and die."

But he wasn't getting off that easy. He was invisible to some spirits, but to others he was as obvious as a bull's-eye on a shooting range. One night he was watching television and heard the front door open. Assuming it was his brother, he didn't say anything or look around to see who it was. When the show ended, Stanford turned to behold not his brother but a big white cowboy who stared at him silently and then slowly stood up and walked out the door. He left a smell behind him, the smell of someone dead. He was a spirit, a "poor soul," a visible one who had not moved on. Like many young men with extra time on their hands in the early 1980s, the cowboy watched a lot of *Dallas*.

The woman with the gray hair and her male partner visited as doggedly as social workers or Jehovah's Witnesses. They left little gifts right in Stanford's hand—sage, as well as red paint, which can cure children of chicken pox.

"They were there to help me pull it together," said Stanford. "They started showing me things.

"Hey"—he looked over at me—"could you get me a cigarette?"

This was going to be a duty of mine. I already knew the routine: I put a KOOL in his cigarette holder and inserted its hand piece into his mouth. He took it from there, clasping the hand piece with his left hand, removing it from his mouth, inserting the filter end of the cigarette between his lips, and waiting for me to light it. He could also use the phone, punching out the number sequence with his upper lip. He could hold a plastic mug and sip coffee through a straw; he could feed himself with a plastic fork, but if the meal needed to be cut into pieces, someone else needed to do it.

I lit his cigarette with his lighter, and he took a long drag.

"What things?" I asked.

"I'll tell you later," he said, exhaling smoke. "You ain't ready for that. Not yet."

I was relieved. I needed a break.

The Winnebago lumbered through a pastoral patchwork of hills and cornfields and hardwood forests. This part of Iowa really looked like Europe.

Stanford had more to say.

His family had kept the old ways. Even though the police had cruised the reservation back in the 1960s and '70s, Stanford's parents had gone to Roma, Texas, and picked peyote, and at home they never stopped holding sweat lodges and peyote meetings.

"We were way out there," Stanford told me. "The BIA cops [police from the Bureau of Indian Affairs, who had jurisdiction on the reservation] would have a hard time finding us."

Stanford's aunt Myrtle had dragged him to enough Catholic masses that he'd learned to avoid her house on weekends. And even though he'd driven his father to all-night peyote ceremonies and enjoyed the old men and their stories, he participated only now and then. "They were kind of boring, praying for two, three hours at a time, trying to stay awake." He attended occasional sweat lodges, too, but only to prove to himself how much heat he could take. The Catholic priests had told him Native spiritual practices boiled down to devil worship; his schoolteachers insisted supernatural phenomena didn't exist.

Influenced by both traditions, the young Stanford Addison was convinced by neither. When the jealous Navajo shaman-in-training had pulled out some of his hair in that fight in Albuquerque, Stanford hadn't given it a second thought. When the nurses back in Seattle had thought his visions of spirits were signs of brain damage, he was inclined to agree.

So when he found he was watching television along with a cowboy he knew for a fact was not a live human being, or when he found medicines in his hand and knew full well he hadn't put them there himself, he did the best thing he could think of: He drank. Since he'd failed at killing himself, he'd let reservation life kill him. It was good at that. He started volunteering to ride along when his friends drove to the liquor store. But no matter how drunk they got, they kept arriving home safe and sound. So he tried another strategy: He'd roll up to the meanest, drunkest guys he could find at parties and try to antagonize them into killing him. He found the perfect candidate at a party in Riverton. A guy Stanford didn't know was bragging loudly that he'd just knocked someone out with a hammer. Stanford rolled over to him and started mocking him, telling him he was lying, that he wasn't brave enough to have done it. Instead of igniting into violence, the way Stanford had planned, the man started telling Stanford about how hard his childhood had been. He'd always felt like an ugly kid whom nobody loved. People had always pushed him around. Then he started *crying.*

This kept happening. Children and animals would pad up to Stanford's motionless feet that dangled down from his wheelchair, climb into his lap, and fall asleep.

"Something," he said, "was up."

We had arrived. We entered the Meskwaki Settlement the back way, the way that didn't pass the tribal headquarters, in order to prevent anyone from watching Stanford arrive. This seemed overly cautious to me, but what I didn't know then was that in comparison to my Native American companions, my sense of who or what was drawing near was about as well developed as an oyster's. Time and time again at Stanford's, I'd be taken aback by how people sitting at the kitchen table and looking like they were studying the pattern of the plastic table-cloth would suddenly say, "Someone's coming," when I hadn't heard a thing. What they meant was someone was coming in a few minutes. Once I was talking to Stanford when there was a knock on the front door.

"Can you feel the alcohol?" he asked me.

"No."

When the door opened, a man stood there, swaying on his feet.

Stan lay on his stomach on his foam mattress, propped himself up on his elbows, and looked out the Winnebago's window at the pastoral Iowan scenery of the Meskwaki Settlement.

"I feel real lonely," he said. "Things are real lonely here. It's in the ground. It's in the people, and it's contaminating the earth with all this negative thought. Tonight remind me to give you safety medicine."

We parked under some walnut and maple trees. It was shady, leafy, still, lushly green and birdsongy in a way that made Wyoming feel very far away.

In white America, the Meskwaki do not carry the historical cachet of Plains tribes like the Lakota or, for that matter, the Arapaho. The siege of Detroit—in which the Meskwaki attempted to starve out a garrison of French soldiers—just doesn't burn in the Hollywood-fed imagination the way Little Big Horn does. But the Meskwakis didn't take European settlement sitting down. In fact, they presented it with such fierce resistance that during the Fox Wars of 1701–1742 the French king called for the tribe's extermination. He never got his wish, but in the face of white settlement throughout the Midwest, by the mid-1800s the Meskwaki were consigned to a desolate reservation in Kansas. The tribe resisted, eventually buying their own land in Iowa in 1857.

For decades, the federal government didn't interfere with the land-owning Meskwakis as it did with tribes on reservations. The Meskwakis nested on their settlement. They hunted deer and squirrels. They lived in hardscrabble poverty, but they were also the owners of a verdant wonderland. Meskwaki children were routinely taught the old ways, praying to the Creator, learning about edible plants and medicinal herbs.

Then, in 1993, the tribe opened a casino, located about an hour west of Des Moines on Interstate 80. Each of the fourteen hundred enrolled Meskwakis started receiving a monthly check from tribal coffers, which at the time of our visit amounted to $1,700.

The money was nice, but interfamily squabbles and tribal politics are one thing when everyone's dirt poor and entirely another when there are millions of dollars at stake. By the time we rolled onto the Meskwaki Settlement that day in May 2003, an uprising had occurred right here in the middle of what looked like Norman Rockwell country. A group of Meskwakis who opposed the elected tribal council had taken over the tribal building and had been occupying it for weeks. Death threats were being left on answering machines. Guns were being stashed under car seats. The rumor mill on the Meskwaki Settlement made my small town's look like it was powered by a collection of deaf-mutes. The county and state governments had backed away from the situation so fast they had almost tripped over the back of their pants. Things would probably get a lot worse before they got better, because a federal judge was weighing whether the casino should be shut down.

Stanford's Winnebago nestled underneath a walnut tree. I set up my tent nearby, underneath a maple. I remarked to the jovial Meskwaki man who had let us camp on his lawn how nasty all the recent events sounded, how un-Iowan.

"You're not in Iowa now," he said in a voice containing not one iota of irony. "You're in Indian Country."

We would be here for ten days. Our host's big house was open to Stanford, Mark, Cody, Robert, and me. Unlike Stanford's house, where the food supply fluctuated wildly, our friend's kitchen consistently overflowed with jumbo-size boxes of cereal, packages of bacon, orange juice in pitchers, milk by the gallon, eggs by the flat, brightly colored soda in big plastic bottles, rolls of paper towels, and cans and cans and cans of coffee.

This kind of bounty was unheard of before the casino was built.

"I told my kids, 'You've got it easy,'" our host told me. "In my day you had to haul water, cut wood, hunt. I remember using kerosene lanterns. And then the casino came, and everyone's got new houses, nice cars, electricity, running water, appliances."

The wealth wasn't necessarily a good thing. "There's more money for alcohol and drugs," he said. "And you don't need to get a job."

Then he went outside to mow the expansive lawn with his riding lawn mower.

On our first night on Meskwaki land, Stanford gave me the promised protection root. He instructed me to touch the ground, touch my tongue, and nibble a tiny piece of root. Then I "fixed" myself—spat little bits of chewed root into my palms and waved my hands over my head and torso, whooshing my root-infused breath all over myself. Stanford said the Arapahos had used the root since before the time of Christ.

"It's for your spirit and your body, so they don't get damaged," he said.

Good enough. I put the remaining root in my pocket and slept with my jeans on so I could keep the root close to me.

Our lives took on a pleasant rhythm. In the evenings, Stanford ran sweat lodges that provided physical protection and spiritual renewal for our hosts and their friends. By day, people visited. Stanford's presence caused people to condense out of thin air. They brought their public problems and private torments to the man lying in the Winnebago. They came in an almost hushed manner, as if Stanford were the pope or the Dalai Lama. One day a motorcycle club arrived, a black leather-clad gang composed entirely of former alcoholics and drug addicts. They were clean and sober now, slim under their leathers, with creased faces. Cody carried Stanford out of the Winnebago and lowered him into his chair, and he chatted with the motorcyclists kneeling in the dirt and grass. Their bikes were Harleys with stickers like RIDE IT LIKE YOU STOLE IT. But they were really like a pack of declawed kittens. Afterward, grinning like a little kid, Stanford said, "I got my own motorcycle gang!"

The rest of us found our own niches among the Meskwakis. All of us except Robert, who smoldered around the Winnebago, his long hair in his face, playing video games. One day I mentioned to him that I thought he'd look great with blond streaks in his hair. This somehow cracked open a door into the part of him that was a sweet young boy. So I got a kit at the store and streaked his hair in a cloud of ammonia. When he washed it out, it looked great.

Cody either played videos with Robert, drove around in the Chevy Suburban with Mike the Meskwaki, or hung around with his brother Sass, who worked here in the casino.

Mark rumbled around, dispensing a full-on Washington D.C.–style political commentary to the Meskwakis. I listened. The Meskwaki men talked each morning, reminding me of a group of old farmers in a coffee shop. I kept waiting for someone to notice I was a woman, a white woman at that, and point me toward the door, but no one seemed to care. For the first time in my life, I felt the magic that is a bunch of non-working adults gathered around a large pot of coffee for days on end.

The political situation was so confusing and dramatic that after a week or so of hearing about the unfolding controversy, I possessed only a single reliable fact: These people are pissed.

I decided I should take a walk and interview people across the settlement on how they felt about the controversy. Sitting in our host's kitchen, I asked what seemed to me a perfectly reasonable question: Would anyone like to give me a ride somewhere closer to the action? A man sitting next to me barked that no, he would not give me a ride. I looked at him, surprised at the tension in his voice. Maybe I could walk, I suggested, then noticed that the woman sitting on the other side of me had blanched white. She told me it wasn't safe to walk across the settlement. Her eyes were wide.

Her fear, and the obvious horror with which my companions viewed my planned excursion, formed a sharp point that moved very close to the big balloon of my white complacency. These people weren't crazy. Things were genuinely tense on the settlement, and it seemed possible that bad medicine might somehow, somewhere, for some people, be real. It was, in fact, excruciatingly real for the people in the room with me now, people who had been unfailingly kind and generous to me.

I felt very meek and small. I didn't know who, if anyone, was in the right in this tribal imbroglio. But if bad medicine actually existed, I didn't want to get any on me, and I certainly didn't want to bring any back to Stanford's friends.

The premise of our trip to Iowa, it now slammed into my consciousness, was that bad medicine is real. The point of this trip was not my entertainment or education; it was the protection of Stanford's Meskwaki friends. They locked their doors every night. Stanford and company all jammed together in the Winnebago. And me, I went to sleep in the middle of the lawn in a tent, protected by two layers of nylon, one layer of white skin, and many centuries of cultural denial of this sort of thing.

I felt disoriented, in serious need of getting off the settlement for a white girl's night off. I wanted to get on the phone and talk to Peter and my mom. Several people immediately offered me rides. I was escorted to the Super 8 motel in Tama like a little girl with matches being escorted out of a fireworks factory.

CHAPTER 8

LITTLE WHIRLWIND

A couple of nights later, I sat next to Stanford in the sweat lodge as he writhed and moaned, attacked by what he said were the bad intentions flying around the Meskwaki Settlement. He did this in his usual position, lying on his stomach and propping his torso up on his elbows. Afterward, he said he'd been scratched on his back.

Uh-huh, right, I thought, looking for proof.

A playing card–size patch of his skin was reddened, as if by sunburn. The burn was in the shape of a three-clawed scratch. My heart froze for a moment. I'd been sitting several inches from Stanford the entire time. I would have known if anyone had scratched him. No one had even touched him, except for me, when I adjusted the towel he draped over his head, and the men who carried him out when he needed some cool air.

Let me give a little background here. In the few days since I'd gotten over my fear that Stanford would use his powers on me, my attitude about his spiritual prowess had become one of detached respect. When he told me stories about being shepherded out of dangerous bars by ghosts back when he was a teenager, or what a spirit told him to do to cure someone of cancer, I did what a journalist is expected to do: I wrote it down in my notebook, the same way I'd written down the opinions of someone running for governor, or someone who had just won the lottery. It wasn't my job to find out if these guys were telling God's Honest Truth.

But when I saw the scratch-shaped burn on Stanford's shoulder, my centuries of conditioning that spirits don't exist wore just a little thin. A few days later, I had an experience that wore it nearly completely through.

I was standing on a lawn chair outside the window in the Winnebago that looked onto Stanford's bed. He was lying under the covers and we were having the morning chat that had become a regular part of our day. He told me he had invoked a spirit called Little Whirlwind. Her job, he said, was to relieve people of their grudges. I opened my notebook and wrote, "Rx for grudges: Little Whirlwind." Good idea, I thought, in a place where people harbored so much ill will.

A couple of days later, I set out on my daily jog down the side of a cornfield. It was a spectacular late-May day: still, warm, sunny, with a few plump white clouds sitting in the clear blue sky. I ran down the driest part of the field I could find, rounded some trees, and nearly ran into a very large whirlwind. A sub-tornado, actually. About forty feet high, the size of a grain silo, it ripped cornstalks and little branches into the sky.

My first thought was "Wow! Little Whirlwind! I should run in there and get rid of all my grudges!" But that was nixed by a second thought: I could dislocate a shoulder or lose an eye in that ripping, spinning pillar of flying debris.

I skittered around the erratically moving twister, ran back to camp, and reported what I'd seen. Iowa was tornado country, wasn't it? I was surprised to find that none of the Meskwakis had ever seen such a thing on the settlement. They'd never seen anything bigger than a dust devil.

Stan was smiling quietly. "Got any really big grudges?" he said.

"Only about six hundred and thirty-two of them," I said.

Meaning, ha ha. Meaning, not really.

Not long afterward, a Meskwaki friend of our host who was deeply involved in the controversy saw a big whirlwind, too. This made perfect sense. He had been threatened with violence; he was angry and hurt. Little Whirlwind seemed like just the ticket to help him move through the next tricky weeks in an unvengeful, constructive way.

But no one else had seen a whirlwind. Not the Meskwakis whose jobs, social standing, safety, and casino income were at stake. Not members of the tribe who were regulars at the sweat lodge. Not even the people, Native or white, who had been incarcerated or had regular run-ins with the law. Nobody did except us two. Why me? Was the spirit world showing off for the white media? Or did I have a grudge I wasn't aware of?

I spoke to the man who had seen the whirlwind. It had been several days since he'd seen it, and now he had bigger things on his mind, like the fact that he'd ended up in the emergency room a couple of nights before when he'd been burned in a fire he'd built to incinerate a pile of thistles he'd cut from his yard.

"As soon as I lit the match, I was blown back," he said. "I smelled burning hair and flesh. I had secondary burns on my nose, cheek, and ear."

He fell silent, and we looked at the hills and fields. It looked like Hobbits could live here.

"To me it's obvious what's happening," he said. "There's always been bad medicine . . . It's what the people were given to protect themselves years ago. Now we don't fight other tribes. We turn it on ourselves."

A few days later, we packed up the Winnebago and went to our next destination—a medical conference in Rock Island, Illinois, where Stanford was one of four Native healers scheduled to speak.

As we barreled down Interstate 80, Stanford told me the sweat lodges had helped the Meskwakis. Things were safer and more stable now than they had been before. It made sense to me. After that much praying, that much sweating, that much time next to this gentle man, I felt changed, too. The heat of the sweat lodge is so intense, your skin burns if you don't cover it. During the ceremonies, my heart pounded with its biological commitment to getting my blood to my skin to cool it, except that the surface of my skin was where the heat was the most intense. My blood careened back and forth, filling my capillaries with hot blood. Hot blood, it started to dawn on me, laced with something else. Stanford was leaking faith in the sweat lodge. He leaked divinity. I wasn't used to the struggles with bad medicine that were swirling around me, and I wasn't used to their cure, which was prayer. But Stanford's faith was leaking onto me. My heat-softened cells, my nerve endings searching blindly through the heat for relief, received his prayer instead: Creator, have pity on us. Keep these people healthy and safe. Bring peace back to this place.

Stanford had also held sweat lodges for the Iowans' personal problems. One couple who smoked a lot of pot came in.

"Man, I feel like one big eyeball," Stanford told me afterward. "My eyes are real dry, like when I smoked dope every day."

Another time he turned to me and said, "Cancer tastes real rotten when I get it out of someone. But then I spit it out."

"Where do you spit it?" I said, instantly apprehensive. "Like, somewhere someone could step on it? Or somewhere I could pitch my tent?" I pictured a little pulsing piece of cancer moving my tent floor minutely up and down, up and down.

"I don't know where it goes," he said. "Maybe it goes to outer space."

Even Stanford didn't fully understand everything that happened in the sweat lodge, which didn't bother him at all. Stanford was noninsistent to the core, and the sweat lodge fostered that kind of surrender. My years as a journalist had made me pretty insistent, but I didn't feel any need to ask questions about the sacred objects that I handled for Stanford in the sweat lodge. I didn't care. They were instruments. So were the people who prayed in the lodge, including me. I did what I was told. It was restful. I would listen and pray for the person the lodge was being held for, as well as the people in my own life who were suffering.

The morning after the last sweat, Mark and I had taken a walk, a habit I was trying to instill in him so he could slim down and better deal with his diabetes. I liked talking to him; he was friendly and avuncular, and I felt he was key to my growing understanding of Stanford and the Native world.

"I think my heart became totally whole in that sweat," I told him as we batted away mosquitoes and headed for the river. "I think I can take anything now."

"Oh, Lisa," he said. "Be careful what you say."

CHAPTER 9

A TERRIBLE PHONE CONVERSATION

For the next leg of our journey, we moved into a big old hotel in Davenport, Iowa, just across the Mississippi River from Trinity hospital. I had my own room with a phone and a shower. It smelled moldy, but it looked great. And it was wonderful to have easy access to a phone.

Of course, phones can deliver any kind of news. On my second night there, I returned from an evening watching Mark win $140 in gas money playing blackjack at the casino, and I got a phone call from Peter.

"Hi, honey!" I hollered with the happiness of someone having a damn good adventure.

"Hi," he said quietly. He didn't sound like himself. He sounded dismayed and sad. He was, he told me, seriously attracted to another woman.

This seemed impossible. Peter was about as flirtatious as Thomas Merton. Nothing like this had ever happened in our four-year relationship. He sounded as shocked as I felt. He had met her at the Tibetan Buddhist retreat in California.

"Did she come to Paonia because of you?" I gasped.

No, she had another friend there who was going to install a new part on her car. The chemistry between Peter and the woman, whose name was Mariel, had started a few days ago. In our own kitchen. My kitchen. I'd painted its cabinets yellow and tiled the floor black and white. The whole thing had come out of nowhere, Peter said.

We sat for a moment in mutual astonishment.

"Is she pretty?" I choked.

Yes. And they liked to meditate together. She had spent years in Nepal. She had lived in an ashram in India. She was a Tibetan Buddhist with years of experience.

I took a breath. "A car part?" I said dumbly. "To *Paonia*?"

"Yeah," he said. "A transmission." He paused. "She wants the same things I do. I think our lives could be a perfect fit." He sounded like he was describing an unwanted medical diagnosis.

"I should fly home right now," I said. There was an airport here, wasn't there? But I would be home in three days anyway, and my car was in Wyoming.

I felt like I was spinning through space. I was somewhere in the Midwest with a bunch of Native men I had known for about two weeks, and the relationship with the man with whom I wanted to spend the rest of my life was on the verge of falling apart.

I barely slept that night, and the next morning the thought of spending the day alone in my musty hotel room was unbearable. So I went with Stanford to the conference: "Developing Awareness of Native American Traditional Healing Practices."

Oh God. This conference. This hell. Either my day was going to be one of the worst I'd ever lived through regardless of what I did, or this really was the most dreadful conference I'd ever attended. Its too early start (eight A.M.), its supermarket Danish (pineapple), its not quite ripe strawberries that skittered away from the jabs of my plastic fork and dropped onto the orange carpet, the two women who had organized the event in a bitter, silent feud.

But the event organizers had the right idea. About fifty nursing students and medical staff at Trinity hospital heard about the potential for conflict between, say, a medicine man holding a bunch of smoldering sage and a nurse who didn't want an oxygen tank to explode next to her patient. Or between a medicine man afraid of the destructive power of a woman who was "on her moon" and a nurse who didn't think her menstrual cycle was anyone's damn business, and certainly no reason for her to stay away from her patients. Trinity was forward-looking. It already had a staff member whose job it was to pray during operations in the surgical theater.

The presentation started with a pair of brothers from a tribe in Oklahoma. One was an office-equipment salesman, the other a motivational speaker. They talked about how everything is connected to everything else, how their parents' tribes traditionally walked in different directions around a fire, how God blew into a shell and created someone called *anish-na* man, how Western medicine just wasn't to be trusted.

"I had acupuncture when my arm got hurt!" the motivational-speaker brother nearly shouted. "I distrust Western medicine *that much*!!! So I went to Chinatown, and a Japanese man put needles in my arm!"

His speech roared and bubbled along like a river, and the heads of the nurses and radiologists bobbed along with it, their pencils hovering over notebooks with well-intentioned expectancy, but failing to find a statement with sufficient gravity to make those pencils land.

Preston Duncan was next. Everyone leaned forward in their chairs. Preston appeared to have been selected from a casting call for most gorgeous older Native male in the Midwest. He was sixty-two years old, and each one of those years seemed to be working for him. His square, muscled frame topped six feet, and he wore new jeans, a blue shirt with a feathery design, a brightly beaded medallion, and polished cowboy boots. His eyes and nose were pure poetry, and his long gray hair was pulled back in a ponytail that looked strong enough to bind bridges together.

He was a Meskwaki, but he started his presentation by saying his names were Scottish; his first name meant "dark warrior," his last, "golden warrior." Wanting very badly to write something in my notebook, I recorded this.

Then he said, "But I don't have any Scottish blood in me at all."

Boredom rose in my chest the likes of which I hadn't felt since junior high school. Could I jump out a window? Could I run out the door? But I could see the barely suppressed thoughts about the state of my relationship with Peter inside my head, and my mind snapped back to the safer environs of Preston's talk.

Preston broached the subject of menstruation. Many Native healers considered it a potent enough source of "dark power" that they didn't allow women in the sweat lodge when they were on their cycle. Stanford mostly followed that rule, but tactfully attributed it to the belief that women "were too powerful" at that time of the month. Preston said that even some canneries wouldn't allow women to work while they were on their cycle, because they were so full of dark power.

"I hope you're not mad at me," he concluded, drawing a tense laugh from the nursing students. I had known Preston for a couple of weeks now, and I knew he was capable of evoking uncomfortably opposing feelings in women. On one hand, the words coming out of his mouth were, from a feminist perspective, straight out of another century. On the other hand, he was friendly and well intentioned, not to mention possessed of a physique so harmoniously constructed that just looking at him made the universe seem like a less confusing place.

Preston sat there looking compassionate for the painful feelings women seemed to experience so often. He was used to it; he hadn't asked to be built like Michelangelo's David, holding strong into his seventh decade, but there it was. He hadn't asked to be a spiritual healer, but he had been given medicines years ago that he couldn't give back. He wouldn't even sit next to Stanford out of respect for what he considered Stanford's superior powers, and he called himself Stanford's little brother even though he was eighteen years his senior.

Then Stanford was introduced. Neither slick like the Oklahoma brothers nor glamorous like Preston, he sat in a borrowed wheelchair, his thin legs poking out from a pair of cobalt-blue nylon Nike shorts monogrammed with STAN. His shirt was a white nylon hockey jersey emblazoned with blue, yellow, and red corporate logos—Ford, Tide, M&M's. Snow-white ankle socks covered his motionless feet, which were propped stiffly on the footrest of the gray wheelchair.

"I'm Northern Arapaho," he said in a soft voice powered by his single lung. "I'm kind of nervous and don't really know what to do."

A surprised, sympathetic chuckle swept through the crowd. Then the room fell silent and attentive.

He sat quietly for a few moments. "They say we're not supposed to separate our everyday life from the spirits," he said. "It's easy to talk about, but it's hard to live."

Preston tilted the clean lines of his profile toward the ceiling, looking as if he were searching out the face of God in the fluorescent lights.

"Because of all the activity and how fast Grandmother Earth is moving, it's getting harder to interpret the old ways," Stanford continued. "A lot of different situations in your everyday life mess up the balance; how we're supposed to act with creation. I don't know what to do or what to say."

That, it appeared, was the sum of his speech. He couldn't have spoken for longer than a minute. Everyone seemed astonished. They had come here for him, the real deal, a powerful healer straight from the high plains, and they'd been handed a couple dozen words and a lot of quiet. I laughed softly to myself. I had experienced this already, my white synapses tripped up by Stanford's affinity for silence.

Indian time, people, I thought.

Stanford told me he was nervous about the hospital presentation. I remembered way back in Wyoming how I'd laughed when he'd told me that. Back then I had helped Stanford draft a letter about his credentials for this conference as well as for a visit to a federal penitentiary in Wisconsin, where he had been invited to do a sweat lodge.

I had told Stanford that the prospect of sitting in the boiling dark with a bunch of murderers and rapists sounded a bit scary. Stanford was much more concerned about this medical conference.

"You're kidding!" I said.

"I've been a outlaw before," he said. "I never been no doctor."

The conference broke for lunch, and Stanford collected his nephews, who had spent the morning in tragic postures of boredom. Cody had popped an empty water bottle loudly for two hours, and Robert had sat outside the conference room in an upholstered chair with his head in his hands. Stanford took them to eat in the hospital cafeteria. Then he rolled out of the hospital, stopped about two feet past the no smoking sign at the curb, and smoked three KOOLs. The brothers from Oklahoma joined him, lighting up gratefully.

That afternoon, when the same speakers proceeded in the same order, everyone strained forward when it was Stanford's turn to speak.

"I was raised on the rez," he said. "I seen some things that should've woke me up, but I didn't pay attention, and now I see the things I should've paid attention to when I was walking.

"There's things we lost; the Catholic missionaries stripped us of a lot of our culture.

"They [the spirits] started showing me things I should have done. And I started doing the things they asked me to do, that they wanted me to do. Now I got a better understanding of what's important in life. In the medical field, Grandpa used to tell me, we need to be as kind as we can. To our heart, mind, body, and spirit. When these are in balance, that's when our prayers are strongest for the people who are hurt or sick.

"So when I came over—my brother Preston asked me to come over and speak—I wasn't sure what it was about. What I see we need to do is understand and communicate and trust each other. The Creator's the one who showed us what we need to know. Whether through the medical field or through spiritual healing. I want to thank you guys, because I don't have much of a story. So, thanks."

The audience clapped. His brevity wasn't such a shock this time. But his truthfulness and sincerity were inarguable. The crowd loved Stanford. I did, too.

That night, back in his hotel room, Stanford said, "I could have talked and talked and talked and talked, but I didn't see the point of it."

"Did the grandfather answer a lot of questions with you?" Mark asked.

"Who's the grandfather?" I interjected.

"A messenger from the Creator," Stanford said to me. Then he turned to Mark. "Yep," he said. "He was right there with me."

CHAPTER 10

LITTLE WHIRLWIND
GETS TO WORK

I called Peter to talk, but he wouldn't say what I wanted him to say—that I'd just had a bad dream, that the whole thing with Mariel had been a silly mistake—and when he hung up, I couldn't bear not talking to him, so I called him back. Three times. He begged for mercy. He was confused and exhausted, too; he needed some sleep. But Mariel was in Paonia. Not at our house, but close enough to prevent me from sleeping, and in the morning my stomach was sealed tight against food. This made the day's activity—accompanying Stanford as he escorted some ghosts out of a beautiful historic building—seem stranger than it already was.

The building was full of large windows, chandeliers, long, broad Asian carpets, huge plants, and a grand piano. Nicely framed black-and-white photographs lined the wall.

A beautiful, impeccable woman in her thirties owned the building. Her name was Rena. She had come to the hospital the day before and visited him later in the hotel. She owned a big old building nearby that she was convinced was haunted. She wore a floral skirt with a white transparent tank top and a white scarf draped artfully over her breasts. Her cell phone rang often, causing her to clatter out of the room in an exaggerated knees-together-high-heels-out feminine trot. Then she'd come back in, wind her long legs around each other, and resume talking about evil spirits. Stanford shied away from calling them evil. The spirits that inhabited her building weren't evil, he said, they were just lost. He had compassion for them.

Rena suggested she come and get Stanford at ten or earlier the next morning. He said, "I don't *do* earlier than ten tomorrow."

"So, ten," she said, rearranging herself into her final pose before leaving.

The next morning, Stanford said he felt something like nausea as soon as he rolled through the front door of her building. He took the elevator up to the third floor. Up in a spacious room lit by large windows, he faced the woman—dressed today in an elegant red skirt, bangles, and matching lipstick—and gave his report.

"The spirits aren't so bad on the first floor," he said, accepting a burger from a bag I'd just brought in. I liked the smell of the food, but I couldn't stomach more than a couple of bites. "They haven't found anything they're real attracted to, but when they get weak-minded people up here, they'll come on up."

Stan rolled his wheelchair around the room. A picture fell off the wall as he passed it, causing Rena to exclaim in a sugared voice, "You are such a lightning rod!"

Oh GAWD, I thought, making a mental note to bring this up with Stanford later so we could laugh about it. But when I asked him later what had happened, he said simply, "When I went by that picture, the bad spirits headed on out."

My mind flickered between Peter and Mariel back in Paonia, doing—what were they doing?—and the outlandish scene unfolding before me here in this well-appointed room. Who was this Rena? That morning I'd been crying in a phone booth in the hotel lobby when Mark gathered me into his arms to comfort me just as Rena walked in the door.

"What's wrong?" she demanded.

I didn't have the strength to hide my feelings, I told her.

"Men," she shot. "You must outwit them; lie to them if necessary."

And now here she was, gushing all over Stanford while he replied in straight, quiet little sentences. Growing up, I was the middle of three sisters; I befriended women more easily than men. But suddenly, the female world seemed strange and hostile. Who was this woman trying to seduce Stanford? Who was that woman in Paonia, circling my life like a hungry shark, trying to snatch Peter?

I picked up a Coke I'd bought along with the hamburgers and went to play pool with Cody in the next room. Around his quiet friendliness and rounded benevolence, I felt instantly better. Cody was twenty-one. He had two kids at home with his girlfriend Nicole, and she was pregnant again. He was an enthusiastic father, leading his kids around on horses during Stanford's clinics with a quiet smile on his face. Stanford depended on him.

"He helps me out," Stanford told me. "Not only that, he'll stop his own fun to help me out." Cody had been an intrepid driver on the long stretches of our journey. He'd fixed the sewage pipe when it detached from the Winnebago tank while Mark and Robert and I stood near the splattering sewage, giggling with embarrassment and horror. At a gas station a few days before, Cody had asked if I would buy him a *Maxim* magazine. He didn't have any money. I hemmed and hawed, trying to get out of it, but I relented when I realized how homesick he was. He read me some of its jokes. They were funny.

We played pool in merciful silence. After a while I went back to the conversation in the next room. Rena wanted Stanford to come back in a few months and smudge the place while she charged people to come and watch. He backpedaled out of it with such soft language it was hard at first to know what he was doing. But he'd changed direction like a breeze. He never charged for his services; he sure wasn't going to let someone else do so. He wasn't coming back here.

That night Stanford held a sweat lodge for some of the participants in the hospital conference. The heat clobbered my body and my sadness crawled through my heart. I lay in the fetal position and cried.

"You're doing real good, Lisa." I heard Stanford's voice over my sobs, above me in the dark. "You're gonna be fine."

The next morning—after my second sleepless night in a row, and after Stanford stopped to smudge a house to help a little girl living there get rid of her nightmares—finally, blessedly, we started driving back to Wyoming. Mark peeled out of Davenport so fast he smashed one of the Winnebago's side mirrors on a post and didn't slow down. Stanford and I looked at each other and laughed. As soon as we hit the interstate, I seat-belted myself into the passenger seat and fell asleep for fifteen hours.

I called Peter from a pay phone in Wyoming. He'd taken a long walk with Mariel by the river near our house. She wasn't right for him after all. They hadn't even kissed.

"Oh," I said, numb as a snowman.

I climbed back into the Winnebago, fell asleep again, and when I woke up we were just a few miles from Stanford's.

I went to the back of the Winnebago where Stanford was lying. Robert got up and left without a word. There was nothing left to be shy about. These guys had been so gentle with me when I needed it I felt like part of the family. I lay down in the spot Robert had warmed.

Stanford launched right in: "That woman Peter messed around with, she's nothing," he told me. "But he ain't there for you, either. Not when you really need him. And he ain't gonna be, either, not unless you're really patient."

"How patient?" I said.

"A couple years," he said.

A hundred yards from his place, the dirt road was abruptly teeming with kids running, welcoming us, looking a lot like the third-world kids Stanford's nephew had imitated three weeks ago.

I helped unpack and became absorbed in the surge of nieces and nephews and mother and sisters flowing around Stanford, all happy to see him safe, proud of him, beholding him home at last. It was midafternoon when I woke up to the fact that I wasn't actually staying. I still had an eight-hour drive ahead of me, and no idea what kind of homecoming awaited me in Colorado. Reluctantly, I got into my own car and pointed it south.

When I got home, Peter and I greeted each other calmly and started negotiating a way to be together. He had told Mariel he wanted to cut off contact completely, and she had agreed. He was committed to me but still shaky about what had happened. One morning I noticed he was at his computer for an awfully long time. This was unlike him. As he tapped away, I realized, Oh my God, he's e-mailing her. I waited for my chest to swell with the anger and self-righteousness I had felt every other time I'd been in this sort of situation, but instead, I felt as if I were wearing someone else's nervous system. It was as if my heart and mind had been colonized by Mother Teresa. I could only think calm and charitable thoughts. I thought, Well, he's got to have some kind of resolution with her. And he's not seeing her or talking on the phone. I went to our front porch and sat in the sun.

Stanford called me later that day to see how I was doing.

"Stan, did you put a spell on me?" I asked. "I'm being way nicer than I really am."

"I didn't put no spell on you," he said. "I just gave you some protection. The whirlwind was to get you through a tough time, and the protection root was so you wouldn't hurt yourself by saying things you don't mean."

Oh. I thought all that had been for the situation in Iowa. But I'd been wrong. So. A protection. A spell. A whirlwind. The earth raised itself from its axis and readjusted itself. I could feel it.

CHAPTER 11

STANFORD'S EDUCATION

I'd gone through my life thinking I was open-minded, that I embraced mystery and new experiences. But what I meant was that clouds are mysterious. I meant that death and oceans are mysterious. Biking through Costa Rica was the kind of new experience I really liked. My sense of adventure did not include replacing my personality with someone else's.

But I didn't need to worry. The change wasn't permanent. My usual self was fully in charge in about four days. When Mariel let Peter know she might move to Paonia—even though she didn't know a soul here beyond the friend she'd come to visit in the first place, and Peter—I stopped channeling Mother Teresa and started channeling Wyatt Earp. Ours was a town of fifteen hundred people, twenty-five miles from the nearest traffic light. Herds of sheep occasionally trotted down Grand Avenue, and a couple of miles from town mountain lions took down ranch dogs in the full light of day. The community was closely knit; you couldn't hide from anyone. I called Mariel and told her—and I think I actually used these words—that the town wasn't big enough for the two of us.

"You're so hostile," she said, all innocent and taken aback.

"You are correct!" I shrieked, like a demented game-show host. "I am really, really hostile! I am glad you get how hostile I am! Now get out of my town!"

She did.

I felt shaky. Recent events—Mariel and, to a greater degree, the whirlwind that had helped me negotiate the effect she'd had on me—

were messing with my sense of sureness. I felt jackknifed in the middle of the logical progression of ideas and events that constituted my life. I started saying no to party invitations and taking a lot of walks.

I called Stanford. New and unknown experiences were his specialty. He told me about his twelve-year transition from a rageful, suicidal young quadriplegic to someone who healed people, physically and spiritually. "The doctors told me I'd be dead in twelve years, so after twelve years, I started trying," he said. "I really started applying myself."

During those confusing months after he came home from the hospital and played the unwilling host to spirits at his parents' house, he turned to his uncle, a medicine man named Three Bears. Three Bears would visit Stanford and tell him not to be frightened. He would assure Stanford he wasn't going crazy. These visits from the spirits were just that—they were visits, and they were from spirits.

Three Bears took Stanford to fast in order to get a clearer message about what his future would hold. That meant he would stay in a specially constructed little willow shelter for four days and four nights, praying and touching neither food nor water. As soon as Stanford went near the shelter that Three Bears had built for him, "You could just feel it. It was real. Another presence, boy, that you couldn't see."

Three Bears prayed, lit a sprig of sweet sage to clear the air of negative spirits, and then, with the help of three of Stanford's brothers, carried him in. The floor was covered with long, tough weeds that Three Bears had cut in a swamp and laid down so Stanford wouldn't have to sleep on the bare dirt. Stanford was joined by his brother Glenn, who fasted along with him and helped when he needed it.

"As soon as Three Bears left, man, the spirits were shaking the lodge, hitting it, shaking the weeds up to my face real quick, to startle me," said Stanford. He felt calm. "Like I had nothing to lose. I was already paralyzed. What the hell else could happen to me?"

Three Bears had instructed Stanford that if he heard anything or got scared, to offer the spirit his pipe.

"So that's what I did," Stanford said. "I offered the pipe and prayed, and the spirits told me things I needed to do."

"What things?" I asked, the phone cradled between my shoulder and ear, tapping away on my laptop, hitting the numeral 1 so we could start the list.

"Things about my life and about how things were going to be," he said. "It was kinda like I started moving forwards instead of backwards, not like planning or plotting or nothing, but just accepting what comes."

It sounded exactly like what I needed.

"Do you think that's what I should do," I asked, "or try to think things through in a rational way?"

"If I tell you what's going to happen, you won't believe it," he said. "It's a lot stronger if you find things out for yourself. I can just help you with the direction you're already going."

We were quiet. I thought I was just writing a book about you, I thought, but now I feel like I'm falling backward into space.

"Okay," I said, propelling us back to the known world. "What happened next?"

After Stanford fasted, he was sitting in the sweat lodge one evening with Glenn, Three Bears, and Three Bears's wife. Three Bears told Stanford that he wanted him to run the lodge that night. There was no one else in there. Feeling expansive, he said sure he would.

Moments later, a whole truckload of people showed up, ready to sweat.

Stanford panicked. "You run it!" he said to Three Bears.

Three Bears stood up, walked over to where Stanford was lying on the floor and sat next to him. "You said you would run it, right?"

"Yeah."

"So what's the argument?"

There are some places where a person might have continued trying to wiggle out of this situation, but Three Bears's sweat lodge wasn't one of them. When Arapahos give their word on a spiritual matter, it isn't taken lightly. "Our word is more powerful than our body," Stanford told me later. "That's how we communicate with the Creator. We need to get our word as true as we can, or our hardship's gonna just keep going on and going on."

Stanford prayed shakily for guidance. It came. He led prayers and talked to the spirits. As the evening progressed, he was filled with a feeling of rightness.

"I think I darn near cried the whole sweat, because I was happy." he said. "Because I knew I wasn't insane."

Stanford held thirty sweat lodges in thirty days. A Crow basketball player named Beau Little Light came to Stanford's with a bum knee. Beau was enthusiastic; he cut wood for the sweat lodge every day. The sweat lodges lifted Stanford's spirits, and they cured Beau's knee.

"I'd been doubting myself and doubting the spirits, and everyone— my white teachers in school and even some elders from other tribes— was telling me Arapahos didn't have spirits, but we did," said Stanford. "And so I went in and felt them, and it made me feel good that the Creator still heals us. Seeing Beau Little Light's leg get better, that made me feel good. It kind of made everyone know, you know, that there is help. Help from the Creator."

CHAPTER 12

BEAUTY AND RUIN

JUNE 2003

I wanted to go back up to Stanford's. Peter wanted to come with me. This surprised me, but I was glad he was interested and even gladder when they seemed to hit it off, giggling at each other's jokes like a pair of gnomes. He, Stanford, and I were in Stanford's room on our first night there, chatting and watching the Food Network, when Mike came in and said he'd hit a horse in the driveway. Stanford started to pray. He prayed it wasn't the horse he had been training for Ed Underwood. It had shown so much promise. Mike said he didn't think that was the horse, although he couldn't be sure in the dark. After the accident, the horse was limping but still walking, Mike said. Maybe it would be okay, he ventured. Stanford finished praying and gave Mike his rifle.

Mike went out, found the horse with the dangling leg, and shot him dead. Then he and Cody tied its carcass to the car, dragged it a mile into the sage, and left it for the coyotes.

Peter and I traced the whole thing the next day, led by Jay-R, Stanford's younger brother. Jay-R was an inveterate walker, and had been one since shortly after he survived a car crash two decades before at age twenty. The accident left him in a coma, but then Three Bears came into the sweat lodge and sucked a clot out of Jay-R's forehead without making an incision. Jay-R had made an astonishing recovery, although he lived with his mother and sometimes took such long walks in the desert that sometimes he forgot to come home.

"When he don't turn around, we call the BIA cops," Stanford told me.

We set out in the general direction of the dead horse with Jay-R and his four-year-old nephew, A.J., who was wearing a Superman suit he hadn't taken off for four days straight. We looked at the angling tire skids, the hoof prints and the long, straight marks that looked like they'd been drawn by a stick but must have been made by the hoof, which presumably dangled straight down no matter which way the stallion held his broken rear left leg.

It was a windy day. Thin clouds arced above us. The Wind River Range hulked and glimmered to the west. A.J. jumped through the sage in his blue suit and red cape, yelping when he found drops or smears of blood—which meant the horse had walked there sometime between being hit by the car and being shot—or pools of blood, which meant he'd stopped to rest or perhaps tried to make sense of his useless leg. After we got to the place where the dead horse had been dragged behind the car, there was no more blood. We walked down the parallel tire tracks the car had followed, looking at the plants flattened by the horse's downed weight.

We walked a mile up onto a plateau so beautiful that my heart involuntarily lifted. Sage and rabbitbrush streamed for miles in all directions. The thin clouds sped by and came apart in the fast, dry wind. Then, on the ground far ahead, we saw a still black shape.

"Oooh, it's scary," said A.J., standing in the tire tracks, staring straight ahead. "I'm gonna stay here."

"Yeah. You stay right here," Peter and I echoed, eager not to traumatize the little boy. We kept walking toward it.

When Jay-R reached the carcass, he called back to A.J., "He's moving! He's gonna git you!"

Peter and I walked to the horse and around it. He lay on his side, his brown eye staring westward, its surface covered with a film of dust. His hoof, attached to about six inches of leg, angled down like a plumb line. A pool of blood the size of a dinner plate had congealed on the dirt under his muzzle.

My stomach clenched like a fist. This wasn't just any horse—this was the black stallion I had ridden in Stanford's corral the summer before. The sweet, scared little stud. The one who'd reared up and sent me flying into a new part of human experience. That day he had moved so beautifully with his best buddy, the paint. His black hide, once so shiny it looked wet, was now dull with dust. I'd stood over his downed body on the day we had thrown each other, but he'd struggled to his feet and we'd made our peace. Then I had brushed him, thanked him.

His leg was snapped as simply as a pencil, and his handsome, fine head was going to turn to bone and rest on the dust right where I stood.

Three dogs that had followed us up from Stanford's started licking at the bloody mess beneath the stallion's nose. Then they milled around in a tail-wagging way, and soon, with apparent satisfaction at their great providence, they discovered the horse's anus. They started pulling at it with their teeth.

The last time a nurse drew blood from my arm, I looked at the test tube for too long and fainted right there in the plastic chair. Now I was over forty years old, and I didn't have a place to put the sight I saw before me. Life on the reservation was too harsh for me. I was too damn sensitive: too sensitive to break the horse in the first place and certainly too sensitive to watch his lower intestine be dredged in the dust like a chicken breast through flour. I turned to look at the mountains and crossed my arms over my churning abdomen.

"I've got to get off this reservation," I mumbled to Peter.

He found my hand and held it.

I was happy when Peter and I turned our car back to Colorado. A pattern was forming. In the sun-blasted spaces of Wyoming, I'd be hit by nearly unbearable waves of fear and joy. In Paonia, in our old house mercifully shaded from the Colorado sun by two huge trees, I'd recover.

One morning in August, I walked into Stanford's kitchen and found Moses Stark sitting at the kitchen table. A big white cowboy with his legs stretched out in front of him on the bench, he was hand-rolling a cigarette. The only other white people I'd met at Stanford's were horse clinic participants who came a few times a summer and the home nurses who drove up in their Subaru, changed the dressings on Stanford's pressure sores, and drove off again. White people—or maybe it was just me—were prone to scuttle through Stanford's house, apologizing with their whole bodies for their presence and the events of the past. But Moses wasn't passing through. He had no Subaru; he had a huge, mechanically corrupt yellow GMC pickup parked with an air of permanency outside the house. He was tall, with Wrangler jeans and a thinning blond ponytail. His face was half burned. Not sunburned, although he looked fair enough to get a good sunburn. No, Moses's face had been half melted in an eye-socket-altering way in a 1989 truck fire that had also killed his best friend. My eyes kept flitting from the unscathed side of his face to the burned side, trying to register an average. But there wasn't one. There was unscathed golden skin over an enviable bone structure on one side, and there was a pocked, scarred mask on the other.

Beauty and ruin. Ruin and beauty.

Moses had spent the better part of the last decade in and around Stanford's house, although for the past two years he'd been home in Washington State to help his stepfather, who had been dying of cancer.

Moses looked back at me with a steady and appraising gaze similar to the one Stanford had given me a few months before when I met him for the first time. What was that look? Was it a reservation thing? No, I remembered, I'd also received that look from ranchers, who regard journalists who had taken the trouble to find them at their isolated homes with the quiet and unblinking attention they directed toward a dog that was behaving strangely, or a malfunctioning irrigation pipe. It wasn't shy or coy or angling. It was more practical and inquiring. It was a look that asked, with equal parts curiosity and equanimity, Are you going to blow under pressure? Are you in heat?

There was a copy of *Smithsonian* magazine on the table next to Moses. The article had just come out, a year after I'd worked with the horse. A positive, straightforward piece, yet I still felt a little nervous about how it was going to be received.

"So you're Lisa," said Moses. "I just read the story. I think you're the perfect person to write about Stanford. It's kind of hard not to see you as some sort of goddess savior."

Well, I thought, my mind bunching up in surprise at what I had just heard. Hello, yourself.

He got up and went to the corral, mounted a horse, and rode off.

*   *   *

Back home, Mariel had left town, but her influence endured. Her stories about the years she'd spent with Buddhist teachers in Nepal and gurus in India had made Peter realize he wanted to go to Asia, too. This news brought us down to something we'd both been avoiding: I wanted to get married, but he couldn't make that kind of commitment because he couldn't rule out the possibility, however tiny, of someday being ordained as a monk. Meaning a guy who was working all day on removing "the three poisons"—greed, hatred, and delusion. Meaning a guy who shaved his head and wasn't allowed to be alone with a woman.

To say I resisted Peter's attraction to monasticism would be an understatement. I forgot about it, then denigrated it, stomped on it, wanted to obliterate it. It was one thing for natural introverts, I argued, but hadn't he recently sung a whole lot of Prince songs in falsetto to a row of stunned coal miners on karaoke night at the Paonia bar? He loved to talk, he played piano in a local jazz band, he could make me feel so much desire it hurt. I couldn't imagine him as a silent celibate. But I also knew that no one can stuff down dreams with any real success.

As great a threat as pretty, slim Mariel had been, she was nothing compared to the plump and smiling Buddha. She was bound by attachment and had everyday flaws. Not Siddhartha Gautama, the Indian prince who had left his family and a life of wealth and comfort to pursue the truth of existence.

I was worn out. "You should check out a monastery while you're in Asia," I said.

"That's not the point of the trip," he said.

"Make it the point," I said. "I want to get married. You can't because of the possibility of wanting to be a monk. Figure it out. Quit wasting my time."

We spoke to a counselor. She asked me how I felt about Peter.

"I adore him!" I shouted.

"I think you're very angry."

And so I was, although I wouldn't realize it until well after the October day when the man I'd pegged as the love of my life took the bus to Denver and boarded a series of planes that would take him to his favorite Tibetan teacher in Nepal. He would rent a room there and attend teachings every day. Then he would see if he could go to Thailand and spend some time at a monastery in the forest, just seeing what it was like. He would be gone for five months.

I spent a good part of the month before he left sobbing that this would surely be the end of us. He looked guilty and frozen, all the more so when his attempt to reassure me backfired: "There's only a five percent chance I'll take robes permanently."

"Five percent!" I howled. "What if I told you there was a five percent chance I'd get kicked to death by some horse? Would that be good enough for you?"

Right around this time, a writer friend of mine pointed out that it wasn't very wise to take one's unmet personal needs into one's journalistic work. I'd never had a problem keeping my personal needs under wraps for the fifteen minutes it took to conduct a newspaper interview, or even the few days it took to get material for a lengthy magazine piece. A book was another story. It required months, at least, in the company of one's subject. And if the book happens to concern a powerful healer with psychic powers, forget about it. Despite my attempts to appear dignified around Stanford, I could feel him reading me as if he had infrared vision. And with my beloved freshly gone to see if he would rather be celibate than spend his life with me, I imagined Stanford could see the shrunken, wincing shape of my heart. Being measured against another person by one's partner is one thing, but being measured against a life of celibacy is another. From a romantic point of view, I felt worse than nothing.

In January I drove to Stanford's for a sweat lodge. Afterward, when a couple dozen of us had polished off ham hocks and fry bread and ginger cake, I announced my intention to camp outside, where the temperature registered 11 degrees. Everyone was surprised. The Arapahos have come a long way from their roots wearing buffalo robes on Colorado's Front Range—on winter nights the kids all ask for a car ride even to go to Grandma's house, which is all of three hundred yards down the road—but they have retained a strong code of hospitality.

Stanford was baffled by my rejection of his offer of a warm bed in favor of Wyoming's January deep freeze. What I was really rebelling against was sleeping in a bed with a child or any number of dogs, not to mention cigarette smoke. I was expressing my own version of a basic human right: a clean, solitary, quiet, child-free, smoke-free, dog-free, uninvadable sleeping space.

Moses understood both mind-sets. He came up to me and asked quietly, "Why don't you open your mind?"

The question really annoyed me. Wasn't I opening my mind simply by being here?

"I'm really interested in eight hours of sleep," I replied. "And I really do think I'd sleep better in a tent."

"Maybe eight hours of sleep isn't the most important thing," he suggested.

"Well, a couple of years ago I had a really hard time sleeping for months, so I disagree," I said. "Eight hours of sleep *is* the most important thing. In my whole life."

But it was freezing out there. The dirt was frozen so hard I wouldn't be able to drive a tent peg into the ground. So I got into the same bed I'd slept in before we went to Iowa, only this time Tisha, its owner, was in it. I popped a couple of Tylenol PMs and slept for exactly eight hours. Shortly before I woke up, I had a dream that Moses had pulled Tisha out of bed by her ankles, she yelling her protest. He had helped her find some clothes to put on and cajoled her to brush her hair properly. All of this passed in a jerky, dreamlike way, and when I finally emerged at nine in the morning, everyone under the age of eighteen had left the house, leaving Stanford sleeping in his bed, me stumbling toward the coffeepot, and Moses drinking coffee by the kitchen table, his legs stretched out before him and his usual hand-rolled cigarette in his hand.

"Good morning," I said.

"Morning," said Moses. "Sleep okay?"

"Yeah," I said. "Moses, did you pull Tisha out of bed by her ankles?"

"Yep," he said. "I was trying to get her out without disturbing you."

"Was she screaming?"

"Yep. Sorry if it woke you. She just won't *git* up."

"Wow. Did you do her hair?"

"I can't do it," he said. "My left hand don't work." He held up his scarred claw.

Later, the kitchen started filling with Arapahos and visiting Meskwakis. I sat down next to the one I knew best and peppered him with questions about the latest political news from Iowa.

"Man, you're an interrogator!" said Moses. Everyone in the kitchen laughed quietly into their coffee in obvious agreement. Moses continued, "Just hanging out, just visiting, will get you a lot farther than asking a bunch of questions."

Everyone laughed again, and I did my best guess at a gracious smile as I slugged back some coffee and thought: 1) There is nothing more condescending on God's green earth than a white person who thinks he's got the Indians *all figured out*; and 2) One day I will have my revenge on you, white man.

What I didn't know yet but would soon find out was that Moses Stark had a deeper understanding of the Arapahos than any white person I would ever meet. He'd lived on the reservation for so long that when the police pulled him and one of the Addison boys over on the highway a few years back, he'd exploded, "They wouldn't even have looked at us if we was white guys!"

The Addisons felt the same way about him. One day Moses told a visiting Lakota to clean up the mess in the kitchen, and the visitor had gotten offended and tried to start a fight. ("It was Sara Lee versus Martha Stewart," Stanford said, laughing.) Moses resisted, but when he walked away and the visitor hit him across the back with a shovel, Moses turned around and, with some regret, delivered him a pummeling.

"That Lakota guy," Stanford's mother, Stella, said later, "he wasn't even from here!"

And Moses is? I thought. He's as fair as I am. He's part *Norwegian*.

She looked at me like she'd heard what I was thinking. "When Moses sees me, he says in Arapaho, 'Hello, Mother,'" she said. "And I say, 'Hello, my son.'"

He had injected himself into their culture and spiritual practices, but that wasn't the main reason he stayed. He stayed because they were kind. The Arapaho world was the only place he'd found that had sufficient tolerance for a recovered cocaine addict or a half-melted cowboy attempting to open his furious, writhing, broken heart. Moses Stark was on the reservation for love. The Addisons had taken him in and fed him and loved him and teased the bejeezus out of him. The teasing wasn't light or politically correct, either. Once, when the pilot light on the stove went out, Stanford's sister Frenchie turned to Moses. "You light it," she said. "You're already all burned up."

At first Moses would explode at this kind of treatment.

"Man, he was hard," Stanford said softly. "Yelling around. Going off into the hills to cry."

But eventually Moses softened.

"I started thinking, Why do I think I'm so special I can't be teased?" Moses said. "The Arapahos tease. It's their way. It's from living years and years and years in teeny-tiny spaces together. They have to get along."

CHAPTER 13

MY MOTHER HELPS ME
MOVE TO THE RESERVATION

In February I drove up to stay with Stanford and his family for what would be a nearly five-month visit. I was nervous. So I did what had worked for me when I was nervous in grade school: I brought my mom. Mom was perfect for this expedition. She was adventurous and friendly and flexible and interested. She'd grown up in Sweden, spending her summers fishing and eating berries. Her connection to nature didn't lessen when we moved to Scotland, nor did it change when she rescued ducklings that were swept through a culvert away from their mother at our home in suburban Denver, or during our subsequent move to Scottsdale, Arizona, where she would prowl the huge cement irrigation canals looking for crayfish that she'd bring back in a bucket and cook for our dinner.

I was fifteen by then, and my friends' moms drove around in air-conditioned white station wagons and fed their teenage girls what they wanted—Fresca and Space Food Sticks. The sight of my mother walking through the suburban streets wearing a big hat and carrying a bucketful of squirming crustaceans made me want to die. But fifteen lasts only for a year, and I enjoyed her unabashed naturalness later in my teens when we'd be hiking in the woods of Colorado and she'd announce, "I'm going up there; I'll be back in a minute," then bolt off-trail and return a while later with sticks and bits of dirt all over her shirt, her hands full of mushrooms. Or we would be walking along on a sweltering summer day and she—in her late sixties by this point—

would jump into the river, hat and shorts and shirt and shoes and all, waving as she floated by.

She drove from Denver to Wyoming in her navy blue Volvo, and I drove up from Paonia in my twelve-year-old paint-blistered Toyota. We met in Lander and left my car parked next to the old hotel where I'd rented us a room.

"Good Lord, that was a long drive," my mother said as we continued on to the reservation in her car. "Lovely, though. Antelope everywhere."

It was almost dark when we stuck our heads through the door at Stan's. Moses was wiping the kitchen counter clean. We said hello. He took his baseball cap off with his scarred left hand and put it over his chest before offering his right hand to my mother. It was like something out of another century. She clasped his hand as if everyone greeted her this way.

In the back of the house, Stanford lay on the bed with his brothers Jay-R and Glenn. When we came in, the brothers quickly pushed themselves out of their plastic chairs and left, making me feel more honored and uncomfortable every second. My mother, Stanford, and I sat and chatted. My mom wasn't much for small talk. She started describing how angry she'd gotten at a prison guard who hadn't let her drop off some clothes to the mentally ill son of one of her closest friends the week before. "I wanted to *muh*duh him," she said.

Moses jumped right in, saying that not so long ago he had found his hands around the scrawny neck of a crazy woman who was sharing his mobile home at the time.

Well, hello, everyone, I thought. Now that you have bonded sufficiently over your homicidal capabilities, I think we should retire for the evening. My mother and I left Stanford's and drove to our motel twenty miles away in Lander.

My mom's attributes were inseparable from her most striking drawback, which was that she was drawn to interesting men as if interesting were the only thing that mattered. Perhaps it was the fact that she'd grown up in Sweden—"*not* the most interesting country in the world," she said—with an insurance executive for a father. From a marital standpoint, my mother was like a tireless nature sprite who threw herself pell-mell into hurricanes and tidal waves because they were *interesting*. Even though her divorce from my father was wrenching and she was ferocious about keeping my sisters and me housed and fed, she survived it almost cheerfully. She bounced back from her subsequent divorces as if from an especially grueling hike.

There was a lot of chaos during my teenage years, but there were also sit-down family dinners every night, often with candles and always with conversations in which I, my sisters, and any visiting friends were expected to participate. My mother's emotional generosity and genuine interest in us were infectious. Thirty years later, a high school friend told me, "Despite everything, your mother seemed deeply happy." It was true.

I grew up sociable, energetic, and completely clueless about how to stay in relationships with men. I loved romance and sex, but I could never endure the suspense over how it was going to go bad, so I'd end it myself.

"You're so *cold*," said one of my boyfriends—a kind, loving, funny, musical, intelligent man—as we broke up after seven happy years together. He was right. Things had become difficult, so my heart had turned to ice. I couldn't do anything about it. I couldn't feel anything.

That wasn't my current problem, though. The dynamic that had prevailed in my youthful romances had reversed itself. Now I could feel too much. Peter was in full flight from me, I was sure of it, and his 95 percent chance of a permanent return from Asia looked to my eyes like a bunch of platitudes over a 5 percent chance of doom that throbbed and grew with a vigor only I could detect.

The next day Mom and I returned to Stanford's and made spaghetti and garlic bread for the family. We were chopping olives when Stanford's mother, Stella, came over and sat down with us to tell stories about the old days. When she was young, she picked potatoes in the fields alongside German POWs. "They were real nice," she said. She also told us about the years she spent working in the kitchen at the elementary school, and how she was friends with everyone there.

"I've always liked people," she said, a smile appearing on her face the way an earthquake fissure would crack open a field. "All kinds of people. I like visiting."

She told us that sometimes the young Addison family would all go to the ditch so the children could swim in the shallow water. Or Stella and Mervin would yell, "We're going!" and the kids would pile into the car without asking a single question about what their destination might be. When they got close to the Riverton drive-in, the kids would all get into the trunk of the car, packed like sardines, so their parents would be charged a low admission to *Cool Hand Luke* or *The Poseidon Adventure*.

She told us that she never cried out during childbirth—nine times and she did not cry. "It was real bad when the pains come, and you want to scream out and cry. And my grandma was trying to stick a feather in my mouth and make me throw up. This helps birth a baby. I told her to go away.

"When [my oldest daughter] Arilda had hers, I said, 'No one's going to help you if you fuss.' I told her, 'Don't make a noise. They won't help you.'

"Then Arilda was having [her fourth and youngest son] Aaron, so we went to Riverton, and me, I'm crazy for yard sales and I was looking around. And I got some stuff at the yard sale. Arilda was in the car moaning, and we got to the hospital, and the nurse said it'd be a while. I went out and got me a pop. And when I got back, that baby was already there!"

She shook with laughter.

The house filled up with the smell of sausage and fennel and tomatoes and garlic and butter. Then it filled with nephews and soon the whole pot was gone. The next night the nephews and some nieces cooked for us. They served Indian tacos—fry bread on the bottom, meat sauce, cheese, and then tomatoes.

Afterward, Mom went into Stanford's room to chat. I stayed in the kitchen, cleaning up. Moses sat at what was apparently his customary place on the battered kitchen bench. A few months before, I'd seen him branding a young horse, which panicked and crashed into the corral fence, falling on his side, his legs tangled in the rails. Moses was there instantly, grabbing a thrashing hoof, levering the horse up sideways, and releasing him.

Peter had come with me on that visit. We had looked at each other, wide-eyed. "Holy shit," Peter had said. "That guy is *strong*."

The image stayed with me, the man moving directly into the flailing hooves of the panicked horse. What struck me was the lack of hesitation in a person who knew exactly how physically damaged you can get in this world; how easily it can break you.

I squeezed out the sponge and sat down across from Moses, placing my notebook on the table. He looked at me appraisingly. Eventually he said without malice, "You're the enemy."

"Pardon me?"

"I don't want nothing to do with this book of yours," he said.

He didn't want to tell his story. He didn't want to be in it, didn't want to share his life. He shared his life story, he said, only with his lovers. "I'm hiding here," he explained.

"But don't you want to be seen?" I said, leaning forward, completely sure of my craft and goal and rightness. "I believe everyone wants to be seen."

My mom came in and sat down. Her tall-necked, long-backed presence exerted the effect over the male gender I'd observed for forty years. It wasn't just her lovely physical self; she was a gifted listener.

Moses looked conflicted. He wanted to hide, but apparently he hadn't run into too many former gymnasts from Sweden who wanted to hear his life story. He started talking. He had been the oldest of five children. His parents fought a lot. Moses remembered during one of his parents' scenes, he ran out to the corral, hugged his pony, and made a promise from the bottom of his nine-year-old heart: I will never have children if I can't treat them differently than my parents do. He never has had children.

His father left the family and their five-hundred-acre ranch when Moses was eleven. Moses tried to do all the ranch work himself, begging his mother not to move them to town. But she did, and then she remarried. By the time Moses turned fourteen, there were nine kids and four adults living in the house. His youthful chivalry thwarted,

Moses moved out. He dropped out of high school at sixteen, moved in with the first of a series of girlfriends, and started selling cocaine, heroin, pot, acid, speed, and prescription medications.

It wasn't long before he wasn't giving a thought to running into a house, stealing whatever drugs were inside, and running out with the bullets flying. Nor did he mind sleeping with women, and then sleeping with their teenage daughters as well. I looked sideways at my mother, who was taking it all in with the calm interest she'd have shown during a discussion on where the best mushrooms in Colorado were to be found. I was the most prudish person in the room. One night Moses used a car a smitten eighteen-year-old girl had borrowed from her mother for a night's adventure—robbing a pair of small-time drug dealers. The evening ended with the car squealing in circles to confound the drug dealers before the car's getaway, the windshield shattered by gunfire, and the girl calling gamely from the backseat, "We're just like Bonnie and Clyde!"

"That poor girl," he said. "I was a pure son of a bitch."

His youth reminded me of Stanford's. They had been so bad. While the young Moses Stark lacked the extended family and spiritual tradition available to the young Stanford Addison, he did have something Stanford hadn't had—a personal urgency about spirituality. When he was about twenty, he started driving regularly across the whole state of Washington to pick psilocybin mushrooms. On the Olympic Peninsula one morning, he'd downed 149 mushrooms and ended up in his tent in a rainy pasture, ranting to himself about people needing to work their whole lives away for big houses with two-car garages. Right here in this little tent was everything anyone could really need!

He'd wanted only one thing—a woman who could be as happy with tent dwelling as he was. "Where is she, God?" he'd cried. "Where's my blond-haired, blue-eyed babe who can understand this?" He'd started laughing, feeling as if his sounds were reaching across the whole universe and that he had been filled up with a huge cosmic laugh, or sob, or both. He'd thought of Jesus and started yelling, "Lord! Lord! Lord! Lord!"

He said to my mom and me, "I thought how all the suffering in this world was not only necessary, it was the only way for God's perfect plan to play itself out."

My mom nodded. She had been in a Jungian study group for years. She loved this stuff.

Moses's life obliged his vision of God's plan. Over the next twenty-five years, it handed him enough suffering that he alternately felt like an apostle and a raving maniac. It took him until he was thirty to kick heroin and cocaine with the help of a couple of Native American brothers from the Colville Reservation in Washington. Shortly after that, his best friend, Eddie, wanted to show him his new pickup truck. On the way home, a wheel fell off, and the truck rolled up onto the driver's side. Moses heard the sound of gas dripping, and the next second the cab exploded in flames. Eddie screamed. Moses knew if he breathed even once, he'd die. Moses's side, the passenger side, was farther from the roadway and closer to safety. With the last movement he'd ever make, Eddie pushed Moses up toward the window, and Moses helped, grabbing the open door of the glove compartment and levering himself up with such vigor that he shot out of the window and tumbled to the pavement.

He sat at the side of the road and watched the truck burn, Eddie's now motionless silhouette consumed by flames. A car pulled up. The driver, who knew Moses from the bars, turned white as a sheet. Moses got in and told him in a conversational tone that he didn't want to go to the tiny clinic in nearby Prosser, but twenty miles farther, to the larger emergency room in Richland.

"You'll be lucky if you make it to Prosser," breathed the driver, presumably shocked by the specter of this chatty man whose skin was hanging off his arms in charred black strips.

"I was probably still smoking," Moses told us.

Burns are excruciatingly painful when they're healing. Heroin was the only thing that could quell the pain sufficiently for Moses to do the stretching exercises required for his skin grafts to take. With the twenty-five-thousand-dollar settlement he received from Eddie's insurance company, he started buying more. Soon enough, he was hooked again.

Discouraged by his pain, disfigurement, and addiction, he thought, "Hell, I'll just kill myself."

He sent his brother out to get enough heroin to do the job, but he returned empty-handed. A prostitute named Kate had swindled him out of the money. Moses knew her, and he and Bruce went out to set matters straight. He ended up being taken in by Kate and her fellow prostitutes, who nursed him for months. He and Kate became lovers.

Moses and Kate decided to kick heroin together. They quit just before they took the bus to El Paso, Texas, and spent the three-day trip moaning and shaking. Not long afterward, Kate left Moses and Texas and returned to the Northwest.

Moses had gone to El Paso because his father lived there and needed a roommate. His father would take him out to the desert surrounding El Paso, not having a clue why Moses was heading out to fast and pray in the desert, but dropping him off all the same. Moses would walk until he ran out of food and water; then he'd stay still and pray before walking and hitchhiking back to the apartment. He gained an affinity for the desert, finding that despite its desolate appearance, it was far from lifeless. It was a mirror of the scarred body he now occupied: "Not lush, like the northern climes I was from, but still alive; still vital."

If there was one thing this guy was, it was vital. "I transformed," he said. "I got a new perception of myself."

He stayed in El Paso for four years. He read about spirituality and found himself most attracted to kabbalistic Judaism and Native American traditions.

Finally, he made his decision. "I ain't no Jew," he concluded. "And the Native Americans will take anybody."

I laughed. He didn't. It wasn't a joke.

Four years after his accident, Moses was making his way from Texas to the Flathead Reservation in Montana when he ran out of money and retreated into the Wyoming mountains.

"I was up there three weeks, fasting and praying and starving. Some cowboys gave me a bunch of boxes of canned food they were taking to their camp. On my way out, I ran into the toughest man I'd ever seen. I'd only been afraid two times in my life that another man could kick my ass. One was my dad, the other was this guy, Three Bears. Stanford's uncle. There was no doubt in my mind. He could kick my ass."

Three Bears was cutting wood for a sweat lodge. The way Moses told it, Three Bears saw Moses and thought, Who would be out here except a ghost? He studied Moses some more. Moses's long blond hair scattered over the shoulders of his thick flannel shirt as he searched for medicinal herbs.

Maybe that's Custer's ghost! Three Bears thought.

They greeted each other and loaded Three Bears's wood into his truck. Three Bears gave Moses a ride to his nephew Stanford Addison's place. Moses went into Stanford's sweat lodge that night, and stayed around for ten years.

After a few years at Stanford's, he and Stanford resolved that they were both such alpha males it would be better if Moses moved to his own place. He found one about five miles away, right outside the village of Ethete. The house was spacious, with twenty acres of pasture for his Arab stallion, Sinbad, and a couple of mares. The Episcopal church owned it, and they said he could live in it for free if he did some renovations. Moses was happy with the arrangement. At first he cowboyed for a living, then he worked at the tribal detox center. He figured he could save some money and fix the house in his free time.

But he soon discovered there was someone else in the house: a rather high-maintenance ghost. It came to him as a voice. At first Moses was congenial and practical. "You take the back of the house," he told the spirit. "I'll take the front."

The spirit wasn't interested; it wanted to talk. It made Moses feel good at first. He was doing research for a book on a subject that fascinated him—the Indo-European horsemen of the steppes. But soon enough, the spirit turned into a book critic, and Moses found it difficult to distinguish the spirit's messages from his own self-critical thoughts. The spirit made Moses feel hopeless, worthless, better off dead.

Welcome to writing, I wanted to joke, to dispel my own discomfort with the fact that Moses actually believed what he was saying about the spirit. I couldn't join him in his belief, but Moses was a born storyteller. His story, so unwillingly initiated, sprang out as polished and whole as if telling stories were all he did. He was as enraptured as we were. It seemed he was hardly aware of our presence. I stayed quiet.

Because of the ghost, Moses stopped letting Stanford's kids come over. He didn't want them to be exposed to the psychological pain the spirit could induce. He would stay home and deal with it alone.

"I wasn't trying to beat it," Moses said. "I was trying to understand it. The only way to deal with it was to know what was my pain and what was pain from the outside.

"I was getting tired," he added. "The house was getting to me. I was working long shifts as a counselor at the detox center, and I'd come home beat, too tired to resist that spirit."

He wanted some reinforcements. He contacted the church's housing committee, and they agreed to meet with him in their mission, which was just on the other side of the field that surrounded Moses's house. Now that he was experiencing the house's complicated inner life, the committee told him the whole truth: Native Episcopal priests and medicine men had tried but failed to rid the house of spirits. The groundskeeper told Moses that the former resident—the groundskeeper's own cousin—had gone crazy there.

Moses pointed out that he'd removed a lot of drywall. The walls were skeletal and exposed; perhaps it would be easier now for holy men to exorcise the spirit and bless the house. Some committee members revived an old idea of simply burning the house to the ground. Moses disagreed. He thought the spirit was weakening. So they planned a two-day series of blessings for the house involving both Christian priests and Native medicine men.

Moses left the meeting satisfied. He turned the corner to head for home. The house was in flames. The groundskeeper came up beside him.

"It knows you told on it," he said.

Moses stopped talking. The kitchen was silent. Mom and I leaned forward on the table, toward him. He sat straight up, looking past us and the kitchen. We all drew long breaths.

"Why did you stay in that house?" Mom said.

"It was a matter of principle," Moses said.

"What's principle to a guy like you?" I argued. "You don't seem like the type to do things on *principle*. That's for guys in the army, or in a monastery."

"Yeah," he admitted quietly. "You know, that was the first house I've ever had in my adult life that felt like a home."

He was visibly shaken. He walked past Stanford's open bedroom door to his own room to find some pictures from his past to show us, and a few minutes later, when he hadn't come back, I went to find him. He was hunched over a cardboard box, looking so vulnerable that I wanted to hug him. But I held back. He exuded the rawest sexuality of any man I'd ever met.

"Thank you for sharing your story," I said lamely from the doorway.

He looked at me like he'd just walked away from a burning truck.

"Remember," I continued, "you live right here on earth with regular people, too. You have a life and human companions."

"This lady I met once, a tarot reader who would travel out of her body to visit me, she told me that I wasn't just the gatekeeper," he said. "She said I was the fucking *gate*."

"I believe you," I said. I did.

I went to the kitchen, got my mom, and we drove off into the night.

CHAPTER 14

FITTING IN

This wouldn't be the last time my mom would visit Stanford's place. She would take over the kitchen with Scandinavian efficiency or, to the astonishment of everyone in the room, tell Stanford that he was pronouncing the name of the nearby village Ethete incorrectly. The Arapahos said "EE-theh-tee."

"It's Eh-theh-teh," she corrected.

"Mom," I said, horrified, "it's not a Swedish word. It's *Arapaho*."

"For 'beautiful place,'" Stanford added with the solemn respect his culture still had for its elders. I was mouthing "I don't know her" to him when my mom realized what she was doing and started laughing. We joined her.

If the mood struck her, she'd wait for the Arapaho kids to return to the corral on their favorite horse, Chief, and tell them to get off; it was her turn. Then she'd kick Chief into a trot and ride away, looking like she'd ridden all her life, which she hadn't.

"She don't seem like a white lady," Stanford would say approvingly as the woman and horse disappeared down the road. "More like an Indian lady."

Even though we'd had a great time when she was here, I thrived when she left. I rented a room in Lander so I could sleep away from cigarette smoke and interruptions. It was in the Noble Hotel, a historic place where the heads of moose and antelope looked down on the lobby from their places high on its walls. It was a great place to stay, and cheap, but I spent my waking hours at Stanford's, where I slipped easily into the daily rhythm. With a steady tide of visitors and relatives ebbing and flowing, some staying for a cup of coffee, others setting up camp on the couch for a week, I was never really clear on who lived there. There was no fixed idea of normal at Stanford's.

This suited me fine. I had fallen out of step with normalcy years before. I was a forty-two-year-old woman who had never been married or had children. I'd been proposed to several times, and I'd said yes to a couple of them, but then a hand of ice would clutch my heart, while cold lips drew near my ear and whispered, *Run.* I was thirty-seven the last time I'd done that. I broke the engagement, watched the relationship—and my hopes for a family—explode into a million pieces, and when my former fiancé quickly took up with another woman, I left the cabin we had shared.

I moved to my mother's house in Denver and spent months either lying on the floor or taking long walks around town. I held down two waitressing shifts a week at a restaurant where I was ten years older than any other member of the heavily tattooed, studded, and stapled waitstaff. I didn't pay much attention to them. I couldn't. My mind was foggy. I could barely remember the names of the specials. My mother told me I was showing classic symptoms of depression, and she suggested I see a therapist or a doctor.

"I earned this depression," I snarled, "and I'm gonna damn well have it."

I sought neither therapy nor drugs but did my best to read books on Buddhism, which I was just starting to learn about, and to meditate. Every grief I'd ever hidden beneath the sprawling network of activity and relationships that had made up my life until now came calling. All that grief broke through the wall and took a place at the table. I tormented myself with the thought that I would never find love; I kept thinking about how distant I'd felt from my father, how numb I'd been at his funeral.

I walked around the big parks of Denver, usually ending at the Tattered Cover bookstore, where I'd sit and take in the smells of coffee and paper and watch the agreeably absorbed customers. And one day, eight months after I arrived in the city, I found myself chatting with someone in line at the bookstore café. I was reaching the other side. My depression ended almost as suddenly as it had arrived.

I didn't want to go and try to resurrect my old life. I wanted something softer and sweeter. So I headed for a meditation center in Massachusetts that I had heard about. The day I got there to start work in the kitchen, one of the other cooks asked me what had brought me there.

"I destroyed my chance to marry someone I loved, left my job and my house and all my friends, moved in with my mother, and got really, really depressed," I said.

"Oh," he said, waving his hand in a way that neither judged nor diminished what I had said, but seemed to distribute it among all of humanity. "Suffering."

I loved the cool, spacious, accepting, nonjudgmental, incremental flavor of Buddhism. I loved my new boyfriend, David, who maintained the computers at the meditation center and, like an emotional emergency room doctor, made me feel completely loved, although he didn't want marriage and our relationship would last only for the year I stayed at the meditation center.

And then came Peter. He lived in an efficiency apartment with a hot plate, which seemed downright urbane to me. He meditated all the time but still engaged in the world, with a real job as a wildlife biologist and college instructor. We had enjoyed a perfect mix of the spiritual and the secular. That was then. Now he wore white robes and lived in a monastery.

I wasn't like my mother, who, despite her repeated attempts at matrimony, turned out to be happier when she was single. I wanted love and stability and a Subaru Outback with kiddie seats in it so people would stop looking at me funny.

"You want kids in those kiddie seats?" my friends would ask.

"Yes. Maybe. I don't know. I hate the way people always ask me if I'm married and have kids, and when I say neither, their faces go funny. I know I want the respect people give women who have kids. But really, I don't know if I want the kids."

So, kids, maybe not. But a husband, definitely. I wasn't one of those free-spirit hippie women who proliferated in western Colorado, buzzing around serenely, doing yoga every morning, aging gracefully, visiting every flower. I wanted to land on one flower.

*   *   *

In Stanford Addison's kitchen, I quit worrying. As I listened to the stories of my new, interesting, worthy friends, my own twists of fate started looking a lot less like doom and more like The Way Things Are. Here, outside the bubble of good fortune that constituted material reality for most people of my age, class, and race, I could actually learn something useful. This Arapaho man and his friend the cowboy had suffered more than anyone I had ever met. They'd endured physical pain I could only imagine. They had fucked up extravagantly when they were young, gotten hurt, then suicidal, but now they were kind and wise because all their misfortune had pried them away from serving their own egos above all else. They had spun the worst kind of misfortune into something reverent and beautiful and real. They showed me the rock-bottom truth so often obscured from the white middle class: Life doesn't do a damn thing you think it will do.

CHAPTER 15

THE WINTER DAYS

Stanford held sweat lodges on Wednesdays and Saturdays. The women would clean the house and the men would clean the lodge. The teenage girls—Cody's girlfriend, Nicole, or Stanford's niece Suzi—would put the chairs up onto the battered kitchen table, sweep the linoleum floor, and then mop it with Clorox. Plastic bowls of every color would be stacked on top of laminated cabinets already stuffed with coffee mugs and dinner plates. The trash would be emptied into a big hole in the ground southwest of the house.

At the sweat lodge just a few steps outside the house, Moses and Stanford's brother Jay-R would use shovels and pitchforks to take out the rocks that remained in the structure from the last sweat. Then they rearranged them on the cottonwood limbs that they had cut and stacked neatly close by. They cleaned out the ash and rock fragments that remained in the pit and dumped them on the mound in front of the sweat lodge. Then they would pull all the rugs out of the sweat lodge, sweep off the cigarette butts and dust and candy wrappers, put the rugs back inside, and collect the socks and towels that had been left there by participants during the last ceremony.

Then Moses would pat his shirt pocket and find a couple of cigarettes he'd bummed from Stanford the night before, and the brain-damaged Indian and the half-melted cowboy would relax on the row of foam-upholstered chairs that looked like they'd been spirited from Concourse B at Denver International Airport to the middle of the Wind River Indian Reservation by Salvador Dalí himself.

They would sit quietly or tell stories, and when two-year-old

Quamé would come out of the house and make a herky-jerky break for freedom in the general direction of the mountains, Moses would push up from his chair, walk over to the child, briefly tower above him, and say, "I'm taking you back to your mama, you little runaway," just as Nicole would come to the door, yelling *"Quamé!"*

Inside the newly mopped house, it would smell like a swimming pool. Stanford would sit in his wheelchair next to the kitchen table, wearing only a pair of nylon shorts. He didn't wear a shirt in his wheelchair because shirts made him slide around, aggravating the pressure sores on his buttocks that he could never quite beat. He would look out the window at the horses, stroke the side of his chin with his left forefinger, and occasionally break into an Arapaho sweat song. *"Howuunoni Beteen,"* he sang. It meant "Pity us, Creator. Our life is our prayer."

Then evening would come, and between ten and forty people would file into the lodge.

Inside, the person seeking healing rolled and lit a ceremonial cigarette, which called up the spirits. More spirits came when the people sitting in the lodge sang sacred songs. Stanford would refine the spirits' actions when he directed the afflicted people to use sage to drive off bad spirits and negative influences. Or he'd tell someone to sprinkle some powder from a mysterious source onto a piece of red-hot cottonwood from the fire, which would clear the mind and summon only good influences. Or he'd use sweetgrass to call the sickness out of a person, "sickness that the bad spirits are strengthening," he said. "You call out the sickness and those bad spirits so the good spirits can overcome them. Sometimes the sweat lodge is a showdown."

Other times, the spirits would tell him what the Creator saw as the path for healing whomever had come for relief. Once they told him that a woman with cancer didn't really want to recover; she just wanted to be comfortable for the rest of her days.

"Sometimes the spirits tell me what plants I need to get for a person, and the location of where it's at," Stanford told me. "Then I have to go and get it." Once he was directed to a plant that grew by the river and resembled sage. As promised, it cured a man of cirrhosis. "It's not like I carry it in a bag, like a medicine man would."

He considered himself merely a spiritual healer, because his healing powers were available to him only in the sweat lodge. When he threw up to funnel the bad medicine and sickness out of people, none of the vomit reached the ground because the spirits would take it.

After each lodge, Stanford met with the people who had come for help and told them what the spirits had told him the Creator wanted them to do. Over the years I would spend visiting, that advice included instructions for further ceremonies, or an explanation of where their lost child was, or a reassurance that a tumor was gone—"all that's left is dried blood and scar tissue"—or an admonishment that their cancer wouldn't kill them but their chemotherapy would, or—this, time and time again—instructions to stop drinking or using meth, a growing problem on the reservation. Stanford was middle management in the sweat lodge; he wasn't the big boss. He didn't heal people; the spirits and the Creator healed them through him.

"The Creator gives power to me, and takes it away," Stanford said.

He explained that healers could delay death, or temporarily bring someone back from the other side, but they could not stop it. "When the Creator needs you," he said, "he takes you."

One of my favorite things about the sweat lodge was that it felt like a complete experience. During the rounds, there was prayer, urgency, and pain, and then the round would end and everyone would laugh and chat and lie there together, all of us sweaty in the dark, young and old, healthy and sick, Native and white, coming through something together. That's one big difference between white life and the life I observed at Stanford's: Here people seemed to share their suffering. White people bear their difficulties alone, then smile and wave as if everything's fine. The reservation is riddled with trouble, but it felt a lot less lonely than the white world.

Even on days when there was no sweat lodge, a constant stream of people arrived looking for Stanford's help. They came in large old-model American cars, eased themselves onto the bench at the kitchen table, and sat quietly or teased the kids before going into Stanford's room to watch TV and chat or sometimes close the door to talk privately. Eventually, they would emerge, go out to their cars, and procure a folded blanket or a meat loaf in a huge disposable aluminum pan, offer it to Stanford, and drive off as Stanford called to Cody to help empty his urine bag. Cody would look up from cuddling with his daughter, Triston, or from his video game, and do what needed to be done.

Moses helped Stanford by cooking and cleaning and feeding the horses and getting kids on the right school bus. And when Stanford was helping out a visitor, or off smudging a house, Moses was happy to help me understand Arapaho ways. Passionate and talkative, he was well read in all kinds of spirituality, from the Sufis to Joseph Campbell. He wrote poetry and read a lot, checking out books on string theory from the Lander public library. Sometimes, wiping the table after dinner or crunching over a snowy field to see which mares had foaled, I would break into laughter. I felt unburdened, not just from the wondering gazes of my peers back home, but also from the puritanical hand that held my and everyone else's noses right on the grindstone of my culture's definition of success, which was production.

I soon grasped that arriving at Stanford's with a notebook full of questions didn't work. What worked was listening and watching what happened. Moses had been right.

I helped them both, by listening to their stories and cooking dinners and buying a wall clock I decorated with stick 'em rhinestones.

Occasionally, Stanford's house would lie empty, other than Cody napping on the couch and Jay-R coming in to announce he'd just found an arrowhead. But most of the time, between five and fifteen people stayed here.

Stanford's sisters were strong presences at his house. Over the months I lived there that spring, Arilda would come over about twice a day. My friendship with her progressed from tentative to almost sisterly. When I needed a break from Stanford's place, I'd go to Arilda's, help fold laundry, and sit over coffee and chat while her grandkids clambered all over us. Every adult around here had a few extra kids in tow. They'd leave them at one another's houses, and everyone there would take care of them. Stanford loved kids; babies especially. They got onto his wheelchair to take rides, clinging to him like cherubs.

At the end of every brilliantly lit winter day, the Wind River Range looked like a heaped and gorgeous feast that flamed gold and peach in the molten, freezing sunset. Most evenings, whoever was staying at the house would congregate back around the kitchen table or Stanford's bed and digest the contents of the day.

Stanford's house seemed like a version of *The Waltons*; although, unlike the Depression-era Christian farmers who bade each other good night in buttoned-up nighties from different parts of a good-size farmhouse, the Addisons who didn't manage to find space in a bed slept in their clothes on couches or the floor. All together, surrounded by snowy plains. The horses were out there, snug in their fluffy chestnut, bay, gray, and Appaloosa coats, breathing steam in the winter night.

CHAPTER 16

GOT WARRIORS?

The most noticeable residents of Stanford's house were the teenage boys. Some were furloughed to Stanford from the juvenile justice system, some were nephews, and two of them—Beau and Daniel—had been adopted by Stanford as his own sons when they were tiny. Beau was here only now and then, but Daniel was a fixture. He was seventeen years old and skinny when I met him, although it was hard to say for sure because he wore such oversize clothes. When he rode a horse near his home on the Wind River Indian Reservation, he flopped and clinked around in the saddle like a heap of black laundry encrusted with chains.

Daniel was Northern Arapaho Goth. Once I said to him, "It must be really easy to do your laundry, since everything's black."

He looked blank.

I said, by way of explanation, "When all the clothes are black, the colors don't bleed onto each other."

He looked at me quietly for a few seconds, then said with real feeling, "Yeah, but black *fades*."

Once I was talking to Stanford about the spirits when Daniel yelled, "Aaaa!" He was about four feet away from us, scrutinizing his face in the mirror. "A hair!" he hollered. "On my chin!" Being from a European and hairy race myself, I'd grown up believing that for seventeen-year-old boys, finding a hair on their chin would be an occasion for joy or perhaps relief. Not so for Native Americans. Or at least not so for this one.

He came over, thrust his chin into my face, and said, "Can you see it? Can you see it?"

I couldn't. I promised.

"Oh, man," he said disgustedly. "I look like a man who lives on a *island*."

What did that mean? Maybe he meant someone who'd survived a shipwreck. Or maybe, for a young Plains Indian whose life is all about roaming the Wyoming sage in his grandma's borrowed Cutlass Sierra—which Daniel had done with satisfaction until a few months before, when he swerved to avoid a horse in the darkness and totaled the car, emerging characteristically unscathed himself—maybe for a young guy like that, living on an island would be a confining, bad, hairy experience.

I loved Daniel even though he bred pit bulls. He gave them delicate, feminine, frontiersy names—Daisy, Eve, and Nell—but the dogs were still killers in the "I'm just playing, but oops, now I'm killing" way of their breed. They killed my favorite dog at Stan's, a little mutt named Mark that ran with the pack around Stanford's house. Daniel had been there when this happened and had been bursting to tell me about it for months, but he had been sternly instructed to tell me the little dog had been killed by a porcupine. Mark was six months dead when I found out the truth, and I was grateful for the lie.

I loved Daniel even though he wrote violent rap lyrics. A lot of the boys at Stanford's did this. What made Daniel unusual among his cousins and peers was that underneath the Goth clothes, underneath the part-supermodel, part-scarecrow presentation, underneath the rap lyrics, he was serious. More than serious; he was priestly. Other than his clothes and the pit bulls, he owned one thing: a DVD of the movie *The Passion of the Christ*, which he loaned out only with great hesitation.

Conversation:

ME: Daniel, have you ever considered really going for it as a Native American rapper, or using your looks to become a model and help your dad pay to get some decent fences around here?

DANIEL: It is easier for a camel to pass through the eye of a needle than for a rich man to enter the kingdom of God.

STANFORD, FROM HIS BED: Hey, it ain't a bad thing to make some money, if it helps other people out.

[*Silence.*]

Daniel, Daniel. Kicked out of Wyoming Indian High School in the ninth grade for fighting, he'd spent the last two years flopping around the house, borrowing cigarettes, hogging the phone to talk for hours to a girl who lived twelve hours south in Pueblo, Colorado, a geographic distance that required the squeezing of money and rides from not only his own grandmother but his girlfriend's as well.

He could charm his grandma out of twenty dollars in about twenty seconds. "She talks all tough—'I ain't giving that kid another penny!'" Stanford told me, "And then he comes in and sweet-talks her, and she gives him twenty bucks! It's embarrassing."

Stella Addison was tough, but she'd borne nine children, and now she was past seventy. She was tired. Sometimes she had her grandkids and the sundry relatives who lived in her house on a tight leash, badgering them to make pineapple upside-down cake and Spanish rice for dinner. Other times there was a brawl.

I didn't know what part Daniel played in these brawls, but he was never implicated. He was quiet, a Goth priest out in the yard playing with his dogs, moving below the radar of conflict and loss.

But then things started to change.

One night at Stella's, a guy named Luke came in and started picking a fight with Daniel. Luke cuffed him, danced around, delivering some stronger, more serious punches to his face. Daniel leaned out and socked him in the nose. Luke was taken aback.

"Why'd you do that, Daniel?" he asked, hurt.

"Cuz, man, you hit me first!" said Daniel.

It went on from there.

Daniel and one of his relatives told me the story a couple of days later, and I said, "Well, I heard Luke was drinking."

The woman snorted. "We was *all* drinking."

Which made me realize how little I knew about what went on around here, and which gave me a whole new regard for Stella, who had waded into the middle of the fight and broken it up, yelling, "I'm gonna call the cops on you kids!" and then did so.

"She called the cops on me," said Daniel, his eyes lit up with triumph and affection and acceptance of the rightful order of things.

*   *   *

The teenage boys at Stanford's house had the appearance of a bunch of pirates or rap stars from East L.A. Daniel even named one of his pit bulls Compton. The boys' clothes were black. They wore skullcaps and chains, and their hairdos were intricate combinations of shaved skin and cornrows braided close to their skulls. They listened to rap, or traditional Native music, or death-metal bands. Left to their own devices, they would have become completely nocturnal. But there were horses to be fed, and wood to be cut for the sweat lodge. There were probation appointments to be met, and court appearances, and occasional stints in jail for breaching the peace or public intoxication.

At first I positioned myself a polite distance from these boys. And by "polite" I mean "safe." But the house wasn't big enough for the distances I preferred. There was no way to dilute human contact here. As its welcome result, soon enough I found these boys in their raven-colored clothes vulnerable and sweet, and I started hugging them and pulling their hair and loving them.

Stanford commanded an enormous amount of authority over them. If a visitor needed to be smudged to receive spiritual protection, Stanford would call Daniel out of his roost at the back of the house, and he would crouch at the feet of the visitor with an eagle wing. His cousin Suzi would kneel next to him with a metal bowl with some burning cedar inside, and he would use the wing to buff the person with cedar smoke.

If a group of horses escaped, Stanford called on Beau, if Beau was around, and he would saddle up, quiet as a shadow, ride out, and bring the horses back.

Maybe the boys could take direction from Stanford because before he had been paralyzed in a car wreck at age twenty, he had done all of the bad stuff they liked to do and more. His stories of his past were all sheer reckless exhilaration. In the early 1970s, he ran away across the South Dakota border to the Pine Ridge Reservation. Tension was beginning to build around the town of Wounded Knee, which was torn between the tribal government of Dick Wilson (backed by the National Guard and the FBI) and the activist American Indian Movement. The Wounded Knee situation would lead to a shootout in which two FBI officers would die. Stanford loved sneaking over the rough ground to get close to the National Guardsmen on patrol.

After asking his uncles to go pluck Stanford out of the South Dakota grass, his parents decided to send him out of hitching distance from South Dakota—to Oakland, California, where he'd stay with his brother Glenn, Glenn's girlfriend, and their new baby.

This was fine with Stanford. "Home was too hard," he said. "Not much food. Too many people. Too much drama."

But Oakland was Black Panther territory. On Stanford's first day in seventh grade at Frick Junior High School, three black ninth-graders surrounded him and told him that Indians were stupid troublemakers, not just on Pine Ridge—which they knew about from the national news—but everywhere. Why, they asked him, were Indians even in this country?

Stanford weighed the wisdom of answering this question. These guys were big and strong, two years older than he was, on the verge of manhood. He was a skinny Native boy with long hair. So he kept silent and walked away, but the ninth-graders came after him, taunting him and telling him they were going to teach him some manners. Then they picked him up and rammed him headfirst into the brick wall of the school.

He woke up in the school nurse's office. A diminutive Asian man peered down at him: "I am Mr. Toy," he said. He taught gym at Frick. "Do you want to learn to defend yourself?"

Stanford did.

And so every afternoon, Stanford and Mr. Toy would fight. Stanford learned karate. "He was real mean, boy," said Stanford. "Never a compliment. He worked me real hard."

But Mr. Toy was Stanford's savior. He gave Stanford what he needed to survive junior high in Oakland in the mid-1970s. Stanford didn't lose a fight for the rest of the year. In fact, he didn't lose a fight for the next six. He went home, grew to six-one and 175 pounds, and kicked ass whenever necessary. Which was plenty of the time. He got into it with four hostile cowboys at a bar in Shoshoni, Wyoming, when one of them refused to pay the fifty dollars Stanford had just won from him in pool.

"The bartender called the cops, and I ran for the car," Stanford remembered. "And my friends were all in there, hiding!"

His karate background proved useful again when Stanford and a pair of his uncles got into a tussle at another bar. A cowboy rushed him. Stanford stepped back, grabbed the shoulders of the cowboy's jacket, and sent him through a plate-glass window.

He got these tendencies from his father.

"He did all these amazing things, and I wanted to be real tough for him," said Stanford. "He used to calf-rope and train his horses. I think what impressed me the most was the way he trained his horses, and the fighting stories. His brother-in-law was gonna hit him back of the head with a steel pipe one time"—Stanford, who had been watching, was about six years old—"he kept trying to hit my dad. My dad didn't want to fight him, and turned his back, and the man was going to hit him with the pipe, but just when he swung down, my dad turned around and caught that pipe. He worked him over pretty good."

Stan might be a holy man now, with no respect for meanness or senseless violence, but he never lost his respect for toughness. As for the boys' skirmishes with the law, to him they were a modern version of counting coup—the game warriors used to play with each other. You rode in and tapped your opponent and dashed off again, showing your superiority without hurting him.

"That's right," the boys would say from the kitchen table. There were four of them sitting in a row, smoking, looking rapt, as if fighting and brandishing steel pipes were the most fun things in the whole world.

But if Stanford's stories recollected his heyday of macho rebellion, his body showed one logical outcome of the same thing. He was a cautionary tale, and the boys understood that. He reminded me of the metaphorical catcher in the rye—shepherding boys from their late teens into their early twenties, an age range that had been as treacherous to negotiate in Stanford's youth as it was now. Stanford was paralyzed at twenty. Just four years after Stanford's accident, Jay-R reached the same age and had his accident. Two years after that, their younger brother, twenty-two-year-old George, died in a car crash. The following year, the youngest Addison boy, David—father of three-year-old Beau and eight-month-old Daniel, committed suicide. He was twenty.

Two of the six Addison boys of Stanford's generation turned twenty-three unharmed.

The boys who lived in Stanford's house now were interested in his past, but he was interested in their present. "Hey, Daniel, sing that song you just wrote," he'd say when there were visitors in the house. "Listen to this," he would tell the visitors. "It's good."

Once a carload of us parked in downtown Riverton while one of Stanford's nephews went into a store for a CD. After some minutes, which I spent thinking about how it was four in the afternoon and we hadn't even had lunch yet, the nephew came out of the store and leaped into the truck clutching a paper bag.

"Let's see it," said Stan. The boy took out the CD—it was his favorite band, Cradle of Filth.

Gawd, I thought.

"Cool," said Stanford.

He didn't expect the boys to be saints, but he didn't allow any drinking or drugs at his house. Through their silent black exteriors, the boys absorbed Stanford's interest and concern and his sometimes pissed-off commands. In return, they got him his cigarettes, fed and watered the horses, and carried him to the truck and drove him to whichever house needed to be smudged of restive spirits, or helped him go to the bathroom, or stayed awake at his bedside all night when his pressure sores went septic and he got a fever.

One summer, the state parks people called Stanford. They wanted to reenact the 1866 Fetterman Massacre in which Arapaho, Cheyenne, and Sioux warriors ambushed and killed eighty U.S. soldiers. It was the hundred and fiftieth anniversary of the event. They had the cavalry and infantry lined up; did Stanford have any warriors? Sure he had warriors. I wasn't there at the time; we were talking on the phone. I imagined him looking over at the boys sprawled on his bed, watching Beyoncé Knowles dancing on MTV. He was up to his neck in warriors. He had Beau, and Daniel, who could handle a horse well enough. Stanford hustled up these two and four of their friends, plus one kid currently living at the house. In ten days, he got them onto horses often enough that they were ready to drive to Fort Kearny, in the northern part of the state.

In the park museum's bathroom, the boys painted their faces. Beau put black-and-white horizontal stripes on his face. His head was crowned with a coyote pelt, some feathers, and a pair of antelope horns. He looked like something from a Grateful Dead album cover. Daniel painted the right side of his face black and had lines on both sides from his eyes to his mouth. The other boys' efforts to appear warriorlike were less successful: A boy named Brandon painted big red circles around his eyes. "He looked like a rodeo clown!" Stanford said, laughing. "Daniel got mad—'Take it off! I'll paint you!'—but Brandon still wound up looking like a Care Bear."

Then they mounted the five bareback ponies Stanford had brought up in a borrowed trailer, whipped the saddles off the two dude-ranch horses the parks people had provided to round out the Indian herd, and galloped flat out over the rough ground toward the soldiers. The park superintendent told me he was amazed at the bravado and speed of their attack, but Stanford saw three of the warriors fall off, one of them so often that the rider resorted to leading his trotting horse by the reins and running after the infantry, threatening them with his hatchet.

"The soldier guys, I think they wanted to laugh, but then again, I think they were just happy the Indians showed up," said Stanford. "But Beau and Daniel looked good. All they had to do was not smile, and people thought they'd get scalped. Beau snuck up to one of the cavalry guys. The guy turned around and went 'Whoa-oh-oh!'"

He laughed so hard at his own story, he had to rub his eyes with his limp hands.

Stanford had orchestrated all this from a body that could no longer do his favorite thing in the world, which was ride a horse. And while the Arapahos and their allies prevailed in the 1866 Fetterman Massacre, within a few years, it was all over for the Plains Indians. If Stanford had tended toward bitterness, historical or personal, or if he'd have been scared of the Indian riders looking less than stellar on horseback, his group of latter-day warriors never would have left the reservation. But Stanford wasn't bitter, and he wasn't afraid, either.

CHAPTER 17

MOVIES

During my first extended stay at Stanford's in the early spring of 2004, we watched a lot of movies. One night I stayed up in his room until two A.M. watching a Cate Blanchett western about a frontierswoman's young daughter being kidnapped by some thugs led by an evil Apache shaman. Cate, looking understandably stressed, strode up to a homestead with pioneers' bodies strewn on the garden path, left by this guy, who did things like dip eagle talons in rattlesnake venom and then press them into the white necks of his victims. Then she found her dismembered lover swinging gently over a smoldering fire in a leather sack.

I was watching with Stanford, a bunch of nephews, and one niece. I was the only white person in the room. Someone arrived and said into the dark, "Are the Indians the good guys or the bad guys in this movie?"

Cody replied, "They're always the bad guys."

Just as he said that, Cate Blanchett spat, "Indians!" with disgust and fear.

My palms started to sweat. I shifted in my seat. Stanford was on his bed, stroking his new pit bull pup, a silky little female with blue eyes and light brown fur. Her personality ran so counter to the nature of the breed, he'd named her Shy. He turned to me. "She's so soft," he said. "Like one of those slippers."

Stanford kept stroking her, and her leg went into one of those helpless sewing-machine movements dogs do when they're petted just so. Stanford and Cody laughed.

The movie plunged on, and right after the Apache shaman blew some powder into the eyes of a white guy who commenced dying noisily in the dust, I looked at my watch and remarked how late it was.

Stanford laughed. "You just can't take it, can you?"

"Nope," I said, and drove back to Lander and my own bed.

But Hollywood wasn't done with me. A few weeks later, Daniel and I decided to go to the movies in Riverton. Riverton has had its share of troubles. The white supremacist World Church of the Creator relocated there a few years ago. It didn't last long, but the fact that it moved to a town physically located on the reservation (although not legally part of it) says a lot about which race has dealt the suffering in this country and which race has received it.

When I went to pick up Daniel, his cousin Aaron and uncle Jay-R said they wanted to go, too. We were running a little late for the chosen movie—*The Passion of the Christ.* That was fine with me. I wasn't in the mood to see Jesus get beaten to death in slow motion, and *Hidalgo* was starting twenty minutes later.

Perfect. Any takers? Nope.

By the time we walked in, about fifteen minutes late, any hope of seeing Jesus unbloodied and whole had evaporated. I had been instructed to keep a close eye on Jay-R, because of his penchant for taking unannounced, lengthy walks through the high desert.

"*Watch* him," Grandma Stella had told me sternly as we left.

So I watched Jay-R, and Jay-R watched Jesus get peeled like an onion by the Romans. Riveted, Jay-R didn't move a muscle. Eventually, buoyed by gratitude that the end of the movie was near, I relaxed enough to actually watch the crucifixion scene. The cross was hoisted and Jesus delivered the line that clinched the movie: "Father, forgive them. They know not what they do." A single tear dropped from Jesus to the dirt, splashing as perfectly as physics and cinematography would allow.

I was surprised to feel tears in my own eyes. On the way home, the Addisons talked about how they'd loved the movie. I said how much the crucifixion line had touched me. "Yeah," said Aaron. "It reminds me of me."

Of Native Americans?

"Yeah."

Because of what white people have done to your people?

"Yeah," said Aaron. "Yeah," echoed Daniel. "Yeah," said Jay-R.

CHAPTER 18

THE WOMAN OF THE HOUSE

Stanford was in his room with one of the nurses who came every few days to check on the progress of the healing of his pressure sores and change the dressings. The low February sun streamed in the kitchen window, and I sat with Daniel and Jevon. Jevon had been the boyfriend of Stanford's niece Suzi for seven years—since they were ten. They reminded me of Romeo and Juliet, they were so young, beautiful, and passionate. Jevon had recently been released from a group home into Stanford's custody. Today, Suzi was off writing poetry, leaving Jevon and Daniel to work on their own rap lyrics. A karaoke machine did backup, and they rapped on top of it. Rez rap. They were good, in a shy, thuggy way.

Daniel rapped:

> *Yo dawg fuck what you heard*
> *What's the word*
> *I'm a stud keeps my herd*
> *I'm a one-man crew*
> *A one-man army*
> *It'll take fifty SWAT teams to try and disarm me*
> *And it'll take Bruce and Muhammad Ali to try and stop me*
> *I'm the one*
> *I'm untouchable with my twenty-two Mag*
> *Just me and my snag*
> *Bonnie and Clyde*
> *Crossin' state lines*
> *Expressing how I feel in my high school rhymes*

A man arrived, hoping to give Stanford a truck starter he needed. Hearing the boys rapping, he said he'd wait for Stanford and that he had done some rap back when he was in the army in 1980.

"Rap existed back then?" I asked.

"Sure did," he said.

He was plump and black and talkative, wearing a bright red T-shirt over a healthy belly and a floppy hat over a three-hundred-watt smile. He told me he would give his life for Stanford. Stanford had helped him and his wife get their three kids back after they were put in state custody while he served a seventy-two-hour jail term in Oklahoma. The custody battle took three years. It looked hopeless; then last fall he'd come to Stanford, who had told him to do a ceremony in the early morning for four mornings in a row. A few weeks later, he and his wife had their kids back.

We discussed the merits of rap. I said I liked a lot about it, but I hated the way it talked about women. But the visitor was steadfast that it was a good outlet for lost young men.

"Lemme guess," he said to Jevon. "You grew up without a dad, just a mom at home?"

Jevon nodded. No one really knew who Jevon's father was, his mother had died of drinking, although the specifics of the stories varied. Some people said she died of cirrhosis, others said she'd been run over by a car when she was lying in the road, drunk, and still others said someone had hit her on the head when she was drunk and the resulting blood clot had killed her.

The man continued: "And when other guys came around they didn't have no use for you?"

Jevon nodded again.

"These men, man, they're like lost in the woods," he said to me. "They're, like, in the trees, and there ain't no path. And what a boy needs is a *man,* a *father,* and that's what they don't get. And this rap gives them a way to release."

That said, he relaxed. He said he loved being a father to his four kids. "I just wish I'd been more of a dad to the first nine," he said.

I watched him closely to see if that was a joke. It wasn't. I was getting better at this.

He was out of time. I walked him out to his car, and he said, "Man, these people are *lost*. They ain't doing nothing! Can you imagine, a reservation this size given to the black man? Things'd be *happening* out here!"

At St. Stephens Indian School, Tisha's teacher asked who her parents were.

"Stan's my father," she told them, "and Moses is my mother."

This was a perfect role for a macho cowboy who had once been told by a medicine man in the Northwest that he needed to develop some respect for women. He said he'd never really appreciated what women had to put up with before this winter. Stanford was laid up inside. It was too cold to work horses, anyway, so Moses wasn't cowboying, he was cooking and cleaning. He'd effectively become the woman of the house.

"Here we are, me and Stan," he told me, holding a mop and pausing from cleaning the floor. "Two straight men! Married! To each other!"

One afternoon I skied through the flats of sage. I started about a mile from Stanford's. As I set off, Stanford's dogs ran toward me. They were running ahead of Stanford's younger brother Jay-R.

He stumped up to me. "Where are you going?"

I pointed in the direction he'd just come from, toward the swimming hole, which was frozen so solid you could walk across it.

"I'll go up there," he said.

So Jay-R walked and I skied slowly, listening to him talk about his potbelly and his worries about getting enough exercise and his car crash, and how, after Three Bears brought him out of his vegetative state in the sweat lodge, he looked at the women on the other side and said "something about them being beautiful."

"But when you and Stanford told me the story before, you told me you'd said, 'What are you looking at? Are you guys horny or something?'"

He laughed. "I forgot that part."

The conversation turned to Stanford. "If he was still walking, he'd be the boss of me."

"Really?" I asked, my skis creaking along in the icy snow.

"He beat me!" Jay-R said. "Beat me up."

"But Jay-R," I protested, "you've got a good life, with all this beautiful land and your family all around."

"All around!" he said. "They're like snakes! Say one thing wrong, and they'll strike!"

The sun got low and golden. The sky was a bright china blue, the moon a day short of full. We turned and watched the shadows get long and spiky on the gold-lit snow behind every sage bush. The temperature approached freezing. My cell phone rang. It was Michelle, a friend from home.

As I answered the phone, Jay-R turned away modestly, as if I had crouched down in the middle of the trail to pee. Michelle and I spoke for only a few minutes. At the end of the conversation, she said, "It seems like what Peter went looking for, you've found."

CHAPTER 19

A HUGE CRUSH

Stanford's corrals were empty that winter. Like many horse owners on the reservation, he couldn't afford to keep them in hay all year so he let his horses out onto the open range to fend for themselves. We'd see them roaming in the hills, though, and they animated a lot of the stories I heard and read during the long evenings.

The Plains Indians rode the descendants of horses stolen from Spanish explorers and settlements, or rounded up off the plains. Generally unstoppable, with whipping manes, compact bodies and hard-muscled legs, Indian ponies lived close to the edge because their owners did. They were sometimes sacrificed at the gravesides of their owners, but many Indians worshipped their horses. Horses transmitted messages to Assiniboine shamans. Geronimo would dismount his buckskin in the midst of battle so the horse could escape, and later, when the enemy was gone, he'd whistle the buckskin back from a cliff side. A Comanche chief who was offered a handsome price for his buffalo-hunting and war horse replied that he "could not think of parting with an animal so necessary to the welfare of his people," adding, "moreover, I love him very much."

Like many of their neighbors, the Addisons had broken their own horses for generations. Stanford's father had a way with them: "He just had to snap his bullwhip, and four horses would come running up," said Stanford. "Gray Mare—that was her name—would always be the leader. He had them trained pretty good." But if a horse was difficult,

Stanford's father would starve it for three days. Then he'd swing a sack around it, snapping it in front of its face, hitting its sides, scaring it. Hungry and dehydrated, the disoriented horse would go emotionally numb, lose its spirit, and be declared broken.

It wasn't the way the Arapahos' ancestors had done it, but by the latter part of the twentieth century, the Northern Arapahos hadn't only cut off their hair and had their language beaten out of them and their peyote ways mocked by white teachers; now they also broke horses the way cowboys did.

Not long after Stanford was paralyzed, he was in the corral pushing a horse from behind when the horse sat down and broke his wheelchair. This didn't faze Stanford one bit. Another time he left home for the day for a medical checkup. His brothers, an uncle, a friend, and little six-year-old Beau stayed home breaking horses. When Stanford got home, four adults and one boy sat morosely along the side of the house, each displaying a different combination of bandages, splints, and casts.

It looked like there had been a brawl. What there had been was a revolution. A buckskin horse had thrown himself on Stanford's big brother Bill's leg, breaking it. Glenn, the oldest brother, had been bucked off so energetically he'd almost broken his back, and their uncle Tommy, right after announcing he could do anything he wanted on the horse he was riding, had fallen off and broken his collarbone. A mare had bucked off Stewart Blindman, an Oglala Sioux friend of the family, and snapped his rib. Apparently not wanting to be left out of the great equine uprising, a colt had thrown little Beau right over the corral fence. Beau had grabbed the fence on his way over, dislocating his thumb. Stanford's mom had loaded the men and the one small boy into the family's sagging Buick and taken them to the clinic.

Not long afterward, a relative of Stanford's came over to geld a stallion, a deep reddish-colored quarter horse with a small, triangular head, strong legs, and a broad, strong chest. In other words, he was a quarter horse lucky enough to look like an Arab. This was the way to the heart of Stanford Addison, who was about as much of a horse snob as, say, Queen Elizabeth. The owner tied the stallion's rear leg to his neck to immobilize him. This was a common enough technique— some tied it loosely, so the horse could keep all four hooves on the ground but couldn't kick with the tied foot—but this man tied it so the horse had only three hooves on the ground. Then the horse slipped in the mud and broke his pelvis with a sickening pop. He went into shock. The owner loaded him into the trailer and sped him to the Riverton stockyard to sell him as dog meat. When the owner brought a prospective buyer to pick up the horse, he was already dead on the trailer floor, so he took the horse to the dump and left him there.

"I got to thinking," said Stanford. "There must be a better way."

Those were the days when Stanford was still adjusting to his injury. He was plagued by depression, but he started spending his time watching what went on in the corral, what worked and what didn't, how the horses responded better to calm and persistence than they did to the brutal regime Stanford had grown up with.

Then he bought some new horses from a rancher for fifty dollars.

"He started with a few horses," his mother told me, "and then he had lots. I'd say, 'Stan, why not get rid of your horses?' and he'd say, 'Yeah.' And next I knew, he'd have more."

Stanford had started putting together a new set of horse gentling techniques when Moses arrived twelve years before—raging and heartbroken from the fire that had disfigured his face. At Stanford's corral, he met his match: a palomino that was both athletic and homicidal. Palominos aren't the easiest horses in the world. They're flighty and impulsive, and Stanford is wary of them. And this palomino wasn't just difficult; he had killed another grown horse by biting it in the throat, throwing it down, and stomping it to death. Once he was enclosed in Stanford's corral, he would rush the corral fence and try to attack anyone who approached. Stanford wouldn't let the children even get near the corral.

The palomino had gone through several trainers. One local horse breaker, who had been known to tie bucking horses to the back of his pickup truck and drive them down the road to tire them out, had tried to subdue the palomino by hitting him over the head with a two-by-four every time he reared. This kind of treatment had refined the horse's aggression into something resembling criminal genius. The owner, a seventy-year-old rancher, had finally brought the horse to Stan. Stanford did two things. He gelded the palomino, and he put him in the ring with the angry cowboy his uncle had found in the hills.

When Moses and the palomino faced off in the corral, they were both damaged blond creatures who were ready to kill something. When they managed to get a saddle blanket on the palomino for the first time, he ripped it off his back with his teeth, shook it like a killed rabbit, dropped it on the ground, and stomped on it. When Moses finally succeeded in looping a rope over the stud's head, he stood close to the horse's neck, warily watching the next move while fashioning a makeshift halter out of the rope. But there was one knot that required his full attention, and as soon as he took his eyes off the horse's legs to concentrate, the horse kicked him hard on the forearm *with his front hoof*.

"The horse wasn't like a horse at all," said Moses. "He was more like a dog."

A wild dog. Or a ninja. Or a vengeful spirit loosed from an ancient massacre somewhere in the high desert.

Moses's thresholds for fear and pain were higher than those of a regular person, but this horse didn't need to be broken so much as he needed to be exorcised. He scared Moses.

"I would just stand in that ring and pray," said Moses. "I'd just pray."

They "hung" the horse on the center line to calm him down. The center line was central to Stanford's horse gentling technique. What the horse does underneath it—find a way to be calm despite the obstacles with which it's faced—was key to Stanford's whole existence. He called it finding your center.

Physically speaking, the center line is a rope threaded through an apparatus that is suspended above the horse. The low end of the rope has a clip that dangles at the same level as a ring on the horse's halter. Once the horse is clipped to the center line, there is only one area—directly below the ring—where it can stand without having its head pulled upward at an uncomfortable angle. While the horse tests the limits of its confinement, Stanford shoos everyone away from the corral so there is no one for the horse to associate with its distress. Alone in the corral, the horse figures out that the center line is something he can't argue with.

Most horses spend an hour or two on the center line. The palomino was there for a week. Moses would loosen the line each night to let him eat and drink, but the next morning they'd tighten it again. He didn't do the customary fighting and fussing; he *flew*. He swooped around like a kite, like a crazy bird of prey. He assumed positions usually seen in yoga studios. Although his head was held by the rope, he still had 360 degrees for swinging his strong, round butt around to kick Moses, winding him, bruising him, sending him flying. He could have surrendered to the rope by simply standing beneath it. But Stanford and Moses might as well have asked the wind to stop blowing. It just wasn't going to happen. The horse would not stop fighting. He didn't care how much he had to contort his head or strain his neck; he would not submit.

Stanford was just formulating his horse training regime. "We rolled tires by that horse to show we weren't going to hurt him," he said. "They came into his territory and went away without hurting him. If there was hurting happening, he was hurting himself. We were trying to show that horse respect. That's what we're all looking for."

It was 1994. Stanford had married Sandy, the mother of Daniel and Beau, several years before. His new family created money worries, which led to a strong desire to build his reputation as a horse trainer. The palomino was so notorious on the reservation that Stanford knew if he succeeded in gentling it, his reputation would be secure. So he pushed. He pushed Moses. He pushed Moses when there were other people watching.

"This is what chicken shit looks like!" he bellowed at Moses while a group of friends watched. Moses took it for a while. When the horse kicked him, its leg at full extension when it contacted his abdomen, Moses went to the tack shed until he figured out how to breathe again. Then he came back.

Still, anyone who knew Moses could see this was not a sustainable situation. The cowboy had been getting less aggressive since he'd been put in the rock tumbler of the Addison family. But he wasn't exactly mellow. Everyone waited for him to blow. And he blew. He grabbed Stanford's wheelchair and pushed it in front of the horse, screaming, "I'll put you in that corral, and *you* can figure out what chicken shit feels like!"

Stan fought back. He tried to run Moses over, "but my wheelchair wouldn't make little turns."

The spectators watched this turn of events with some alarm. When they realized the men weren't going to kill each other, they melted away. Moses stalked off into the wild rosebushes by the irrigation ditch and sobbed. When he came back, Stanford was sitting in his chair, all alone next to the corral. He had tears in his eyes. They embraced.

"I realized then just how horrible it was for him to be in that chair," Moses told me later. "That's when I realized he was my brother. That's what I seen, my brother in that wheelchair, hating being there. It hurt."

A couple of years later, with regular effort, Stanford and Moses finally broke the horse.

"We had to use a lot of kindness on it," said Stanford. "We had to keep being real calm with it. But we done a lot of horses in between and grew with the horses we were doing while we were still working on the palomino."

They got to the point where Moses would sleep in the meadow to hear the palomino grazing at night. In the morning, he'd hold out a halter, and the horse would come and put his nose right in it. Eventually, the palomino was returned to its owner and became a valuable calf-roping horse.

When they told me the story, one man's memory of training the palomino jogged the other's, the details of the story came spilling out and they laughed for a long time. Stanford laughed so hard he started coughing and couldn't stop. Moses wiped tears from his eyes.

I told them that in my childhood home in Scotland, every year the horsey people in our neighborhood would ride south to the English border, which was not far away, to make sure the English weren't going to come up and sack the abbey the way they did in 1322. My father ran a mental hospital outside of town. "We'd walk from our house to his office to visit him, and he'd give us money to buy candy at the little snack shop, and the patients would say, 'It's Doctorr Jones's gurrrilz!' and hug us and not let us go."

I usually imitated my Scottish accent for people only after a couple of beers. There was no beer here. These guys had been dry for something like twenty years. There was only cup after cup of weakly brewed, heavily sugared coffee. But there was something about the sweetness of that drink, the warmth and comfort of the modular home, that was neither too much nor too little. It was incredibly relaxing. Back home, I tried to stop any boisterous activity by ten P.M. so I could calm down and go to sleep. Here, we drank Folgers coffee with nondairy creamer until midnight, and I slept like a baby.

I loved listening to Stanford talk, to the kids or the visitors or me or Moses. By white standards, just about none of this man's needs were taken care of, but still he met every human around him with kindness. As for the limitations on his own well-being—his poverty, his injury, the jealousy that ran rampant on the reservation and was often directed at him—those he met with surrender. There wasn't a bit of fakery about it. I felt like a better person when I was around him. Maybe it was that I could see what was possible. When I'd read about Jesus Christ or the Buddha, the stories were moving, but they didn't change me. But here was a flesh-and-blood man living in the middle of the dust of Wyoming, giving this much of himself, and somehow that made it more possible for me, in a tiny way, to be like that, too.

I remembered once when I was white-water kayaking and a lot of the men were learning to throw away their paddles while surfing a wave, keeping control of their boats with their hips while the rest of us picked up their paddles from the froth and waited our own turn. I knew I had the necessary physical skill, but I couldn't make myself do it. I had a justification in reserve—I wasn't a man. One day a woman from Argentina came and just did it. So I did, too. She opened the door for me. And it felt like Stanford was opening another kind of door for me, a door toward being kinder and more centered.

Which isn't to say I acted like him or even believed everything he said. He told me that when he was about sixteen, he was taking care of a bunch of little brothers and sisters and cousins in a teepee set up outside their house when, through the fabric, he saw lights overhead, descending. He peeked out and saw a spaceship. It landed nearby, and little pink men about three feet high filed out.

"The first thing I wanted to do was shoot one so I could keep it, but then I thought they might retaliate, and I had all these kids, man. I was babysittin'."

I chuckled. This was going to be fun.

"I thought about moving the kids away and coming back with my rifle." He got on the roof of the house with his rifle, but before he could do anything the spacemen headed for the family's junked cars sitting in the sagebrush, browsed around for a few moments, got back in their spaceship, and left.

Stanford watched me, his face serious. "Maybe they was looking for parts."

He'd gotten me. "That didn't *happen!*" I howled.

"It did," he said, taking a long drag on his KOOL. "I looked at them through the high-powered scope of my rifle, and they had two arms and two legs and a nose that was a slit and a mouth, too, but eyes that were just black holes. There was four of them."

I shook my head. This had to be a joke. I was sure that in a couple of weeks he'd let me know it was. Otherwise, what? Was a belief in pink aliens normal around here? Was it a requirement? If it was, I wouldn't be able to meet it.

Here was what I believed: Stanford Addison had special powers. I couldn't explain them or quantify them, but he had them, no doubt about it. He had conjured a whirlwind in Iowa eight months ago. These days I heard about his powers all the time, in stories about the glass he spit out in his sweat lodge after helping a car crash survivor, and about those he had cured of everything from cancer to mental illness. I could feel it in the way I both relaxed and brightened up every time I set eyes on him.

Here's what I did not believe: that little pink men descend from spaceships.

And then one night starting my car and pulling away from Stanford's at my normal hour of one-something in the morning, suddenly, my shoulders were up by my ears and they wouldn't come down. My heart pounded. Something was in the backseat of my car, I was sure of it. I looked around and saw nothing in the near-dark. I couldn't turn on the interior light because my car was thirteen years old, and the light had not worked since it was ten. But I knew the thing in my car wasn't anything I could see, anyway.

Later, my friends would grill me: How did I know it was a ghost? I told them that to start with, I wasn't looking for a ghost. Even though my experience with Stanford and the whirlwind had expanded my world, in my conscious mind, anyway, I still defaulted to the person I'd been my whole adult life: a journalist in control of her own destiny. I wasn't scared of the dark; I'd camped and traveled all over the world. I'd hitchhiked alone. I wasn't a New Ager; I had been a Presbyterian as a child and a Theravada Buddhist as an adult—traditions from the frostier end of the spiritual ecosystem, relatively free of mystical imagery, ghosts, or apparitions.

Prior to meeting Stanford, the only experience I'd ever had that made me give more than a passing thought to the supernatural had occurred about twelve years before. I was driving away from the Navajo Nation in southeastern Utah on a reporting trip, looking for a campsite to spend the night, when a low-rider car started tailgating me. I wasn't a nervous traveler, but I was seized with an unusually strong desire to get away from this car. Heading up a hill, I pulled right and slowed down. The low-rider impatiently vroomed around me, hitting the top of the hill at about sixty just to make its point. After it disappeared over the crest, there was a hideous crash. I got there a few seconds later. An enormous deer lay motionless on the shoulder of the road, and the low-rider sat diagonally across the center line, its hood accordioned to half its original length. I pulled over. The air was thick with dust and hair and a horrible silence. I ran to the car. The occupants—two teenage Native boys—were alive. They looked at me blearily.

"Are you okay?" I asked. "What do you need?"

They didn't look bleeding or broken. They looked shocked. They told me they were okay and then, astonishingly, drove off back down the hill toward town, the car squealing and clucking.

I was shaking. This was a four-lane highway. If those boys hadn't tailgated me, I would have been going just as fast as they were when I crested that hill. I was not driving a low-rider with an endless hood; I was driving the smallest Toyota you could buy. I looked at the huge deer that had been thrown off the road and thought, something is looking out for me.

But experiences fade. Sameness will have its day, every day. We wake every morning pretty much the same as we were the day before, because that's how we like it, and because anything else would be scary. Little Whirlwind appeared in Iowa eight months ago, but that came from Stanford, and energies he was responsible for were a lot more believable and a lot less disturbing to me than what I was feeling in my car during the wee hours of this freezing morning—this freelance energy, this random ghost, who just decided to get in my car and *sit right behind me.* Crap. Something was definitely in my car. I could not get my shoulders away from my ears.

That was how I knew it was a ghost, I told my friends—my body didn't lie. I considered stopping right there, driving back to Stanford's, rousing him, and getting him to clear out whatever invisible being had hopped in for a ride. But it was late. Stanford was already in bed, and I was tired.

I used my Buddhist training: How did I feel in my body? I didn't feel scared. I felt annoyed. The ghost, or whatever it was, wasn't bad. It was more like a little juvenile delinquent, a ghostlet, wanting to go to town for some action. So I drove to Lander, my shoulders eventually making their way to their normal position. When I stopped outside my rented room, I opened the car door wide, glanced up the street to make sure no one was around, and said, "Okay, you've had your ride. You're on your own now. Out!"

When I told Stanford the next day, he said, "'Course there's spirits around here. There's spirits around my house because I use good spirits, and bad spirits come over to try to mess them up. You could have just taken 'em to Grandma's and made 'em get out there."

Ghosts and spirits apparently weren't always either entirely evil or entirely good. My ghost was okay, a little sneaky-feeling, but okay. I kept thinking about the cowboy ghost who used to watch *Dallas* with Stan: a bored young ghost who didn't really know what to do with all his time now that he was dead and couldn't wrangle anymore. In his boots, I'd have watched *Dallas,* too.

But now would I start seeing ghosts everywhere? How about pink guys coming out of spaceships? No! So I'd felt a ghost! Who didn't feel some unarguable, invisible presence at some point in life? I wasn't the believer type, like my mother, who would walk down the parkway near her house, hugging trees. Of course, when all this started, Stanford hadn't been the believer type, either.

I called Laurie, my best friend from college. "You should come out here," I said.

"No way," she said from her elegant house in California.

"Why?"

"It's not the ghosts that scare me," she said. "It's Stanford. He would see right through me."

"So?"

"I come from such a different world than Stanford and his tribe. I'd feel too ashamed about the things I focus on in my life, you know? For my 'problems.'"

"I know what you mean, but that stuff's just the skin of the apple. The rest, what there is to share, is just huge," I said.

"But I have more to be ashamed of than you do."

"Why? Because you have more money than me?"

"Yeah, and a cushier life. I'd feel too naked there."

"But Stanford can look right through you and see the goodness in you that you can't see yourself, and right at that moment you'd become a happier person."

"Cool. I'm coming," she said.

"Really? Great!"

"I'm kidding."

I was happy. Stanford made me so happy. I was only three weeks into my stay, tipsy on the sense of possibility that was starting to saturate every moment. I said, "Stanford, have you put a spell on me? I feel like I'm in love, but not romantically. Not even with a person. I don't want to go home at all."

He laughed and said for the second time in eight months, "I didn't put no spell on you."

*   *   *

I found that Stanford, Moses, and I were all within two years of each other in age. The year I was editor of the yearbook, in the honor society, and on the soccer team, Stanford had already tried to strangle his math teacher and Moses had dropped out of school to sell cocaine. What would it have been like to walk across my high school parking lot with my friends Pam and Ellen, coming upon teenage versions of Stanford and Moses hanging around under a scraggly elm tree, making no move toward the building although the second bell had already rung? We'd giggle about how cute and dangerous they were with their long hair and cigarettes—they were natural athletes, but except for Stanford's short tenure on the Wyoming Indian High School football team and Moses taking second in the high hurdles at a track meet he entered with purple chalk around his eyes while he was high on acid, they weren't the team type.

Yep, we'd giggle and scoot right past them into our AP chemistry class.

The discussions between Stanford, Moses, and me eventually reached our love lives, none of which were exactly thriving at the moment, what with my prospective husband in his monk's robes, Moses with his Internet flirtations, and Stanford a couple of years out of his divorce from his second wife. When he and Sandy had split up in 2001, Stanford married again.

"It lasted a month," said Stanford. "That's pretty much all there is to say about that.

"Right now the biggest battle is having a companion," he added. "I could hook up with someone. I know these medicines would be stronger if the circle was completed. A man and a woman. And I know there's women who want to be with me 'cause of the medicine. Moms have offered their daughters to me for the medicine. I know there's women who are fascinated. But I guess I don't trust myself. Women are the easiest thing to get tempted by. Booze and that, it's no problem. The temptation is with girls I meet through sweat lodges. I don't want to take advantage of them 'cause they're looking for help."

This was not the way he treated women in his youth.

He had fathered five children by the time he was twenty. "I'd tell the girls, 'If you wanna get rid of me quick, tell me you're pregnant,'" he said. To this day he hasn't met a single one of them.

His own heart had been broken. He'd found the love of his life, Jackie, at a powwow in Minneapolis when he was seventeen.

"I looked over to see who I was next to," he recalled. "She was light-skinned, long, light brown hair, green eyes. She was a beauty. It wasn't like 'Jump her bones!' It wasn't even like that. It was pretty much instant when I met her. We didn't want to be apart. I didn't need to impress. With her, it felt real natural, like we already knew each other all our lives. I really wanted to stay with her."

They had been together for about six months when Jackie's father, who was German, decided it was time to get his daughter away from this rebellious Indian boy. So Jackie, her Chippewa mother, and her dad moved to Chicago.

Stanford was bereft. He had never experienced this depth of feeling before, or this kind of loss. He drank for a week, lay in bed for another, and took months to feel like himself again. "After that I was like 'To hell with women.'"

I have a copy of a photograph of him from around that time. He was surrounded by six of his brothers and friends. He sat in the middle of the hood of the Maverick he'd bought with two hundred dollars he'd made doing construction in Riverton. He'd called the car Gatorade for its green color. He was all long hair and rangy limbs and perfect skin and chiseled features with an unfettered broad smile, sitting smack dab in the middle of the hood in the middle of his friends in the middle of a bright Wyoming day.

"Oh, he was one pretty man," remarked a girl from New Jersey who got to the Wind River Reservation in the 1970s on the Rainbow Family's school bus and spent her early twenties with the Addison brood, drinking and jumping off bridges, stoned, and having a wild time. Stanford was a few years younger than she was. "He was cocky as hell, a great, great horseman, oh, with hair right down his back."

"I had a harem," he said. "Any party I'd go to, there was a new one. I'd just go in there and make eye contact."

* * *

Now he was the vulnerable one. The fact that some women were after his powers, he said, "always makes me look for the real intention, and it makes me not trust so much. It's really hard to give your heart fully. It's easy to be hurt."

"Yeah," I said. "I know."

"The woman thing is part of the reason I had the accident," he said. "In one way it was a punishment, for disrespecting the ones that carry life. I used to be real angry, too. Everything used to get on my nerves. It was always my way. I try not to do the things I used to do. I used to take advantage of women—in just about every way I could. I don't want to revert to my old ways. I don't want to use people."

"Did you ever use your powers to get a girl?"

"No. Just to heal people. Those powers were given to me for other people. Being paralyzed helps. It's harder to mess up. I have the edge over you guys because I can't go out and screw up."

I thought of the power in his little house, of how it was and was not being used. Stanford never wanted to overpower a woman again. Moses never wanted to abuse power again, period.

"Before I got burned up, I used my popularity," he said. "People hear about you, know about you before they even meet you. That power is very corrupting. I was too weak to withstand it. And so I came to a place where it doesn't exist."

Powerful men who had sworn off the abuse of power had welcomed me into their world. Lucky me. Peter, Stanford, Moses: All the men in my life were renunciates.

I wasn't. I was just dying to use my own power. I wasn't aware of this, though. All I knew was I was developing a huge crush on Wyoming, on the Wind River Reservation; on its harsh-lit beauty and the sweet Folgers that ran through the veins of its brave and accepting people.

Peter called me from his guesthouse in Nepal, where he had lived for nearly four months, taking teachings from his Tibetan teacher. He had just found out that the monastery in Thailand wouldn't let him ordain for less than three months, which would mean he'd have to stay in Asia for two months more than we'd agreed on. He was willing to forgo the monastery and come home as planned.

"You should definitely stay," I told him.

"Really?" he said.

"Oh yeah," I said. "I'm good. I'm fine. I'm having a great time. Come back when you're really ready."

Spring had come. One evening a dozen or so of us sat outside Stanford's house, eating an unusually lavish dinner in the late, slanting sun. We were silent. We had a fresh fruit salad and barbecued steak and burgers. I sat on an upturned plastic bucket next to Stella, who occupied a folding chair.

"There were these white women that got kidnapped by the Arapahos," she said suddenly. "They married Arapaho men. And when their families came to get them, they didn't want to go back."

I ate a forkful of fruit salad. I'd read about a woman named Lizzie Fletcher who married a man named John Broken Horn. When her sister identified her, Lizzie denied being white and stayed with the Arapahos until she died.

"Were they happy?" I asked.

"Happy?" Stella said. She chewed a few times, considering the notion and looking over the propane tank at the mountains. "Yeah, they were happy."

Sarah Kariko

PART 2

CHAPTER 20

STANFORD LOSES HIS HEALTH, MOSES LOSES HIS HOME, I LOSE MY DIGNITY

If the fool would persist in her folly she would become wise.
—WILLIAM BLAKE

What's bad is good. It helps you find your center.
—STANFORD ADDISON

I thought I was in heaven the way a goose flying on the fine salt breezes near La Guardia Airport thinks it's in heaven right before it flies into the landing route of a 747 from Kansas City.

Everything looked golden to me. All things swelled with loveliness. One day Moses was talking to me about training horses. He was wearing a tank top and had his hands on top of his head. I interrupted him: "Where did you get those great arms?"

"I dunno," he said. "Where did you get that nice round butt?"

What was I doing? Outside of my relationships, I had never been a sexual provocateur in my life. I could see Moses's flaws, his short temper, but I could also see his devotion to Stan. And I loved the fact that he liked to talk to me so much and knew so much about spirituality and the Arapahos. I wasn't blind, either: I could see those arms.

I wasn't feeling anchored enough in my relationship with Peter to fully withstand the spark between Moses and me. Not by a long shot.

It would be more accurate to say I was flapping in the wind like a kite with a broken string. But the attraction between Moses and me wasn't the most powerful thing happening to me that spring. Beneath it, other engines of unfathomable joy had chugged to life. I got rushes of ecstasy from Stan, the only person I'd ever known who constituted a conduit to the divine. Then there was the happiness that comes from living in a tribe. I'd never felt it in my life, but I knew what I liked. Plus, it was dawning on me that I, too, had been native before, although I'd forgotten all about it. I once lived on a rocky outcrop in the North Sea where people who looked like me had made their homes for thousands and thousands of years.

Let me be clear: I didn't go to the Wind River Indian Reservation wanting to be Native American. I hadn't gone to Wyoming to get an Indian name or a pipe or a sacred feather. I never envied other white people who got those things. But when I heard Cody say his people had occupied pretty much the same ground for ten thousand years, I actually shivered with pleasure. I knew what he meant. I had been homesick, not to mention heartsick and Godsick, for thirty years. It wasn't that I wanted to stride into some modular home dressed in a kilt and throw my arms around whichever grandmother I found making fry bread in the kitchen or watching TV in the living room and shout, "Sistah!" Well, that's a lie. That's pretty much what I did want to do. I wanted to know people who had a sense of home, and if they didn't have it, at least knew it was missing.

So when I came to Stan's and felt the pull for home and whatever lay beyond that, my heart lunged for it with a clumsy passion. I described it to Stan and he nodded:

"It always stays with you after you start touching it and knowing it and seeing it," he told me. "And then it'll ease off and you'll think it's temporary. But it never leaves you."

Right around this time, a friend of mine who, like me, had been a journalist for over twenty years, warned me: "You're getting too close to your sources."

"Sources?" I said to my friend. "You have no idea."

Which isn't to say I had the remotest idea of what was going on. My nervous system was flooded. Wires were crossed inside me; messages were being deposited in the wrong in-box. Rushes of divine love were being put in the box marked HOW ABOUT TAKING OFF YOUR CLOTHES AND LYING DOWN RIGHT HERE? Unbuttoned responses to divinity had happened throughout history; even Catholicism had produced some pretty luscious writing. "Kiss me with the kiss of your mouth . . . My God and my Glory, Your breasts are better than wine," wrote Saint Teresa five hundred years ago in the lusty language of the bride in the *Song of Songs*. "May we all be mad for love of Him who for love of us was called mad."

She had a vision of a beautiful male angel standing beside her body:

> I saw in his hand a long spear of gold, and at the iron's point there seemed to be a little fire. He appeared to me to be thrusting it at times into my heart, and to pierce my very entrails; when he drew it out, he seemed to draw them out also, and to leave me all on fire with a great love of God. The pain was so great, that it made me moan; and yet so surpassing was the sweetness of this excessive pain, that I could not wish to be rid of it.

Well, yeah, Teresa, I know what you mean.

I didn't know what moved me most: Feeling connected to a large family that had a sense of place? Rushes of divine love? Moses, with his devotion and his arms? Stan, who redeemed the human condition beyond anything I'd ever seen, who filled me with such gentleness and love? Whose very brokenness made his beauty so obvious?

I lacked experience with beautiful angels or conduits or the Creator; my life experience, however, had contained plenty of men. Which is to say that on top of the glorious churned-up swill of subconscious muck sat not a beautiful angel but an attentive cowboy with terrific arms. But when it came to literally lying down and taking off my clothes, I was right there with the chaste Teresa. It wasn't going to happen. I was going to stand by Peter, even if he was on the other side of the planet in a white robe in a monastery, watching his breath, seeing the ephemeral nature of pleasure.

But just as Saint Teresa had been known to levitate on the strength of her religious passion, the kind of energy I was suppressing was bound to start pushing things around. This was a household of very sensitive people. Although it took too much energy and Stan considered it plain unfair to do as a regular practice, the man could read minds.

On the day I asked Moses about his arms, Stan mentioned to me in the most casual tones that Moses was terrible with women. Then he asked me to drive thirty miles round-trip—to Lander—to get him some cigarettes, then thirty-five miles in the other direction—to Riverton—to get groceries.

"I thought it [the growing attraction between me and Moses] was going to be a disaster," Stan told me months later. "I thought you were going to get hurt. I didn't want it to happen."

But Lord, it had been a long winter.

"We're all a little needy," Moses told me one day when we walked back from the corral as the sun set and the air made its rosy, frozen plummet past freezing.

I understood needy. I was made of needy.

A few days later, a foot of snow fell on the Wind River Range and the reservation. I put my skis in my car and drove to Stan's under a flawless blue sky and a wincingly bright sun. I skied up and down the road a few times, enjoying the rhythm and speed of skiing on a flat place. Then Moses came out and hitched a couple of ropes to the back of his huge yellow Chevy truck. One we tied to an inverted car hood, weighed it down with car tires, and piled children and blankets on top. The other I held in my mittened hands. And off we whizzed, through the powdery new snow and sagebrush, screaming and laughing. We whumped through streams. We sped over flats at dangerous speeds. We did doughnuts, falling and getting plastered with snow.

I loved it. It was so reckless.

A few nights later, after midnight, the moon was blue with a big ring around it. The air outside was cold and dry. One breath and the hairs inside my nose stuck together. But my car was idling with the heater on; it was warm and comfortable. Moses and I were inside.

"Tell me what to do," Moses said. "I'll do anything you want. Tell me what to do."

I told him. A few seconds later, I told him to stop.

I couldn't do it. I was cursed with being old enough to know better, knowing from experience how damage spreads, of how it chars the future. Behind it all, the cursed weight of my love for Peter.

I drove away from that house at a speed that was quite unsafe, and two days later, I retreated to Colorado, horrified, fascinated, confused. I hadn't been home a day when Stan was admitted to the Lander hospital with a bedsore gone septic, a potentially fatal condition. His temperature had hit 102 degrees, and he had been rushed off in an ambulance. I sped back to Lander and Stan's hospital room, getting a speeding ticket in the process. By the time I got there, his fever had been controlled by intravenous antibiotics. But his hip hurt. He asked for morphine. A nurse arrived and gave him a shot. I could almost see his woes melt off him as he turned his untroubled gaze upon the pattern of the ceiling.

Stan's house was never what you'd call a tight ship, but without him there, things got a lot looser. Boys who had walked the straight and narrow for some time went on three-day drunks. Police cars rolled up the road. Stan started getting phone calls at the hospital: Someone stole a stereo, someone slugged someone else. Somewhere in the growing kerfuffle, Moses was accused of being too hard on the kids. Stan told him to get out.

Moses agreed to go to his friend Ivan's. He waited up all night for Ivan to pick him up, but he never arrived. So after breakfast, Moses called Stan. "I'm not moving out," he said, "and I hope it pisses you off, you big bitch!"

Stan laughed. But it wasn't over. A couple of nights later, Moses visited the hospital, and Stan said, "This bullshit has got to stop."

"We can end it right here," said Moses.

"Fine," said Stan.

"Okay," said Moses, walking out of the room, right past my gaping mouth, which was covered by the sterile mask suggested for people visiting patients who, like Stan, harbored both staph and strep.

The next day, with Grandma Stella, Nicole, and Daniel standing by, Moses moved his stuff out of Stan's house. Stan directed the evacuation over the phone to Nicole, who, in turn, instructed Moses.

Stan had a final question: "Can you feed the horses on the way out?"

"Of course," Moses said.

I saw him later on, in Lander. He told me he had been kicked out before.

"What happened?" I asked, my heart swimming straight upstream against the current of difficulty that had beset this misunderstood man. Moses told me shortly after he and a girlfriend had split up, he'd seen his ex-girlfriend's car parked in Stan's driveway. He thought Stan and his wife were trying to set up a reconciliation between him and his ex, so he got in his truck and rammed the woman's car. So Stan kicked him out.

"Oh," I said. "What? Really? You rammed her car?"

Another time Stan kicked Moses out on Christmas Eve, and Moses slept by the river in his truck.

"Ten degrees when I woke up!" Moses told me. "Merry Christmas!"

I didn't know about the past, but I thought it was unfair for Stan to kick Moses out so readily, and I told Moses so.

"Don't take that energy up there to the hospital into his room," he replied very seriously. "He doesn't need it."

Who was this guy? How could he be capable of such violence and then this enormous loyalty?

"I'm just gonna step back and not get hurt and be here for him," he said. Tears had sprung to his eyes. "Even with all that driving him down, the boredom, the pain and isolation, he's still there carrying other people through their lives. They lean on him, call on him, visit, call for help, and he's there every time giving them something they need to make their lives easier, better. It's amazing. Even in his condition, I don't know anybody, *anybody,* that's carried that many people.

"I wish I had a fraction of that strength; I'd lose strength, I'd lose patience," he said. "I'd say, 'Why don't you fucking deal with your own problems?' I'd bail."

*   *   *

I needed a reality check. I called my best friend, who was Peter. I stuttered my confession, explained how abandoned I'd felt when he left for Asia, and the feelings I'd had for Moses, and how I'd almost made a serious mistake, but hadn't.

To my astonishment, he didn't fly off the handle. He was actually tender with me. He stayed my friend, my partner. A renewed appreciation rushed into my heart for him and for Buddhism and the kindness it fosters. For the first time ever, I felt a tiny bit of appreciation toward his relationship with Mariel. Because of her, Peter knew how far a bit of forgiveness could go. I loved talking to him. Most of the conversations we had every two or three weeks while he was in Asia took about four hours, the last couple of which were usually spent giggling at one thing or another.

He told me about the musical comedy he wanted to write about Buddhist monks, with a theme song that took the music from Kool & the Gang's "Celebration." He sang in his two-toned voice:

> *Celibate good times, come on!*
> *It's a celibation.*
> *Getting up every morning at three!*
> *227 ways to clean my bowl, that's me!*
> *No sex with mud or geckos*
> *No masturbation.*
> *It's a celibation.*

I'd end up in one of the old-fashioned phone booths in the lobby of the Noble Hotel with a couple of empty cans of Diet Pepsi under the little bench seat. Peter would be on a public phone on the street in Thailand, shielding his eyes from the sun while concerned shopkeepers ran out every hour or so, bringing ice water to the laughing, singing, talking American monk with the shaved head who was clearly not the silent type.

I wasn't going to stray again. I was sure.

Because I was so sure, now that I was confronted with a homeless Moses, broke and with only a saddle to his name, I offered him a place to stay in my room. I had two beds, after all. Growing up in Colorado with friends who backpacked and kayaked, I'd shared hotel rooms and tents with all kinds of male friends over the years. I'd been attracted to a few of them, but all we did was share the space. Right? Right.

The Noble Hotel had once been a block of apartments with a rowdy bar frequented by the likes of the young Stan Addison, but it had been purchased in the 1970s by the National Outdoor Leadership School, or NOLS, which took young people into the wilderness all over the world to teach them how to climb and camp and canoe and get along with one another while doing so. I'd gone to Alaska with them for a semester while I was in college and loved it. And now my status as an alumna had lucked me into a dirt-cheap rate on a very nice room.

So Moses took up residence in the bed my mom had slept in just six weeks before. He thought he would end up in bed with me. But I was steadfast. My attraction to him was still powerful, but now, thankfully, I could manage it. It wasn't going to eclipse my connection to my Thai monk or my attentions toward Stan, who was, after all, the reason I was in Wyoming. Even in the thick of my crush on Moses, Stan was still the most interesting person I knew.

Moses was a light sleeper. Before I'd wake up, he'd go to the kitchen at the end of the hall to make coffee and meditate. I shared the kitchen with maybe a dozen NOLS instructors who were between courses. I'd gotten used to Moses's appearance and manner, but that didn't mean the NOLS instructors would cotton to a half-melted cowboy twice their age sitting in their kitchen next to their bags of organic espresso blend with his eyes closed, chanting in Arapaho.

Moses had spent two mornings in the kitchen when a note appeared for me on the bulletin board downstairs. The manager, who was just about the nicest person in the world, told me that the instructors considered this hotel their home. Who was this guy?

I blubbed and glugged my excuses, explaining that I wasn't aware guests had to pay, assuring them he'd be out that day. Our not sleeping together wasn't working for him, anyway. He'd hocked his saddle to start paying the monthly rate at a nearby hotel.

I felt embarrassed. In the process of blurting my excuses to the

hotel manager, I had lost status. Even though I was telling the truth—
Moses really had been just a guest—I was slipping. I was now associ-
ated with the underclass. I was losing my place in the world. I had
never noticed before how elite NOLS was. Heck, I'd never noticed
how elite I was. I hadn't ever felt elite, not since early childhood, anyway, when our tennis court and hired help embarrassed me among my
friends. I was a writer, so I didn't have much money to speak of. I was
paying off my own house, but it had only half a foundation and was
covered in asphalt shingles. I did my laundry at a Laundromat. For a
while I had commuted two hours and one mountain pass each way to
clean condominiums in Aspen. Sometimes I had health insurance,
sometimes I didn't. I lived frugally, which allowed me to make my living writing about what I wanted to write about for magazines and have
plenty of time left over for friends and the outdoors. But mine was
bohemian poverty, chosen poverty, it's own kind of privilege.

In my thirties, I'd spent two months hitchhiking penniless across
the Deep South with my boyfriend at the time, just to see what it
would be like to be homeless (it's not bad at all if you're a woman in a
nice winter coat accompanied by a bearded man six and a half feet tall).
Even though once we were kicked out of a truck stop that didn't allow
hitchhiking, in my real life I was far from a member of the underclass.

In the midst of Moses's relocating from the Noble to his own room
in town, my purse disappeared, and with it all my ID, money, and
credit cards. I had lost, as Moses later pointed out, my identity. He
didn't know how right he was. My credit card was as essential to my
identity as my driver's license. More so. On the reservation, Stan would
give me cash, and I would pay his bills with my credit card. I'd call the
customer service number for his DirectTV or electric company and
give them my numbers, then hang up and say, "Done!"

Tisha would take my credit card and examine its raised silver numbers, the hologram of the eagle, like, What's in there? Having a credit
card *was* magical, if you thought about it. It was my ticket to the Fat
of the Land, to the great clearinghouse that is America, that great
producer and importer and seller of everything you could think of. I
had a ten-thousand-dollar credit limit on that card. I could buy a car
with it.

I'd been in Wyoming for six weeks without a thought of going home for a breather. But now that I'd lost my credit card, I felt incredibly vulnerable. I wanted to go home. And I needed to replace my driver's license.

Is that what vulnerability was to me—abruptly not having ten thousand dollars anytime I wanted it?

Before I drove back to Colorado, I stopped at Stan's house. He'd just returned from having some bone in his elbow surgically removed after the infection in a pressure sore had spread to the underlying bone. His left arm was in a huge white cast. He looked debilitated and deer-like. He was in pain.

"Remember," he told me as I prepared to leave to find my home and my identity, "What's bad is good." He reminded me of the knight in *Monty Python and the Holy Grail* who got his arms and legs cut off in a sword fight but kept telling his opponent to come back and fight like a man. I must have looked incredulous.

"It is," Stan insisted, sounding muffled, looking trussed, thin, and brown with the huge white loaf of a left arm. "What's bad is good. It helps you find your center."

CHAPTER 21

DUMB BAD LUCK

A few weeks later, I was back and it was spring. The glaciated mountains gleamed with new snow, but down here on the plains, shoots of new grass lay underfoot. When I looked at the cottonwoods down by the river they had a faint tint of green.

With the exception of the roundup the day before, the young Addison men had been lying on Stan's bed watching MTV since Thanksgiving. Now they put down their supersize Cokes and walked into the corral. They were young and their bodies were forgiving and their family had owned horses, lots of them, for more generations than they could count. The family was related to the bronc buster depicted on Wyoming's license plates—the guy was half Native. Straight and tall and unfailingly muscular beneath their winter fat, the men moved slowly, blinking in the bright sun. The horses swirled around them. The animals had spent the last six months on a winter range of half-frozen rivers and bunchgrasses that poked through the snow like fields of porcupines. They wanted out of the muddy corral, now. But the two-leggeds were the keepers of the law and those horses weren't going anywhere.

They approached the fence, then flashed sideways like a school of fish. Four grays, four chestnuts with white blazes on their noses and white socks on their feet, assorted bays. They looked alike. They were alike. They were siblings, all bred from the same stud—an old white Arab named Wizard. The men waved and hollered some of them into a little round corral, the horses turning and stopping to face the gate they'd just run through, their faces a perfect line, each as lovely and wild and expectant as the next. Moses guarded the gate in jeans and a sleeveless olive-green T-shirt, jumping and barking Indian-sounding monosyllables.

When they ran for it, Moses slammed the gate into their knees and noses, bolting it shut in a cloud of dust and hooves. Despite his regionally famous hemorrhoids and his burned-up eyesight and his claw of a left hand, he inhabited his body as smoothly as water inhabits a glass. He and Stan had reconciled after their argument; he was back at the corral, although not yet at the house.

Stan came out of the house and bumped over the ground in his wheelchair, his black braid swinging behind him. When he arrived at the corral, the men stopped milling and waited for instruction. Stan didn't look like himself. He looked angry and scared. It wasn't because of the day's task, which was not training horses but cutting off their testicles. It was because his nurse had just inspected his pressure sores and found that one was tunneling in a new direction. He'd been laid up in bed all winter. The nurse's discovery had dashed Stan's hope that he'd heal up and avoid the elaborate surgery planned for him by Dr. William Wyatt—one of three plastic and reconstructive surgeons in the state of Wyoming, and a man so committed to his job that he spent his vacations repairing cleft palates on impoverished children in Honduras. First, Dr. Wyatt would insert a pump into Stan's abdomen to drip a constant supply of muscle relaxant on his spine, to prevent spasms in his legs that could rip open the postsurgical stitches on his butt. After that was stable, they would shave off some pressure sore–infected ischial bone (one of the pair of bones on either side of your spine that bears your weight when you sit down), then close up the wound and pull up Stan's hamstrings to build him a new butt. He would be in the hospital for about eight weeks.

Stan hated hospitals. Twenty-five years ago, in the Seattle hospital, the doctors had told him that his life expectancy was twelve years. "Everything's gonna break down," they had told him. "Your muscles are going to turn to mush, you'll break down into sores; infection leads to staph and more serious infections like MRSA, and that's what quadriplegics die of."

Stan gave as good as he got. When he left Lander for the bigger hospital in Seattle, his lung was so congested he couldn't utter a word. But when his lung cleared enough for him to speak, he did not have pleasant things to say. He'd yell at the medical staff, tell them to fuck off.

"What's the matter with you?" Stan had snarled at one of the male nurses. "You not man enough to get a man's job; are you some kinda faggot?"

"I was hurting and nobody could understand what I was feeling," Stan told me. "The worst part was when they tried to make me feel better. There was no heart in it. That's what got me mad."

He imitated them in a high, squeaky tone: "'We know how it is; we seen this a lot.'" His face was pinched and pained and furious. "But they didn't know. That was the hard part."

His hormones got off kilter, and the medicine they gave him made boils break out over his shoulders, neck, and face. The medicine they gave him for that left his teeth so brittle, he'd bite an apple and leave some teeth inside. Only six remained.

And now he'd have to go back to the hospital. Stan's terrible winter was extending right into spring, into this glorious day, with its blue sky and calm white clouds. Yesterday's storm left snow on the mountains, dusting them for prints. Down here on the plains, heavy, cold rain showers had left the air smelling like sage and ice, but the sun was shining now, inscribing a warm spot on everyone's back.

Stan turned his irritation on his husky, wanting-to-help twenty-one-year-old nephew Cody. "Open the gate!" he yelled.

Cody struggled in the ankle-deep mud.

"Open the gate!" Stan shouted. "Lift it! Lift it!"

An enormous, jumpy sorrel was biting the other horses. "Does anyone know how to rope?" Stan shouted. "Rope that big-ass sorrel right there!"

A man got a rope. His body spoke volumes about not really wanting to rope the sorrel. When he threw the rope over the horse's neck, the horse started rearing and making a fuss. Moses took the rope from him, and the horse calmed down. Moses led him out of the corral and tied him to a post.

There were now seven horses dispersed through three corrals, all screaming their disapproval of the new arrangement.

"Aw, shaddup," Stan hollered at the one closest to him, without a trace of humor.

I looked at him. I had never seen him in such a bad mood.

Moses stood in the round corral with the young white stud that had been picked to be gelded, frowning at a big blue pickup truck coming down the road. The men immediately tabbed its driver as Butch. When he got out of the truck and walked up to us, he looked like the happiest man on earth. He was a tall, lean Sioux with one glass eye, an ancient baseball cap of indeterminate color, aviator shades, and a wide, gap-toothed, shit-eating grin.

"He's gotta be in seventh heaven that I'm in here, a sitting duck, in this corral," said Moses to general laughter. "Now he can really terrorize me." As the token white guy, Moses took more than his share of razzing on the reservation.

In the corral, the little white horse waited calmly. The men looked nervous. Moses put a purple nylon halter on the stud's head and tied him up close to the fence.

"You guys get in there," said Stan. "You know what to do. There's a white bucket of Clorox. I mean Lysol."

A nephew poured, then set the bucket down with distaste.

"Cody," Butch said, "*you've* done this before."

Cody stood in his snow-white T-shirt and baggy denim pants, looking like he'd been accused of a crime. "No, I haven't."

"Yes, you have."

"I have not."

Butch exhaled patiently. He took a length of rope and dropped it over the horse's back, looped it around the belly, then slid it back over his butt, the loop tightening as it slipped down the horse's legs. But it didn't tighten enough. The horse stepped easily out of it. They tried again, and by the time it got to the hooves, they were tied together, tight. Moses was still at the horse's head, petting it.

"Moses," said Stan, "get away from the head."

Moses did, joining four men at the other end of the rope, which extended fifteen feet beyond the horse's rear end. They counted to three and yanked it hard, pulling the horse's hooves straight out behind and belly-flopping him to the ground. Stretched out. Tied at both ends. His back hooves pointed like a ballerina's, his neck and head extended at an unnaturally wide angle.

Stan's son Daniel, his lean warrior's body clad in baggy black MTV wear, said, "Man, I'd hate to be that horse."

"Well, you ain't! So get over it!" snapped Stan.

The horse was rolled on his right side, belly and genitals exposed. Butch said that when horses are in this position, it signals to their brain that they're done for. Specifically, it means they've been hamstrung by packs of wolves or other predators and are about to be disemboweled. Fair enough. They give up, presumably borne to the next world on a cloud of endorphins.

Stan said, "We gotta work fast."

Butch had one eye, so he wouldn't be doing the cutting. And neither, of course, would Stan. A guy stepped forward and used a rag to wash the horse's balls with disinfectant and water, working as tentatively as if he were defusing a bomb. The horse struggled like a kidnapping victim. Butch elbowed the guy aside impatiently and sloshed great heaps of water on the horse with his hands, rubbing it around. Then the man grabbed the testicles and held them tight. The sac looked like black rubber. The balls were the size of oranges.

Butch and Stan gave explosive commands.

"Cut it!"

"Grab it!"

"Do it hard!"

"Cut it!"

The man made tentative swipes at the sac. Everyone yelled at him to do it deeper and better. But he didn't break the skin. After a few minutes, Moses howled, "Someone take this rope!"

One of Stan's nieces detached herself from the fence and took his place.

Moses took the knife from the man, and cut harder. But there was still no blood. "This knife is dull!" he shouted.

Butch took his pocketknife, dipped it in the disinfectant, and handed it to Moses, who drew a red line of blood on the black sac.

Then the testicle popped out. It was white and pink and blue-veined. A little wave of blood leaped from the sac onto the horse's white inner thigh, staining it like menstrual blood.

"I need a cigarette," muttered Stan behind me. "Man, I picked the wrong week to quit."

"Goddamn!" yelled Moses from the corral. "How do I make this thing come out?" He couldn't grab the second testicle because of his crippled left hand. With Moses still struggling to get his grip, the horse started sighing with what sounded like extreme resignation, as if he were exhaling but not inhaling. Then he started singing with each exhale, a one-toned note. It sounded like a death song.

Stan rolled back up toward the house. Then he turned around and came back to the corral.

This was all wrong. Not just that the horse seemed to be dying. Not that these men seemed to be killing him. What was most wrong was that something was going so very awry under Stan's direction. Stan helped people and horses; I'd never once seen him hurt anything.

"It's good to take one testicle and throw it on the horse's nose, so he knows he ain't a stud anymore," said Butch. One of the boys picked the testicle out of the dirt and winged it like a pitcher throwing a baseball. The horse's muzzle flinched when it struck, but his eyes gazed straight ahead. Butch said, "Man, that was mean. Now he's going to come and kick your ass."

No one laughed.

Moses eventually got hold of the second testicle and cut the cord that held it and its neighbor. The cord was thick. It sounded like he was sawing through a hemp rope. The second testicle came, too, and they threw it behind the horse for speed, as tradition dictated.

It was done. The men undid the ropes binding the horse and stepped away. The horse lay still, singing quietly. Tiny the dog moved in, delicately picking up the testicle from behind the horse with her little mouth. It was almost the size of her head. She carried it outside the corral, sat down with it between her dainty paws, and ate it. My stomach was in full flight by this point, batting around my abdomen, looking for a way out.

The horse stayed down. The men stood quietly, watching. Eventually, he started breathing normally. In a few minutes, he pulled himself onto his front hooves and got halfway up. But Daniel's black-and-white pit bull, Eve, rushed him in the face. He recoiled and fell down again.

After a few minutes, he got up again and staggered around, but soon he lost his bearings and fell over sideways in the dirt, breathing hard.

Everyone was quiet.

Daniel, hanging on the corral fence, said, "You should just put him out of his misery."

"He'll make it," said Stan, his voice muted and distant.

Later, the horse stood up and walked. Stan commissioned one of the nieces to get him some oats. Butch held court by the corral fence. First he teased Moses about how he was in better shape at fifty-three than Moses was at forty-six, because "I'm outside, livin', while you're inside doing e-mail." Then he imitated how Moses would walk after his hemorrhoid operation—knees together and feet out.

It was coarse, but it was humor, and the men gulped it down as if it were pure oxygen on the surface of the moon. The boys laughed, and Stan and Moses did, too, although their eyes stayed worried.

Then they discussed other ways of gelding horses. Butch described one way as "the yoga position": the horse on its back with its rear legs tied to its neck. This would put its back at risk.

Butch said, "I even have that date-rape drug."

All the boys laughed.

"But I only use it for horses," Butch added.

More laughter.

The next day they found the gelding lying, still as a stone, about twenty yards from the corral. The boys pulled the dead horse out into the sage for the coyotes.

Butch was sick for days. "You can't do that to a horse and not get sick," he said. Moses wept, blaming himself and his crippled hand. As for Stan, he stayed in bed for most of the summer—the first of several times he would scare me to death with the thought of losing him.

I couldn't even look at him for a couple of days after the gelding died. But Moses and then Stan filled me in on what I needed to know:

You have to geld most of the young studs, because geldings are much easier to work with than the more aggressive stallions. There isn't enough money for anything around here, and paying a vet to geld the horses wasn't even close to the top of the list of unmet priorities. The guys at Stan's corral always gelded his horses; this was the first time one had died.

The unfairness of the horse's death felt crushing, and so did its component parts: the dumb bad luck of knives gone blunt, of human eyes and hands and spinal cords ruined in accidents, of being a paralyzed, impoverished man in charge of a complex horse operation. Worst of all, the awful, unforgivably bad luck of the little white stud.

CHAPTER 22

KEEPING THE
MEDICINE CLEAN

A few days later, in Lander, Moses insisted we take a walk to what he considered "our bridge." He had a surprise for me.

"Oh, Moses," I said as we walked up to it. "Don't propose to me."

He laughed, got down on one knee, and said, "Lisa, I would be so happy if you would marry me. You can be the boss."

He had a little box in his hand. I opened it to reveal a gold band set with a little diamond.

I sat down on the bridge, and he sat next to me. God, this man moved me. Our attraction for each other had diminished into something controllable, but our friendship had grown. I heard the snow-swollen river tearing along underneath us and felt the sun on my back and smelled the lilacs everywhere. It was beautiful here. And so far from home. And there was someone on the other side of the world I wanted to marry so, so badly.

"I can't marry you," I said. "I can't. But I am flattered and honored that you asked."

I tried to get him to take the ring back, and he refused, even though it cost him every dollar he owned.

"In case you ever change your mind," he said.

Later, I called Stan. "I tried to get Moses to take the ring back," I said.

"He ain't kidding" was all Stan said.

When I was alone in my room with the ring, I put it on. It fit perfectly. I loved it. I would wear it every night for weeks, thrilled to be wanted this way.

The next morning I walked up to the Lander park and sat in the sun. I felt an ocean of pain, not just for me but for all of us: Stan, Moses, me, the gelding dead for no reason. The rest of us all wanting and not getting. Me wanting a future with Peter. Moses wanting one with me. Stan wanting to live in a body that didn't reject him at every turn, a paralyzed body with, as Dr. Wyatt put it, "no healing efficiency—when his wounds heal, they break down again, and the cycle repeats itself over and over. Pretty soon you've got a scar. Scar begets scar."

I wondered how much of my pain, and Moses's, was really that we couldn't bear the thought of losing Stan. We could talk for hours about life, and God, and Stan. We were so much alike—impulsive and analytical, constellated around a man with a genius for peace and gentleness, whose best shot at describing his approach to life was this: "I try to stay real calm and careful." A small statement, but if we lived by those words, our lives would be totally different. Moses and I were more like siblings, really, acolytes on the same path.

We were terrified Stan was going to die. It would be the first death of someone I felt close to. My father had died fifteen years before. He was a brilliant, charismatic psychiatrist who spent his career helping people who were mentally ill and destitute. He was revered by lots of people, was the subject of documentaries and at least one Ph.D. thesis, and had received a medal from the queen. He was also an embarrassing, humiliating father. If only he had been sent sons instead of daughters, he might have thrived as a parent. But he'd gotten baby girl after baby girl, and he didn't know what to do with females he couldn't seduce or impress. That's why he gave us model airplanes as if we were little boys, and when we started developing into women, tended to direct his gaze at our chests and say things like, "You're growing up nicely." There was always a stack of *Playboys* in his bathroom. He was seventy when he married his third and final wife, who was twenty-six. They had come to visit me when I was a freshman in college. Dad's new wife was in the next room when, over cocktails, he stuck his hand down the shirt of my best friend, Laurie, who had come with me to meet my family. The sight hurled a ball of fire through my heart, fire so hot it could only be answered by ice. So much for trusting my dad. So much for beating back the glaciers.

I was old enough now to know that my grievances were not unusual. I was not the only person who'd had a strange relationship with her father. Like so many other fathers, he was mostly unattainable. He had not been all bad. He had not been mean or malicious. And toward the end of his life, he tried. He grew fond of Catholicism and pondered the existence of the divine. He called me to apologize for how he had disrespected women. And there was his struggle of a childhood to consider, with no money and no father and a strict, ambitious, Presbyterian mother.

But I didn't listen to my father's entreaties. Throughout my twenties, I maintained a steel wall between us. When he started to go into serious physical decline, I was working as a newspaper reporter in Central America. I flew to see him three times that year at his home in Nova Scotia. His heart was a little weaker every time. On my way back to Costa Rica the last time, I called him from the Boston airport. The end was near and we both knew it. I was calling to say goodbye. I didn't need the glaciers or the wall anymore, but I didn't know what to say.

"I hope I've been an okay daughter," I said awkwardly, starting to cry.

He paused. "Of course you've been a good daughter."

That was it. Not exactly a ringing resolution. Not a healing moment. I never saw him again.

Weighed down by my distrust for men in power, particularly for great healers, as my father had been known to be, I pretty much avoided romantic partners with any pretensions toward power or healing. In my younger years, I'd had a taste for charmers, flirts, adventurers; guys with a tendency toward debauchery and enough honesty to admit it. Men who would cheerfully agree with me that they were base and selfish creatures. Moses was right in there. "I'm a beast!" he'd told me. That outdoor dog.

But here I was with Stan, the greatest healer and, wheelchair or no, the most overtly powerful man I had ever met. I knew I was the butt of a cosmic joke here, but I didn't care. I would take my healing where I could get it. This was probably the only place I *could* get it—with a man who completely outgunned me in the power department, like my father had when I was a child. A man who had mistreated women in the past. I had to take the risk to enter Stan's magical world with him, and he had to treat my openness with immaculate respect.

And I did. And he had.

From the beginning Stan had been rebuilding a foundation underneath me, simply by handing me his trust as if I were a person who knew the shape and weight of such a thing, as if I could hold it without dropping it. I rarely touched my father. For him, bodies were things to be controlled. When I was around him, I hid mine under men's shirts and overalls. But there was nothing to do with Stan's body except care for it and love it. If he needed his hair brushed, I would brush it. If he needed it washed, I would do it on the porch with him leaning on the railing. When he started to slip, I caught him. He knew I would better than I knew it myself.

I was stiffer and less touchy than some of the other women around Stan, but he had gotten to me. Despite his powers, his vulnerability was the first and last thing you saw. I loved him. I trusted him. And the cutting edge of that was the thought of losing him: It was unbearable.

I'll work on it, God, I thought, feeling the serious hand of the sun press between my shoulder blades. I'll work on it, God, but please dammit don't take him away now. Do it later.

Stan had told me recently, "I get sick so my medicines can stay clean."

I hadn't understood.

"When I'm sick, it starts people praying for me, and me praying, too," he said. "It's like laundering money. Bringing bad money and making it clean."

It was true. Praying for Stan was the sweetest part of my life.

Give me something to carry, Stan, I'd pray as he struggled beside me in the sweat lodge. Give me your burden. Let me take some of it.

We all suffered in the heat, but the heat was what I loved.

The truth was, part of me still felt cold inside, even after years of Buddhist practice. Buddhism had let me feel the pain I'd ignored for the first decades of my life. Buddhism was still and spacious. It had made me more honest and had calmed me down, but it hadn't warmed up the wedge of ice buried in my chest. In Buddhist retreats, we sat silently, wrapped in blankets, watching the contents of our minds rise and fall, or wishing well to others or ourselves. Alone.

Here, Arilda was about to go in for a biopsy of a growth in her stomach. Funny, warm, inviting, talkative Arilda. In the sweat lodge, with sweat coursing down my skin, I prayed, Arilda, give me your burden. It got hotter, and for the first time instead of shrinking down into the cooler air, I sat taller and dropped the towel I usually clutched to my head as a barrier against the heat. I plowed into the heat and misery, soaking my T-shirt and shorts with sweat, letting the pain shoot through my head. I wanted the connection with Arilda and Stan and everybody. I wanted to lessen Arilda's anxiety and make whatever was in her stomach go away, and I didn't care if it laid me flat.

"What's bad is good," Stan had told me.

I was starting to understand what he meant. In the sweat lodge, the act of voluntarily sacrificing my own comfort for someone else's well-being was just a paper's width away from the sweetness of union.

I'd been sitting on the park bench for two hours. Above the lacy canopy of leaves, the sun was straight overhead. A pair of joggers went by with a husky on a leash. I stood up and started walking through the park, still ruminating.

Stan healed people of disease in his sweat lodge with an alchemy I couldn't understand. But what he'd done with me was no less astonishing. He'd healed me by letting me love him, letting me warm up around him. He had set that love expanding inside me when I worked the black stallion two summers ago, and it hadn't stopped.

Romantically, we all wanted things that probably wouldn't make us happy. I would never make Moses happy. We both hurtled through life. Together we could hurtle right off a cliff. I'd been clobbered by my attraction to him, but I needed somebody more stable for the long haul. I couldn't even imagine us together in the white world. I suspected that for Moses, I was a whiff of cellular remembrance, of Mommy or hope or a horse he'd broken once or a woman he'd visualized when he'd eaten all those mushrooms twenty-five years ago.

Peter. Well. He'd been so gone for so long I couldn't even remember his face. We'd spoken the night before, and I'd told him Moses had proposed to me that day. Peter said he'd break his three-month commitment to the monastery and come home early, as soon as possible.

"Why?" I'd asked, surprised.

"Because I don't want to lose you!" he'd said, as if it should have been obvious.

"Hunh?" I'd said. I was shocked. "Okay."

I called Stan to say hi and that I wasn't coming out until the sweat that evening.

He said, "How are you doing?"

"Pretty off center," I said. "Confused about everything."

He said "Hmmmm . . ." Then his voice went high, and he said, "Man, my stud keeps driving his mares back into the corral."

I said, "Maybe he doesn't want to be a stud anymore. Maybe it's too lonely at the top."

Stan said, "Moses is supposed to be here with his truck. We need sweat wood."

"I haven't seen Moses today," I said. "Maybe he's on his way."

I did not want to go and ask favors of the man whose marriage proposal I'd rejected the day before.

We sat in silence for a second.

"I'll see you later," I said.

"Later," he echoed.

We hung up.

I sat there a while longer, not wanting to go and find Moses but thinking I should do so anyway. I thought about how, if you sponsor a sweat lodge, your prayer can't be for yourself. It has to be for someone else. I thought, Stan really needs that wood. The evening's sweat lodge depended on it. Moses didn't have a phone. I was at that moment within one mile of him. Stan was about twenty miles away with a car that might be broken and, if not, was likely being driven by some nephews to the Ethete store to get a pop.

I thought, I'll do this for Stan.

CHAPTER 23

WHAT IT'S LIKE TO BE
AN INDIAN

I walked to Moses's rented room. He wasn't there. Relieved, I was walking away when I passed the Laundromat. Moses's monstrous yellow truck was parked there. I went in, and there he was, putting clean shirts on hangers.

"Hi," I said, my discomfort making me rush. "Stan needs your truck."

"I don't want to be *busy* today!" he barked. "I'm tired! Fuck Stan!"

He groused about how Stan's medicine was getting messed up because he let people have sweats who didn't bring their own wood. Then he called Stan and said he'd bring out the truck after he finished his laundry. This meant he'd need a ride home. Meaning I'd need to follow him out and bring him back.

He finished hanging up his clothes. I was starting to feel roped into the nonlinear pooling of resources that eat up days and days of people's time when they don't have any money. Poverty is a lot of things, but mostly it's inconvenient.

"I want to check my e-mail at the library first," I said. "Meet me there."

We caravanned to the library, did our business, and got back into our separate vehicles. Moses's truck wouldn't start. I watched his head jerk up and down with frustration. He swung back and forth off the steering wheel, looking small in the giant Chevy.

He poked his head out of the window. "Let's try to pop the clutch," he said. "You drive."

I put it in reverse, he pushed, I popped it too soon, and he said, "Whoah! You were supposed to wait for me to say something!"

We were halfway out in the street. We tried again, lurching all the way into the street before stalling again. I felt exhausted. Clouds moved in, and it became a perfectly still, muggy, malevolent-feeling late-spring day. Wasps banged against the windows of parked cars on the side of the road, trying to get in. Occasional cars inched by.

There was no way out. A sheriff's deputy drove by. Moses had no driver's license, and the county sheriff's office had recently notified the Lander cops about his lack of documentation, resulting in sixty dollars' worth of tickets. Another Lander police car drove by. It would be back.

I turned to Moses. "Is this the way life is?"

"Yep," he said, characteristically not missing a beat. "When you're poor and don't have a good truck and don't have no good driver's license 'cause you're all burned up and when Stan doesn't have any sense about how to run a sweat lodge. The people sponsoring should get the wood."

"In my world, it's not this hard," I said. "We all drive Toyotas. They work."

We sat. I knew I should move over to the driver's seat so when the police stopped, I could tell them I was driving the truck when it stalled. But I didn't have the energy to mention it or do it. Then things got inexplicably more companionable. Suddenly, I felt the same as I had two months ago, outside the library, when Moses told me about getting kicked out of Stan's, and that his hemorrhoid operation had been delayed, and that he had eighty-five cents to his name. We'd started laughing our heads off, helpless in the sun.

I giggled. "It doesn't get any worse than this, does it?"

Moses giggled, too.

The cops came by again, did a U-turn just past us, and pulled over. A young, towheaded, fresh-faced sheriff's deputy approached Moses's side of the truck and said, "Sir, may I see your driver's license?"

"You know damn well I don't have no driver's license!" Moses yelled. "You guys e-mailed the Lander cops just the other day!"

The deputy, who apparently hadn't been in on this particular e-mail, said, "Sir, what is your name, and how do you spell it?"

Moses started spelling it, "S-T-A—you guys all know just who the hell I am! Don't play around with me! And of course that's why I don't have a driver's license; you know I can't see well enough to get one!"

Another officer walked to my side of the truck, his hand on his gun. Hooboy, I thought.

Moses's cop said, "Don't get an attitude with *me*. Now, how do you spell your name? S-T-A—"

I shouted, "R-K!"

Moses let loose a string of invective.

"Moses!" I hissed. "It's not their fault! Leave them alone!"

Moses apologized, but the policeman was scared now, and he said again, "Don't cop an attitude with *me*."

"Sorry," said Moses. "I do have some ID." He handed it over.

When the policemen walked back to their car to check, I said, "Jesus *Christ*, Moses! They're the *law*! You can't win with them!"

"But they were pulling stupid bullshit on me!"

"Well, you outstupided them, for sure."

Finally, they came back, and the little one said, "Mr. Stark, I'm gonna give you a break this time. But you need to move this truck."

Moses said, "Will you help us?"

So the two white deputies, and one reservation cop who'd been called as backup, and Moses got behind the truck and pushed while I popped the clutch. It didn't work. Moses said, "Did you turn on the key?"

"No," I said. "Oops!"

At which point the Native American officer said to Moses, "So *that's* why you were in the driver's seat, huh?"

This ignited a spark of camaraderie between all the men. Women drivers: the bane of all males, regardless of which side of the law they happened to be on. At last they pushed the truck into a parking spot, and the cops went away. I waved goodbye with a good deal of friendliness. So did Moses. So did the cops.

"Oh my God, Moses, you are such a dummy," I said, starting to laugh.

The shot of adrenaline and the laughter cleared the air between us. I wanted to confess how strange I'd been feeling. I hadn't been up here

gliding into an intimate understanding of Stan and his spiritual abil-
ities. Instead, I'd fallen into the oldest diversion on the planet: I'd gotten a wicked crush on Moses. I was working my way out the other end
of that, but I'd wasted weeks of time. I didn't understand a damn thing
about how Stan worked. I'd spent most of my time falling on my face.
So much for being a competent writer, much less a faithful girlfriend.
Plus, I was worried about Stan. He was getting physically weaker, and
I wasn't being a help at all. I felt like I was somehow contributing to
his downward spiral.

As a Buddhist teacher once told me, "It's easy to feel like the piece
of shit the world revolves around."

There would be no truck, no sweat wood, and no sweat lodge that
evening. But we drove my Toyota to Stan's and told them all about our
encounter with the law.

"I thought I was gonna get shot," I said, "and we weren't doing anything except sitting in his truck!"

Cody sat on the couch, cracking up, and Stan lay on his bed, laughing. When the laughter died down Stan said to me, "Now you know
what it's like to be an Indian."

CHAPTER 24

THE MONK DISROBES

It was hot the day I left to pick Peter up at the airport. I squinted into the sun all the way south to Denver, pulling over regularly to buy Diet Cherry Cokes with ice and blaring the new CD player I'd installed in my car months before as a foil to the emptiness of the Wyoming landscape.

I called an old friend who happened to be married to Peter's brother. She had worked diligently to get us together, and she still felt responsible for the increasing frailty of our union.

"I don't know what's going to happen," I said into my cell phone. "I feel nothing. It's been too long."

I walked into the echoey white mosque-like Denver airport and stood next to a noisy fountain, enjoying the cool vapor and the clatter of water hitting water. I had been there only a few minutes when a thin, bald man with Peter's face walked up to me. We embraced. His ribs stuck out beneath my fingers. He had no eyebrows. At Wat Pah Nanachat, the monks eat once a day, and even their eyebrows are shaved in order to beat vanity into submission. We went to the Motel 6 on Federal Boulevard, and my monk disrobed. As soon as I touched Peter's skin, my world snapped back into a shape I could recognize. Bodies clear up confusion with a speed and authority the mind can't touch.

We had two days of remembering, clarifying skin on skin. But as a feeling of expansiveness asserted itself throughout Room 214, pain would have its say. I remembered that this person I loved so effortlessly had hurt me just shy of unforgivably, and he remembered the same. One night somewhere in the middle of our stay, we yelled at each other for hours, reviewing every painful thing we'd suffered in the past year at the cruel, thoughtless, self-involved hands of the other.

"You let it go way too far before you told me!" he said.

"Why? Because I didn't tell you every little detail right at the beginning and totally destroy your peace of mind? Spare me."

During a water break, we noticed that the blinds were starting to glow. It was morning. We decided to go and get some breakfast at a twenty-four-hour place two parking lots away from our door. Through senses undone by emotion and sleeplessness, we eventually noticed that not only was everyone else in the restaurant eating piles of ribs for breakfast, they were eating comically large piles of them. We started to giggle. Then our own food hit our systems and exhaustion set in. We walked quietly over the tarmac back to our room, arm in arm.

"I'm sorry about Mariel," he said. "Really sorry. I can't imagine the pain I put you through. That was a huge mistake."

"And I'm sorry about Moses. And about how I've been dissing Buddhism. I just hate that it takes you away from me."

If we didn't throw any new wrenches into the machinery, we would come through this. Peter was the one who helped me to stop hurtling, the one who balanced me. He was the one I could navigate life with, even through the difficulties of the last year. He provided space and laughter. He met me at the bottom, the middle, and the top.

CHAPTER 25

LIFE MOVES AS IT IS TOUCHED

Peter and I spent most of the summer at home in Paonia knitting our relationship back together. Moses stayed in his pay-by-the-month hotel in Lander, so when I went up to Stan's, I didn't see him. My visits to Wyoming took on a simple, peaceful feeling.

One day a horse clinic attendee—a sunburned Dutch man who had picked out a nervous mare to gentle—got up at dawn, climbed into the corral, stuck his butt out to let two other, calmer horses sniff it, then offered his rear end to the nervous mare. She sniffed it, too.

He told us about it over breakfast. "I felt my anus relax," he reported in his strongly accented English. "Away from the way I was when I was a child when I got spanked."

I put my fingers on my lips, forcing them not to smile. Stan looked straight ahead, thoughtfully fingering his sparse mustache. Arapahos don't generally talk about their body parts at breakfast.

"Jay-R," Stan said to his brother, "take out the garbage."

Jay-R picked up the plastic bag and stomped toward the battered door. When he opened it, the barks of the pit bulls and mutts down near the pasture filled the room. Either they'd caught a rabbit or they were just excited to see the door open.

"Leave it alone or kill it!" Jay-R shouted at them, stepping out and slamming the door behind him. End of subject.

Another time I brought my friend Mary to Stan's. She was twenty-five, and could have been a model but preferred tending bar and shooting all her own meat from horseback in the Colorado mountains. She also punched out men who made passes at her at the Packing Shed bar in Paonia. When I suggested we drive up to Stan's in my little Toyota, she snorted softly and said it might not have room for her saddle. The next morning she pulled up in a big white pickup. When we got to Stan's, she filled his freezer with elk steak she'd wrapped in butcher paper and proceeded to the corral, where she broke horses while wearing jeans and a pink camisole that fitted so accurately it dropped the jaw of anyone who came near. Including Stan.

I was just dimly aware of this because I got an upset stomach and spent most of the visit lying in the only shade I could find—under a truck parked in the weeds. Once, when I was on my way back from the bathroom to my patch of shade, a two-year-old bay stud stuck his nose through the fence at me. I went over and put my nose on his. We smooched each other for some time, and then I went in and put a halter on him and led him around. He was as gentle as a kitten. We took a longer walk around the pasture together. Then I tied him up and groomed him, for which he seemed truly grateful. I finally left him and walked over to the big corral to tell Stan.

"That little bay is the sweetest horse I've ever met," I said.

"That's 'cause you're finding the sweetness in yourself," he said without taking his eyes off Mary.

I got hit by another wave of nausea and went back to my place under the truck.

Out in the corral, Mary quickly gentled a gray horse, then turned to a huge, aggressive palomino. Stan sat outside the corral and prayed, and when the horse let fly with a carefully aimed kick, his hoof somehow snapped a pole Mary was holding rather than her leg.

"I prayed to the horse spirit," Stan said. "It's a guardian."

Mary told me later, "A spirit was right there with me, giving me the backbone I needed, and the support and safety and confidence. It's almost like—I don't want to say Stan could use my body to will his actions, but it was something like that. In such a gentle and safe kind of way. I think Stan is superintuitive and that he can really see what people need. He's really good at sending his clear images. He's really good at sending his thoughts to other people when they need them, or his blessing, or his prayer."

CHAPTER 26

ONE EMBARRASSMENT
AFTER ANOTHER

Stan suggested I do a fast. It gets you down the road toward the Creator more quickly, he said mildly. In the Northern Arapaho tradition, that meant three days and three nights in a lean-to hut without food or water, followed by a sweat lodge. Only after the second round would I be allowed to drink.

I swallowed hard. I wanted to do it, but I was intimidated. I mulled it over with Peter on the phone, and I sent my mother an e-mail.

She responded:

Dear Lisa,

I hope you are well and happy.

Have you decided yet when you would do this very scary and frightful thing? I think the absence of water during the heat is really disturbing and potentially dangerous for a northerner with genes intended for fat and cold and lots of water. Indians with their dark skin can do things that we fair-skinned people simply are not intended to expose ourselves to. Witness Sven Hedin's adventures when more or less all of the expedition died somewhere in Asia after having resorted to drinking urine.

Love,
Ma

P.S. My mother knew Sven, who was a famous explorer.
Pay attention to your genetic makeup and respect it. You are not
an Indian. Maybe you need to be respectful of that.

I laughed. My mother. Then I called my doctor. I feared dehydration more than I feared breaking horses, not finding love, finding love, whatever. I drank bottle after bottle of Gatorade between rounds at the sweat lodge. I heard a story once—I'm not sure if it was a joke or not—that one of my Swedish ancestors got stuck in a sauna and died there.

"You have a strong constitution, and you could last until you're ninety," my doctor said. "But you could end up on dialysis in your fifties if you do this."

That brought up the obvious question: What did I believe in, really? Stan had surrendered to the Creator. He had powers possessed by no one else I knew. I had benefited from that power and seen other people benefit, too. I believed if I believed as strongly as he did, I would receive protection.

Trouble is, I didn't believe that way. I wasn't Native American. I hadn't been visited by spirit after spirit in the hospital after getting paralyzed in a car accident. I had not gone through the years of grieving and denial that ended with me completely surrendered, close to egoless, and a full-time employee of the Creator.

I told Stan I didn't think I was going to do it.

"The Creator would protect you, you know," he said.

I wanted to be braver, but I was not. "I'm gonna take my time on this, Stan."

And I haven't done it.

I was no Carlos Castaneda, that was for sure.

One afternoon Stan's son Beau got up from the table and came back with a jar of brackish liquid. It was peyote tea. He sipped some and offered it to me. I took it, sipped, and instantly got a delicious bright yellow dancing feeling in my forehead. Peyote, it is said, was discovered by an Indian woman exhausted by her fight for survival. She went into the desert to die, and when she got there, the peyote plant showed itself to her and she took it. It gave her the strength to go on.

Around here they talk about peyote as a spirit they call That Old Man. As in, "Take that question to that old man. Take that prayer to that old man. He'll tell you what to do."

Not long after I tried the peyote tea, there was a peyote drumming at Stan's. Like a peyote meeting, it would go all night, but it was a less formal ceremony—if we needed to throw up or go to the bathroom, we would be allowed to get up and do so. The occasional ducking out for a cigarette would also be okay.

I went to Stan's with a friend I had met there. Neither of us had ever done a peyote ceremony, and we were nervous and excited and fussy. She'd heard you weren't allowed to move in a peyote meeting, so she'd brought an excessive number of pillows. I heard we'd probably get sick, so I'd brought two changes of clean clothes. We did a U-turn in the middle of the street in Lander to buy two gallons of water at Safeway, even though I'd been drinking the water at Stan's for months.

The ceremony started at about midnight. There were seven men. My friend, who happened to be African American, was the only woman other than me. Stan lay on a couch with me at his head and my friend at his feet. The peyote was powdered and tasted like burned toast mixed with horse poop mixed with dirt mixed with something really bitter, like piano varnish. I took a big dose. Luckily, there was a whole jar of peyote tea to wash it all down with.

After a few minutes, I got a crawly feeling in my brain. I closed my eyes and saw the cellular structure of a woody plant or a series of trusses in a vaulted brownish ceiling, like one you'd find in a wooden medieval cathedral. And then a boat filled with a lot of slender red rectangular people. Then I fell off a waterfall and into blue, blue water. A long waterfall. Free-falling. I opened my eyes and watched the man leading the ceremony and Stan's son Beau drumming and singing and thought I had never seen such beautiful men in my whole life. The leader was a plump jowly man of about fifty, wearing big eyeglasses and his long hair in a ponytail. He was totally serious and focused. Beau was twenty. When my mother came to visit, she told him he ought to be a movie star. She should have seen him now, his face tilted up, his arrow-straight lacquer-black hair pouring off his head, his eyes closed, his voice, a smooth, dependable tenor that reminded me of polished wood, pouring through the room.

I thought I might throw up, and that second Stan said right into my ear, "Don't think about getting sick! Pray! Pray for the people you know!"

So I did. I prayed for Stan, looking back over my shoulder to see his body lying on the couch when I couldn't visualize him correctly. I did a simple Buddhist prayer: May you be safe. May you be happy. May you be healthy. May you live with ease.

The men sang. I prayed.

It all went beautifully until right around dawn, when my friend and I were told we would make breakfast and serve it to the men. We weren't asked, we were told. And breakfast wasn't going to be just a pile of toast and a pan of eggs; it would be a ceremonially served progression of corn, fruit, and meat.

My friend and I walked the ten feet or so into the kitchen and went from religious devotees to stoned coeds in the blink of an eye. We laughed. We bonded. We rolled our eyes at the order that had been leveled at us, my rebelliousness compounding on contact with hers. Giggling our heads off, we looked for can openers and spatulas with hands that felt all thumbs. It seemed to take forever to get that breakfast together.

And when we brought the food back into the living room we were met with a solid wall of disapproval. Stan looked at us softly, then around the room. Beau looked at us, then at the linoleum floor. The leader looked straight at us. He didn't mince words. Our boisterousness had offended the spirit of the ceremony. We had offended that old man.

"Lisa," he said, "put on that blanket. Kneel at that bucket of water. At the end of this song, I want you to pray out loud. Speak from your heart."

I was shaking with confusion and shame. I wrapped a thin fleece blanket of a vaguely Navajo design around my shoulders and looked sideways at my pal, who had thrown herself into Stan's arms, sobbing. I looked around the room at everyone, each carrying his or her particular burden, a particular suffering. Everyone looked so vulnerable, so easily bruised. I felt like I could see everyone's racial pain so clearly: red man, black woman, white woman. None of them was easy.

I don't remember what I said when I spoke. But what I meant to say was this: "White people have been messing up in Indian Country since we got here, and what I just did in your kitchen was just the most recent time for me. I'm very sorry. I apologize to all of you. I didn't mean to be disrespectful. But I'm ignorant. I'm trying to learn, but I'm still a stranger here."

A Buddhist sage once said, "The spiritual life is one embarrassment after another." He was right.

Not long afterward, I was sitting in a sweat lodge when a baby was brought in to receive her Indian name. The English translation of the name was Woman Singing in Sage.

"I got a name for you, too," Stan said later. "They told me." He meant the spirits had told him. I was surprised. I hadn't sought or expected an Indian name. Stan had once told me about a white woman who had introduced herself to him as She Who Walks Upon the Far Blue Mountains, and he had replied, "Can I just call you Blue?" I'd laughed. I pretty much avoided white people who introduced themselves by their Indian names.

But holy cow, the spirits had told Stan my name. I must have earned it. She Comes Far would be kind of nice. That would confer some gravitas on all the energy I'd expended up here. It wouldn't be all that far off.

"It's Little Girl," he said.

So much for being a spiritual adept. I plodded along, doing every sweat lodge I could. Other people—even white people—would come and fast, or work the horses, and go home. I liked to stay. My talent was staying.

CHAPTER 27

JEVON

Like every summer morning at Stan's, it was a hot one. There wasn't a single shade tree near the house, not a leaf to break the constant ministrations of the sun. Air conditioners and swamp coolers tended to die of exhaustion way before their time. In the kitchen, flies proliferated and energy levels sagged as we took turns with a swatter. Two table fans were aimed at Stan, and occasionally a niece squirted him with a spray bottle.

Conversations that morning were short.

"Stan, do you have any dental floss?" I asked after vainly trying to dislodge a piece of bacon from a back tooth with my tongue.

"Dental floss!" he said. "I don't have any teeth!"

Everyone laughed, and the silence reasserted itself.

Eventually, Stan said, "Let's go swimming. Go cool off."

No one responded.

"Let's *go!*" Stan repeated, and we all got up and walked into one another in the tiny kitchen and at last made it out the door and into the bed of Stan's pickup truck, which Cody drove a mile up a dirt track, bumped down the bank, and parked at the edge of the beach. What a beach! It was real, buff sand fronting a deep blue eddy that wheeled slowly off the north bank of the Little Wind River. The beach sloped off steeply and the water was over my head in a few steps. It was a perfect, only slightly fishy-smelling heaven. We all swam. Tisha climbed on my back, and we had chicken fights. Then I swam underwater to get away from the melee to the other side so I could sit and watch and feel the sun dry the water on my skin just slightly more slowly than a towel would.

Cody and another nephew carried Stan from the passenger seat of the truck into the river. He hooked his arms around their necks and they dunked him in the cool water. He floated through the deeps with the big, strong boys holding him up. He cooled off fast—temperature regulation is a constant challenge for quadriplegics—so just a few minutes later, the boys carried him back to the truck.

"That's better," he said. "Now gimme a cigarette."

Another time the drought had left the swimming hole shallow and rimmed with scum. We needed to go swimming, but we had to find another place. Stan said the word, and we all loaded up—three adults in the cab of the truck and at least a dozen kids in its bed. We stopped once at the Ethete store, again at the Fort Washakie store, and then, fully provisioned with baloney and white bread and chips, we headed up into the Wind River Range, to the Washakie Reservoir. The first place we stopped at the side of the reservoir was full of broken beer bottles and toilet paper, so we drove up to a heavily wooded part of the shore right next to where the river fed the reservoir. There was a narrow path through the bushes leading to a three-foot drop-off into the lake. I immediately jumped in with the kids. It felt heavenly.

Stan didn't swim that time but sat in the truck and listened to music, chatting with whoever came in asking for a cigarette. He liked getting out of the house. Once a friend of mine from Denver took him around the reservation in a turbo Audi, hitting 100 miles per hour on certain turns while Stan remembered taking those same turns at the same speed in much different vehicles thirty years before. Every time we went swimming or looking for horses, he could point out every swale and rock and good creek crossing. He knew the country intimately, and just because he couldn't ride into it anymore didn't mean he wasn't going to see it. If not for a swimming expedition or to find some lost horses, at least he'd go to Walmart just to see the country move by, to hear the music the boys brought along: peyote songs for Beau, rap for Daniel, death metal for the other boys. Those afternoons, riding in the truck and hanging out with the Addisons, I felt as capable of simple happiness as a dog.

But Stan always maintained that life isn't about happiness. Good times are followed by bad times; bad times are followed by good. Life isn't about staying clear of pain. Life is about finding your center, even when things get so painful you want to run like hell in the opposite direction.

I was home in Colorado when the news came. Suzi's boyfriend, Jevon, had gotten into a fight on the street in Riverton. He'd been stabbed and bled to death. The funeral was later that week.

Numb, I drove up to Jevon's wake. I got to Lander at about midnight and called Stan to see if he was going. He wasn't.

"It's good you're going, though," he said. "Suzi could use some support. People are talking smack about her."

"Hold on," I said, veering onto the gravel shoulder of the road and pulling the brake. I'd never been to a wake where there was a possibility of violence. I'd never been to a wake, period. I'd never known anyone who'd been murdered. I'd never seen a dead body.

I slowly drove the last couple of miles to the wake, telling myself I could leave any time I wanted.

When I got there, people were sleepy and sad. There was a big aluminum coffee dispenser and portly old folks sipping from Styrofoam cups. I went into a teepee lit from inside. There were a few folding chairs, and a handful of people sitting silently in front of the coffin that held Jevon's body. He lay there looking, well, murdered. His face was bruised and cut. His left eye was slightly open. The air around him smelled of formaldehyde. I sat in the front row.

I remembered one day about four months before, in February, when Stan's sister Frenchie's car—a Mercury Cougar with bald tires and a backseat full of kids—got stuck in the snow in front of Stan's. Moses and Jevon were trying to pull it out with a shovel and a truck and a chain. Frenchie sat in the front seat, spinning her tires and bawling the men out. Frenchie Addison yelling at Moses Stark was about as unusual an event at Stan's as someone making a pot of coffee. But Frenchie yelling at Jevon—that wasn't unusual, either, but Jevon was so much softer, so much younger. His digging got less and less decisive. Then he threw down the shovel and walked over to the sweat lodge and stood there in the snow reflecting the blinding sun and screamed at the sky: "Fuck!"

I'd given Jevon my tape recorder a few days before, telling him he could keep it if he wrote me a rap song. I walked over to the slight, boyish figure at the sweat lodge.

"Here's the kind of rap song I want, Jevon," I said. "One that's about rising above adversity."

He kept looking straight west, toward the mountains.

"Do you know what adversity is?" I said. "It means rising above all the problems life throws at you. Do you get it?"

Now I couldn't remember how he'd responded. Maybe he hadn't. I could visualize him looking down at the ground and mumbling. Maybe that's exactly what he'd done. I wished I'd just hugged him instead.

"Bye, Jevon," I mumbled, getting up from my folding chair and leaving the teepee. Outside, everyone was moving slowly and peacefully. If Suzi was here, she was safe. I got back into my car and drove away.

The next morning I got up early and went to Arilda's. I drove with her and the kids to the funeral at the Blue Sky Center, a gym and community center in Ethete. When we got there, the Addisons hung back on the bleachers, not venturing onto the AstroTurf-covered basketball court, which contained ninety-six chairs. As the service progressed, about half of the chairs were filled and we sat down, too.

After the priest said a brief welcome, we all lined up to say goodbye to Jevon. The pallbearers went first. Wearing low-slung baggy jeans and black T-shirts, they bent over Jevon's open casket, touching him, talking in low voices. They stayed there for a long time. Suzi, who had loved Jevon since she was ten and was now functionally a widow at seventeen, came over to where I was standing in line and gave me a hug. She was wearing white high-heeled platform sandals, a white miniskirt, a white tank top, and a black bra. Her toenails were painted pink. She looked around with a half-smile on her face, as if she were at a party and couldn't find the person being celebrated.

I got to the coffin. Jevon was wearing a black shirt and a bolo tie with a round beaded clasp. His lips seemed full because his face seemed to be sinking. His skin was whitish and dry, and yesterday's bruises were separating into blotches of red and blue. His left eye looked like it had the night before—a tiny bit open, a bit of pupil showing. On his chest was a pack of Newports, a box of Marlboro Lights, a bottle of men's cologne, and a CD. His hand was wrapped around a cigarette. The details hit me one after another, but I was numb inside.

I went outside with one of the little Addison girls and pushed her on a swing near the door. When the pallbearers carried out the coffin, we joined the small crowd, leaned against the wall of the community center, and watched Jevon get loaded up and driven off.

The Oxford American Dictionary defines apocalypse as "an event involving destruction or damage on an awesome or catastrophic scale"—an accurate depiction of what had happened to pretty much all the tribes after the arrival of whites in North America. The Natives had been as oblivious to the concept of land ownership as I am to the concept of sleep ownership or air ownership. After being stripped of what they didn't know could be taken, Native Americans for the most part lived a life that can only be described as postapocalyptic.

Nowadays, the dislocation and violence of the white occupation of the continent still plays out on the reservation. "American Indians are victims of violent crime at rates more than twice the national average—far exceeding any other ethnic group in the country," reported Attorney General John Ashcroft in 2001. Native Americans fall victim to violent crime at about two times the rate of African Americans and two and a half times that of Caucasians, according to 2002 statistics from the Department of Justice. Native Americans between eighteen and twenty-four are particularly hard hit, with one of every four being a victim of violent crime. Federal prisons are "the fastest-growing Indian reservation in the country," according to Leonard Peltier, who is still serving time after being convicted of the 1975 fatal shooting of two FBI agents on Pine Ridge after a still-contested trial.

The specific stories underlying Native America's crime statistics are hair-raising. One day in March, 2005, Jeff Weise, a fifteen-year-old Ojibwe boy living in Minnesota, shot and killed his grandfather and his grandfather's girlfriend, then went to school, killing seven more people before committing suicide. Press accounts revealed that Weise's father had committed suicide years before; his mother lived in a nursing home following an alcohol-related car accident. At the time of Jeff's shooting spree and suicide he was living with his grandmother, spending most of his time alone, playing violent video games, and increasingly retreating into his imagination. His background was not all that different from Jevon's, with an absent father and a mother dead of alcoholism. It was not all that different from the backgrounds of plenty of boys who ended up at Stan's.

I watched the pallbearers load Jevon's coffin into the back of the hearse. A surge of wild thoughts stampeded through my mind: What will happen when white people provoke enough brown people that we get handed an apocalypse of our own? I need to stop being such a beginner at funerals, not be in a constant state of surprise when things don't run smoothly. When peace doesn't reign in the streets of my town; when nature doesn't hand over her treasures so unquestioningly.

I got back into Arilda's car and we took our place in the slow, jolting procession down the bumpy, dusty road to the Yellow Calf Cemetery, where the Chavezes, Spoonhunters, and Antelopes were buried.

At the grave, a group of men lowered Jevon's coffin into the ground on ropes. Half a dozen shovels poked out of the adjacent pile of dirt, waiting for the pallbearers to start shoveling. The priest eulogized noncommittally that he was sure there was room for Jevon in heaven. He sprinkled dirt on the casket, and the pallbearers grabbed the shovels and set to. As the dirt clattered softly onto the coffin, Suzi began to cry. First she fell into her friend's arms, then her sister's, and finally into the arms of Jevon's relatives. Then she started to scream. I looked at Frenchie. Her face crumpled as she looked at her bereft daughter; suddenly she was crying, too. Suzi's younger sisters joined in. They went, sobbing, into the arms of friends.

The pallbearers started to sing in Arapaho as they dug. One of the girls walked up and stood next to me, singing. One of the pallbearers, Stan's son Beau, stopped singing and started to cry. He sobbed, "He was like a brother!" Arilda and Frenchie hugged him. "He was my brother!"

Then he crouched at the head of the grave and started to sing again next to the cream-colored wooden cross nicely painted with Jevon's name. He was flanked by a burly guy who sobbed, tears soaking his face and dripping off his nose and onto the dirt.

I went to sit in the car with lovely little nine-year-old Suzanna, lucky little Suzanna, being raised by Arilda.

"Is this your first funeral?" I asked her.

"No," she told me. "My dad's."

Of course. Her father had been Arilda's oldest son, Adrian. He died in a car crash in October 2001, leaving four kids to be distributed among aunts and uncles.

"What's bad is good," Stan had said. How could this be good?

CHAPTER 28

LANDER

Only a few days after Jevon's funeral, *Outside* magazine published its list of ten best towns for 2004. Lander was in it:

> It's puzzling why even more climbers don't end up in Lander, where the high desert meets the Rockies and calm, sunny days are the norm. Everything from abundant bouldering routes to sandstone and limestone cliffs to multipitch granite peaks in the Wind River Range awaits—plus you can camp for nothing on the banks of the Popo Agie (pronounced Po-PO-zha) River in Lander City Park. If you need a Home Depot, you'll have to head 25 miles northeast to Riverton, but that doesn't mean Lander is a fudge-shoppe-and-wax-museum tourist town. Fremont County ranks among the top in the state for cattle, sheep, and hay production—those guys in cowboy hats aren't poseurs. Throw in rock jocks, instructors from the National Outdoor Leadership School headquarters (on Lincoln Street), greenies, accountants, and lawyers and you end up with a serendipitous blend in this eight-block-wide town.

Outside's serendipitous blend didn't include the Eastern Shoshones or the Northern Arapahos, who are all over the place in Lander, since the edge of their reservation is about five miles from downtown. Lander doesn't have nearly as many Native Americans as Riverton does, but it's got plenty, and they're a lot more visible than, say, the population of accountants who jumped off the streets and onto *Outside*'s radar.

As for the guys in the cowboy hats, on the same day I read *Outside,* I got an e-mail from Moses from his rent-by-the-month room in downtown Lander, next to a room occupied by an entire family. Their daughter was named Debbie.

Debbie's baby died this morning in that room next door . . . So it's just been Debbie and her younger sister staying there and we've all been hanging together, trying to have enough to eat. I haven't ate 3 days now.

A weightlifter works out by steadily increasing the full amount of weight he can handle getting stronger and stronger as time goes by. I have been doing the same with the pain I have been encountering lately. First it was my broken heart over you, then my broken body and life, then my broken core and existence, now the broken core and existence of humanity and what seems to be even eternity's. Letting it bombard me over and over, week in week out, month after month now.

I was there in a meditative confrontation for just a brief moment yesterday but it was long enough to "see" that in that endless black sea of hellish pain and horror, our rotten, broken, condemned cores are as ships with helm, rudder and sail and we can learn to master them as any captain.

The hell's seas are rough and heavy and devastating relative only to our experience of them. One green sailor's insurmountable annihilation is an old salt's petty squall.

Wish I had something nice and good to say instead.

                                                                      Moses

CHAPTER 29

HE GETS TO DECIDE

After Jevon's funeral, Colorado felt like a wellspring of peace and safety. I looked at the cherry orchards heavy with extravagant fruit, and it was the opposite of suffering. I'd go to potlucks with friends: not suffering. Threading morning glories through the wires of our front fence: not suffering. Walking in the morning with Peter along the irrigation ditches, looking for birds in the trees: It was all life, no death. Not suffering, not suffering, not suffering.

I felt more appreciative of my safe, comfortable world than I'd ever been; more conscious of a feeling of choice in all things. I sent out tendrils of understanding for Peter's spiritual aspirations; he reciprocated with the same for my earthly appetites. We experimented with forgiveness, at first offering it by the grain and then by the gram. We took a lot of walks. I tried to understand what he'd seen in Mariel, and as soon as I stopped raving about how pretty she was I heard what Peter was saying: What really appealed to him was her spiritual commitment.

I stayed away from Wyoming for two months—longer than I'd been home at a stretch in two years. And when I returned to Stan's in September, I felt restored. In the peaceful, known territory of Colorado, I'd gotten my legs under me again. I didn't feel like the lurching, stumbling acolyte I'd been.

I pulled into Stan's road feeling like the Mistress of My Own Destiny.

You could almost hear the universe trying not to laugh.

And immediately, damn, there it was. The pulsing, joyous, wild, undeniable presence of a natural order unauthored by humans.

"The will is fully occupied in loving," wrote Teresa of Ávila, "but it doesn't understand how it loves."

I don't go in much for chakras, but my whole core spun and sparkled when I was around Stan. I was happy, deliriously so, to be back.

A couple of days into my visit, Stan, Moses, Cody, and a couple of others took the pickup truck to go looking for unbranded Addison horses running on the reservation range before anyone else took them. I wanted to go with them, but because I had a car and almost no one else did, I got drawn into taking Cody's girlfriend Nicole on a set of errands so slow-moving and frustrating that by two in the afternoon I wanted to fling myself in front of a bus. I knew the men would leave without me, and there I was in the parking lot of the tribal clinic with Cody and Nicole's son, that two-year-old tornado named Quamé, who seemed intent on dismantling the interior of my car piece by piece.

Just as I was about to trade in a strategy of persuasion for one of force, a van pulled up next to me. A trio of elderly Arapahos with empty milk jugs had come to fill up at a water pump that stood nearby. They all lumbered to the pump. Then one of the men worked the handle and found it dry.

God! I thought. *Nothing* works around here.

The two men and one woman turned. Their expressions hadn't changed one iota. Slowly, they moved back to the van. Seeing Quamé and me watching them, the woman smiled sweetly and waved to us. We waved back.

That woman didn't demand or even expect that things go her way. Expectations didn't survive out here any longer than the paint on a porch.

I remembered one night a few months ago, I asked the Addisons sitting at the kitchen table, "What do you guys want for dinner?"

After a silence, Cody said, "Whatever you cook. We're Arapahos."

I remembered Moses had told me once that he'd been fixing a fence with an old man who asked whether Moses thought he should be mad for all the things the white people had done to the Arapaho world.

"Damn right!" Moses had said. "You've got a right to be damn mad."

"But I'm not," the old man had said. "It's the Creator who makes things happen, and if we felt mad, we'd be putting ourselves higher than the Creator."

The light had come on for Moses.

"All my life, I'd been taught to be a white guy and be very pissed off when things didn't go my way," he'd told me. "What I heard that day I've been using for years to deal with my own anger."

The Arapahos had never really been out from under the Creator's thumb. One day they were living from hunt to hunt on the plains. The next thing they knew, white people had taken everything they had and left them to live in poverty on a reservation with their traditional enemies.

So, I thought as the vanload of elderly Arapahos pulled out and Quamé wound a length of webbing around my arm and tried to tie me to the steering wheel, when exactly did my own people decide not to accept things but to dictate? The Industrial Revolution? The invention of the plow? Was putting a wooden blade into the ground the first rejection of what nature and God offered us? The first time we looked at the deer herds and wild strawberries and said, "Not Good Enough. Not by a Long Shot"?

I don't think white people are out from under the thumb of God, either, but because we're so technologically advanced we have been given a slice of time to pretend we are.

My pitch of feeling I had that afternoon had "privileged white woman" written all over it. I was annoyed that the men had left without me, annoyed that I'd had to run all those errands, annoyed that they were late coming home. I was sitting on Stan's porch, grumbling to myself, when they arrived.

Stan's face was contorted with pain. "I'm injured!" he said, rolling up the ramp. "I'm real feverish."

The ride in the truck had been bumpy, and just a month shy of going to Cheyenne to have Dr. Wyatt cut out Stan's sores, those same sores had gotten irritated, and his system had gone into rebellion. His temperature had hit 104. We tried to persuade him to go to the emergency room, but he said the spirits had told him to just lie under a blanket for a while.

When he came out from under the blanket at ten o'clock, his temperature was just under 100. He was through it. That was when he told me that Tiny the dog had gotten lost. She had gone along in the pickup, but she'd kept jumping off and running away. She'd done it at the Ethete store, where Stan liked to stop for deep-fried burritos and Diet Vanilla Coke before an adventure. She'd done it at the post office. Once they were out in the desert, she'd run away three more times. This was unusual for her, because usually, the dog was more attentive and detail-oriented than anyone else at Stan's. Every time a group of people walked from the house up to the swimming hole, Tiny went along, trotting ahead and then looking back with an air of concern over how dispersed the humans had become. Tiny was the only dog allowed inside the sweat lodge. I'd spent many hours sweating away with her smooth, small form curled up next to my leg.

"I think she chased us," Stan told me weakly, "but she couldn't catch us. We were off chasing horses."

So there she was, the size of a tennis shoe, miles from home, surrounded by coyotes and miles of dry dust and crumbling rocks, under a blazing, indifferent sun.

I couldn't stand it—Stan slipping away, Tiny running away and dying in the desert.

"I'm going to go look for her," I said.

"Yeah, go," said Stan from under his blanket. "Take Moses."

That was a surprise. The encounters between Moses and me for the last couple of days had been tentative and gentle, so as not to catch the end of any frayed feelings. There was plenty still between us—the embers of our once-roaring attraction, as well as sorrow and pain. But he'd told me he was feeling much better, much more let go, really pretty fine about the divergent directions we'd taken. He'd done a five-day fast in the desert a couple of weeks before and said it had straightened him out emotionally and spiritually.

But going out to the middle of the desert together at night seemed like exactly the kind of togetherness we weren't ready for. I thought, Well, you're the psychic, Stan. Moses and I got into my Toyota and drove off into the high desert. It was beautiful out, with bluish starlight on the sage. The Milky Way was above us, as distinct as a rough-hewn roof beam dipped in rhinestones, like some resort-town bar's version of medieval Christmas decor. There was no moon. Not yet. We listened to Simon and Garfunkel's greatest hits on the stereo as we drove down the ranch road, two clear ruts of powdery dirt flanking a two-feet-tall, two-feet-wide strip of sage and rabbitbrush. My Toyota, which had nearly two hundred thousand miles on its wheels, scraped its metal belly on the tall shrubs but soldiered on sturdily like the tugboat it had been since its first year, when it had been saved from hitting a huge deer on the Navajo reservation by God Knows What.

Moses was driving because he knew where to go. We stopped at gates made of high-tension arrangements of barbed wire and juniper poles, and he hopped out to open them while I moved into the driver's seat and drove us through so he could close them again. The road got bouncier, and we came to a big, steep hill. Moses gunned the gas, and we headed straight up. My car fishtailed in the latter part of the climb, but in a hail of dust and small rocks, we sailed over the top pitch, catching air like a swordfish. It was thrilling. The whole thing was fabulous, really—the rising moon, the night, our mission, life pressing in on us, so full of mystery and adventure.

"Tiny!" I yelled happily into the night. "Tiny! Tiny! Tiny!"

There was no Tiny. We trundled onward. We were close to the graveyard where Stan's father, brothers, nieces, and nephews were buried. The car filled with sage pollen from the bushes scraping along the bottom of the car. Just about every breath I took ended with a sneeze. Moses handed me a Kleenex and rubbed my neck briefly. And then, out in the moonlit desert, the ruts in the road dropped beyond my car's short reach. We thudded to a stop, high-centered. We couldn't force it out. Couldn't rock it out. We were stuck, good and proper.

I checked the contents of the car. For warmth, we had two thin blankets. For sustenance, we had ingredients for the chocolate birthday cake I was going to make Tisha the next day, and a big bottle of ginger ale. For light, we had matches. Not a bad inventory. But to dig the car out, all we had was a screwdriver.

I was irritated. I'd seen the drop in the road better than Moses had, because with my glasses my eyes are fine and his had been burned so badly in the truck fire he couldn't qualify for a driver's license. He'd been driving because he'd had a decade of experience on this particular stretch of desert. Still, I was a good driver on rough western roads. Why had I let him drive?

Moses made his way around the perimeter of the car. He stepped into a rut, twisting his ankle, and exploded, "Goddamn, I don't need this! My ankle was just starting to feel better. Fuck!"

This made me hate him just a little bit, then hate myself for hating him. But I remembered now the discord between my expectations of this man and the reality of him, discord that I'd felt the shadow of, even when my attraction for him had eclipsed almost everything else.

My delusions about Moses were based partly on the fact that he was a cowboy. When I was a kid, I watched a lot of *Bonanza*. With the horses at Stan's corral, few people acted with more grace or intuition than Moses. Plus, cowboys are supposed to be competent and polite at all times, dealing with problems with unending good cheer and politeness, a hat-tippin' "Now, you take care, ma'am" after they help you over a muddy river or off a scary horse.

Moses had cowboy characteristics—he could stand up to the wildest horses and he wore close-fitting Wranglers and old cowboy boots held together by duct tape wound around the ball of his foot, and he'd gallantly put his cap over his heart when he shook my mother's hand for the first time. But he wasn't really a cowboy. If he identified as anything, it was as an Indian, not a cowboy. And then there was all the time he'd put in as a drug dealer and a cop-beating hippie. As far off as those last two roles seemed when he was in the corral, they were easy to remember right now, with him yelling obscenities at the pain in his ankle and the rutted road.

Soon he got down and started picking away with the screwdriver at the dirt under the car. I listened to Simon and Garfunkel. Things felt companionable again. Really, he was my fellow disciple. It seemed to me that even Teresa of Ávila smiled forgivingly upon what had passed between us: "To reach something good it is very useful to have gone astray," that vivacious mischief maker of a nun had said, "and thus acquire experience."

There wasn't anything for me to do, so I sat in the driver's seat with him working away below me. I felt like the rich girl he sometimes accused me of being. And then I dropped my arm through the open door, my hand resting just above Moses's body lying on the ground. My finger, acting on its own, playfully poked him in the ear, the way I used to flirt with my kayaking buddies when I was the token female all those years ago.

"Hey!" he said, confused and surprised.

"Oops," I said, withdrawing my hand and putting it in my lap. "Sorry."

It was well past midnight. It got cold. I started the car, turned on the heater, and started dozing off. Moses crawled into the passenger seat, and we fell asleep.

Years ago, something felt out of place to my sleeping body, and I woke in my tent to find a skunk standing on my feet. Another time I woke up because an earthquake had rattled my house. That night I woke up because Moses's hands were under my sweater, moving on my belly. I couldn't move.

"Get off me!" I shouted.

He didn't.

I screamed, "STOP! DAMMIT, STOP! STOP!" Moses didn't let up. He kept holding me down. I jerked my body to the right with all my strength, but I couldn't budge his thousand-pound hand. I tried doing the same to the left. I gulped air and screamed, "Moses, God! Let me up!"

His hand bore down on my belly like a block of concrete. I was trapped.

His hand said: No matter how much power you've wielded over me, all that power is trumped right here. Women can do all kinds of things to men's lives and hearts, and you have played some dirty tricks on me, but at the end of the day, men decide the fate of women's bodies. And I am deciding.

Things became extremely simple. I waited to see what Moses was going to do. Rage—his—was in the air like a rare but recognizable smell, like metal striking pavement and sparking. The membrane between life and death was weak here. The gelding had died. So had the stallion. And Jevon. Plenty of people buried in the nearby cemetery had died before their time. Why not me? Arms as strong as those holding me down could disentangle the cutting hooves of fence-trapped horses. And he was right—at the end of the day men could decide the fate of a woman's body. I forgot to breathe, but it didn't matter.

I climbed out of my body and upward, coming to rest slightly above my car. When I think about that night, my memory comes to rest five feet above the car roof. It was beautiful. The desert spread out for miles. The moon was high in the sky now, casting a light strong enough that I could detect my car's blue color. The breeze—which didn't seem cold anymore but just about perfect—nudged at the place where my cheek might have been, and I could hear its slight whomping sounds as it gently shredded itself through the sage and rocks and rabbitbrush. It was peaceful. There was a lot of pulsing moonlit detail—the brightness of the moon itself, the darkness of the distant mountains, the crumpled grays of the nearby shrubs, the fact that below me the blue car was moving slightly.

If your house is burning, you get out and stand nearby. You watch the house and hope it won't be destroyed. But if it is, you can go on with things because you're outside, safe, watching. That is what I was doing.

Suddenly, it was over. He hadn't done anything but hold me down. I was back in the driver's seat of my car, my body clamoring with shock and the whole inventory of emotion I'd have to face now that it was done. The hand was gone. Moses was out of the car, moving out into the sage, fuming. I stared out of the windshield. When he returned to the car, we shouted at each other for a while, me yelling "goddamn" and "what" and "why," him spluttering "goddamn" and "fuck." But mostly, there was sadness. We had shared a powerful bond all these months. Much of it had come from our mutual love of Stan and whatever force was behind him. And now here we were in this ruin.

Later that day Moses would call Stan and say, "I just about raped Lisa in the desert." It would take me months to come all the way back into my body. What he said was true.

*   *   *

We turned our attention to the car, to getting ourselves away from this place. We were an efficient team. I helped adjust the jack on the uneven ground underneath the car. Once we had the car in a good position, I got into the driver's seat and gunned it onto solid ground as if my life depended on it.

As soon as we started rolling toward Lander, I cheered up. Way up. To a dissociated degree. I bubbled and chatted all the way to town, then drove us to McDonald's. Moses said he wanted a superdeluxe breakfast. I didn't hesitate to buy it for him. But after chugging my orange juice, a wave of fresh blood sugar brought me back to reality. I threw my Egg McMuffin in his face as hard as I could.

"You son of a bitch," I spat. "You try that again and I'll kill you."

"That's more like it," he said miserably. He was back in the familiar role of his youth: the marauder, the person who took things and hurt people; who used women and their goodwill. I was in my own past, choking with the feeling of being overwhelmed by a man and flooded with shame, knowing that I'd played a part in the incident with my terrible boundaries and the finger I'd dropped in his ear—and now, as usual, this disgust for men and for myself.

At Moses's rented room, I couldn't clear my car fast enough of the bits of sage stuck in the bumper and Moses's stuff in the back, which I threw at him on the sidewalk. After I pulled up outside my own room and discovered more of his stuff, I returned to throw a second load at him.

In college, I'd had boys stop cars and lunge at me in beer-fueled, inexpert ways that spoke more of clumsy hope than of serious intent. That had been nothing compared to this. Those men had been simply trying for something, taking a gamble. They were stoppable. But Moses had been a solid bolt of archetypal truth, a creature that emerged out of the dirt from another time, his ancient rage with roots reaching far beneath me and the pain I'd caused him. Moses was really good with horses, but when he got angry, they wouldn't get near him. Horses know what prey needs to know—when to get away.

Not that I hadn't been, as Laurie said on the phone, "maybe getting off on your power over this man, just a wee bit?"

Years later, Moses told me about a conversation he had with Jay-R.

MOSES: Lisa is such a liar.
JAY-R: Of course she's a liar! She's a white woman! And you have to respect that. If you don't, you're not respecting the way the Creator made us.

Even though my car's lights had been on only during the drive, several of them had burned out in the desert. I went to buy new ones—a new left brake light, a new right headlight, a new indicator light. Plus batteries for my flashlight. The polite, clean man at the parts store helped me install the left brake light, and I took the rest out to the reservation to install myself while I waited for Stan to wake up. I wanted to tell him what had happened. But he stayed in bed until right before the sweat lodge started at sunset.

I got into the sweat lodge and sat near the door next to a grandmother from a part of the reservation Cody told me was the wrong side of the tracks. She was too decrepit and deaf to join in the banter between rounds. I wanted to hide in the background. But then Stan's youngest sister, Gwen, sat next to me. She had recently moved back to Wyoming from Oklahoma with her kids, and she was laughing and joking about her troubles. Arilda was back in top form, even though recently she'd thought she might have stomach cancer. After a few sweat lodges, when she'd gone in for tests, the doctors hadn't found anything to biopsy. Like the rest of her family, Arilda did not dwell on her troubles. It would make as much sense as dwelling on the bullet they dodged on the battlefield. They needed to be attending to what was going on right now on that same battlefield. She was back in her role as the Oprah Winfrey of the neighborhood, scolding the men, laughing at everything.

Beau was sitting straight across from me, joking in his sideways low-to-the-ground way, even though he'd been in jail the week before for disorderly conduct.

Stan was about to go into the hospital for four consecutive sur-
geries. And he was joking away with everyone there. Suddenly my
Indian name, Little Girl, made perfect sense. I was unwise, impetu-
ous, as needy as a child.

But I was surrounded by laughing Arapahos. Arapaho men started
being tough in kindergarten. Arapaho women were taught by their
mothers not to cry out during childbirth. Then it occurred to me that
I wasn't Arapaho. I wasn't raised in all this. I wasn't raised to accept
or surrender to the world in all its native brutality. I was raised in an
aberrant eddy of comfort and wealth in a stolen land in the late twentieth century. I was raised to consume and be protected, a prize pink
pig raised in safe places, controlled places, in a postindustrial,
preapocalyptic world where police and teachers and doctors and society at large worked for me, not against me. Where men didn't just hold
you down while they decided what to do to you. I wasn't *supposed* to
be good at suffering.

The doors were closed, the heat started, and I got sick. My head
split with pain. My stomach heaved with nausea. My tongue lay in my
mouth like a piece of driftwood, still and dry. I laid bare my misery in
my prayers.

For the first time, when Stan sang the words *howuunoni Beteen*—
"pity us, Creator"—as he did in all the sweat lodges, I was right there
with him. Pity us, I thought. We are helpless. Pity me my blindness,
my lost and destructive ways.

I felt concerned about my elderly neighbor, who was not up to sitting through the entire sweat lodge, nor up to her lot in life—raising
five grandkids in a house that Stan had determined was a veritable
crash pad for spirits. Five sassy, partying grandkids and all those dead
people buried on Beaver Rim above her, their spirits coming to feed off
the kids' drug-weakened souls. And this poor woman, sitting in the
sweat lodge drinking coffee in a way I knew was going to kill her
kidneys.

I kept checking up on her. Stan had told her to attend this lodge to
finish a spiritual cleanup he'd started for her when he smudged her
house of troublesome spirits a few weeks back. I could understand how
weak and hopeless she felt. I refilled her coffee during the break and

did my best to occupy her chubby, talkative eight-year-old grand-daughter at the fire between rounds.

After the sweat, we went inside for the feast. I hoped for chicken noodle soup with its welcome dose of salt and benign soft noodles. But on the menu tonight was elderly and structurally unsound water-melon, and—please, God, no—menudo. It smelled great, like posole, but there was the problem of tripe, which is what? Cow's stomach swimming around like a lacy eel. I took one look and let my own stomach lunge me out the door to the porch, where I sat, steaming, even-tually nibbling on a slice of watermelon. The headlights on the trucks of the people starting the drive home hit my retinas like bludgeons.

My head was beating like a drum, my stomach wringing itself this way and that. I left without saying goodbye.

CHAPTER 30

BEING USEFUL

I sat on Stan's bed the next morning and sobbed. Jay-R and Ivan quietly left the room.

"You'll be all right," Stan said. "You're doing way better than you think you're doing. I ain't been calling you Little Girl for two weeks now."

"I just feel *finished* right now, Stan. I'm so scared, I just want to go home to Colorado and get a job with good health insurance and never come to Wyoming again."

"I know. But he didn't rape you. He didn't."

"I don't give fucking medals to men who *don't rape me*," I snapped.

"We're overwhelming you, you know," Stan said. "Moses has been here for twelve years and he's still learning, so we're trying to overload you so you learn it in a very short time. You're really changing, you know; really growing."

"Stan, part of the reason I've even gotten to be friends with Moses is that he *gets* you, and he's available. And so many people need you, you're available for about eight minutes at a time. So he explains you to me, and I always felt safe with him, and he's white, so I figured he got me, and now I think he's horrible, and it sucks, and I feel so sad and lonely. Nothing's safe up here. Not even you! How am I supposed to be honest with you when I know you can turn me into a toad if you want to? Well, I don't think you could really do that, but I'm about this far from thinking that."

My thumb and index finger were about an inch apart, halfway between my face and Stan's. Stan looked at my fingers. Then he looked at me. I felt like a crazy woman. Neither of us spoke.

"You need a broad view," he said. "That's what you need. That's why you feel so lost. But the way you didn't give in to your feelings for Moses, people saw that: It was real good for the kids to see someone not just give in to their impulses. At the same time, there's some things in your past, your teenage years, that you ain't dealt with yet. And those things don't feel good. And growing don't feel good, either, but you're growing."

"It doesn't feel like it!" I said. "I'm so mad, so scared; I want to go home so badly but I want to be here so badly."

Stan started talking about the sweat lodge. The night before, the spirits in the sweat lodge had used me as a conduit, he said, moving trouble and sickness from the heart and body of the old woman I'd sat next to, to somewhere else, somewhere where they wouldn't bother anyone.

"You helped out," he said.

I started crying again. I truly wanted that to be true.

CHAPTER 31

MAN NURSES WOMAN, COWBOY NURSES INDIAN

At home, Peter put his hand on my leg.

"It's okay," he said. "Come on back. Come on back in here into this nice leg."

Then he pressed one hand to my belly, the other on the back of my spine. "It's okay in here, too," he said. "It's a good place to be."

I put my face in his neck and cried, and he held me tight, rocking us both back and forth.

Two days later, I answered the ringing phone. It was Peter's brother. I carried it in my hand and looked for Peter, following the sound of a rhythmic thudding noise in the backyard. I found him cleaning off our broom the way we always did, by whacking the bristle end on the ground. I approached with the phone; he didn't stop with the broom. He was really punishing it; straws broke off, and the dust rose around him. His face was sweating. He didn't acknowledge my presence. I stood there for a while, waiting for him to finish. When he did, he looked at me, his face contorted with effort and emotion.

"Phone?" I said.

He took it from me and went into the house without a word.

*　*　*

Meanwhile, up in Wyoming, Stan's sores, one on each buttock and an extra one on his right hip, were the size of Chips Ahoy cookies. They wouldn't heal, and they harbored staph bacteria that no antibiotic could kill. They were the same kind of bedsores that had killed another quadriplegic—the actor Christopher Reeve—in October 2004. The day Reeve died so abruptly that his wife barely made it to his deathbed to say goodbye, Stan was lying in bed at the Cheyenne Regional Medical Center, barely conscious. Dr. Wyatt had cut out his sores and the underlying infected bone, then pulled muscle and skin from the back of Stan's leg over the excisions and stapled it all down. There were eighteen-inch seams on each of his legs. Stan made only brief ascents from the dark pull of morphine and Phenergrin and Percocet and Ambien. His weight dropped to 128 pounds, so a doctor threaded a tube through his nose into his stomach through which they fed him a high-fat fluid that looked like white paint.

He always had someone with him. Someone from home, delivered by a carful of relatives who raised gas money by selling Indian tacos around the reservation. First it was Cody, who lay on the sofa watching television and, Stan reported, looking sorrowful. Cody told me on the phone that he wanted to be home. He'd injured his neck and shoulder a couple of weeks before when, drunk, he drove his new pickup truck off the road. The paramedics had put him on Flight for Life to the hospital in Casper, and he'd flatlined in the helicopter before shocking all the medics by coming to. Nicole was about to give birth to their third baby. After two weeks, Cody left Stan's bedside and went home.

Moses replaced him. He animated Stan's room—the whole surgical unit, for that matter—the way a friendly wolf would animate a shopping mall. He'd never been much of a sleeper. He announced that his IQ, which he'd tested on the Internet, was 131, and he was all conversation and cups of coffee and restless questions and appreciative attention to the nurses. The middle of the Wind River Reservation had been a great place for spiritual healing, but it had never been a great place to meet women, and my God the nurses here in Cheyenne were spunky. Moses watched them closely, badgering them about what they were doing with Stan's medications. Then he started playing his wooden flute. The tune would wander down the white echoing halls of the surgical unit, and pretty soon the nurses would be poking their heads into Stan's corner room, even spending their breaks there. Moses was a bridge between the white and Indian worlds. And he'd always been a pretty good bridge between women and, well, himself.

"Moses is henpecking the nurses," Stan reported to me over the phone, not unhappily.

"I ain't met so many women since I stopped going to bars," Moses told me after taking the phone from Stan. "There are some really intelligent women. Stan's started opening up, and the nurses are, too. Everyone's just hanging out in our room. When Stan's himself, people just come flocking."

A month into his hospital stay in Cheyenne, Stan was, according to his surgeon, doing well.

"He looks great!" Dr. Wyatt told me from his cell phone as he was driving 180 miles from Cheyenne to Casper to run a cleft palate clinic. "Stan is going to heal! That is cool!"

Stan's bedsores were removed, but he was emotionally, spiritually, and physically embattled. He had tiny railroad tracks of metal staples going up and down both legs, which were wrapped in ACE bandages, his soft brown curled-over toes poking out, getting cold and tingly because of his diabetes. He grimaced at the dull pink plastic trays of institutional-smelling mashed potatoes and turkey, the miniature pieces of sugar-free ginger cake with synthetic cream.

All that surgery, or maybe all that time away from the reservation and the sweat lodge, had made his diabetes flare up. His blood sugar rocketed, then dropped through the normal zone and off the other end of the spectrum. Once, nearly unconscious when his blood sugar was down, he fought off Moses and a nurse, who were trying to revive him with Sprite. Some nights he had panic attacks that lasted for hours. He'd be overcome with the feeling that he couldn't stay in his skin. Then he'd start trembling. One night—the night before George W. Bush won his second presidential term—Stan's eyes bulged out and he lurched around the bed, unconscious.

"It reminded me of when I was a coke addict and I had drug-induced psychoses," said Moses. "The way he was acting was like some drug experiences I've had. Like trying to commit suicide on an eight-ball." Moses stayed at Stan's bedside every night until he fell asleep. "I'm great in extreme situations," he said. "I feel kind of parasitic that my best depends on someone who's so wiped out and miserable."

Stan was on drugs for diabetes, pain, and anxiety. They put him on Paxil as if he were a graduate student, on Klonopin as if he were a coked-out club owner.

"I'm real homesick, real lonesome," he said.

"Stan, it's the white world!" Moses said to him. "It's lonely!"

Into this atmosphere of anxiety and discontent walked a plump and youthful medical resident who said some things that were so unsoothing that Moses told him to go and get his supervising physician "or I'll beat you to death with my bare hands and fuck your corpse in the ass till you're a shitty bloody mess and then piss on you so everyone knows you're my kill." I could imagine Moses jumping up from the couch where he'd spent much of the past three weeks, filling the room with his long arms and legs, his half-melted face and his raging loyalty.

Stan pulled his sheet over his head.

"They weren't making no sense," he later told me over the phone. "They sounded like kids. And it was my ass they were arguing about. But the doctor ran out of there eventually. He was a little roly-poly guy."

I wasn't there. But I can only imagine that the resident was terrified. I knew Moses's rage. I was still numb from my collision with it in the desert.

After the resident left, it wasn't long before his supervisor came in. The veins in his forehead popped out angrily, reminding Stan of his white neighbor who lost a sorrel horse and found it a month later; Stan's saddle sat on the horse and Stan's nephew sat on top of that, prompting the neighbor to call the BIA police "instead of just talking to me, man," Stan complained to me.

He sounded weak and tired.

"Moses got me in trouble," he said.

Moses said, "I got everyone mad at me, the doctors and the patient.

But I don't care. I can't stand for this kind of bullshit. Stan's mad at me 'cause I got him on a diabetic diet. He's mad at me for getting mad at that doctor. I don't care. It's been seven years of this; it's one thing or another. It always breaks down again. Stan's got Indian nature. He don't stand up to the white man. He says, 'Just let go.' But I seen what Dr. Wyatt did. I seen those flaps, and he did an excellent job. I'm not gonna stand by and let someone screw it up."

The events in Stan's room that morning, along with murmurings among some staff—that Stan was going to be discharged, that Moses was here only because he had no other place to go—combined to bring out the warrior side of some of the nurses.

One came in on her day off. "I just want you to know I'm part Irish and part Lakota," she told me on the phone, by way of showing me her fighting credentials. "It doesn't show in me. I'm blond and blue. It doesn't matter what color you are—we're here to heal people and get them home."

Stan started cheering up. "The nurses are on our side, " he said. "A bunch of women. You don't want to piss them off."

I wanted to visit Stan. The idea was not popular in my house. Peter was wrestling with two equal and opposing forces: He was a Buddhist who was dedicated to not harming anything, but he wanted to strangle Moses.

"What am I supposed to do?" he said. "Beat Moses up? I'm supposed to go beat the crap out of a guy who can lift horses into the air?"

This was good for a pained, shared laugh, but the situation remained: I wanted to see Stan, and Moses was there. I wasn't exactly dying to see Moses, either. So I called my mom and asked her if she'd like to go spend a week with me in Cheyenne with Stan and the guy who had assaulted me in the desert. She said she'd love to.

The day we arrived, I sat with Stan when the time came for his staples to be taken out. He laid his cheek on his right arm and fixed his dark eyes on Cheyenne's flat northern horizon and stopped talking.

Outside the room, Moses was flirting with the nurses—with one nurse in particular, a feisty, pretty, buxom blonde. It was all very bawdy.

I grabbed my mom's arm and said, "Can we go now?" and we drove to a Mexican restaurant where we ate enchiladas and I drank two beers. Then we got into our beds in the motel room and watched *The Stepford Wives,* snuggled up next to each other.

The next day I found myself alone with Moses in the hall.

"I feel really lonely around you," I said. "That's how I felt in the desert, and that's how I feel when I see you operating on these nurses. It's like you don't care about women. You just care about *getting* women."

He was quiet. Then he said, "I'm really sorry you feel that way. I really do care about you, a lot."

And we sat there in silence that wasn't companionable but wasn't inflammatory, either. The visit was going to go okay.

During the five weeks he spent with Stan at the hospital in Cheyenne, Moses would often go outside to visit a three-foot-tall statue of the Virgin Mary that stood in a quiet corner near a dusty ponderosa pine. He'd smoke a Marlboro Light and put a couple of others at her bare marble feet as offerings.

"I pray to her all the time," he told my mother and me. "Can't you just feel the feminine, healing energy of this place? And ghosts! There's ghosts all over!"

I couldn't feel anything except the cold, beating wind that constantly swept Cheyenne clean of dropped gum wrappers, plastic bags, and any likelihood that the city would ever explode into a high-plains megalopolis like Denver.

At Moses's urging, Stan went out to the Virgin Mary once to smudge himself with sage and to pray. He'd gone cold turkey off all the drugs he'd been on since arriving at the hospital, and the withdrawal process gave him occasional convulsions and left him shaken and morose. But he wanted to be completely clean before he went home.

The last person to have convulsions in front of his mother had been beaten with a pair of reins twenty years ago. A friend of the family who didn't have anywhere else to go, a man they all called Charlie Chicken, was in a drunken fit, surrounded by worried peers, when Stella broke in with her reins, yelling "Snap out of it!" He came to immediately. Stan laughed when he told this story, but there was a current of worry underneath his laughter. He didn't want to scare his family. He didn't want to be delivered into the hands of the doctors in Lander, who wouldn't know what he'd been through at the Cheyenne hospital. Pride was at work, too: Medicine men don't get slapped with reins by their mothers.

Stan stayed in the hospital for a total of two months and one day. In the last week, it became clear that he was out of danger and the end was in sight. With no situations left to rise to, both he and Moses got grouchy. Stan was sleeping soundly through the night. Moses took to spending more time with the Virgin. Inside, bored, he spent his time flinging himself into chairs, drinking multiple cups of coffee, farting, flirting, and telling dirty jokes.

One day when the tedium of hospital life was wearing on all of us, I walked into the dining area and found Moses and my mom sitting in a pair of armchairs, tears in both of their eyes.

"What's up?" I asked, instantly on guard.

"We've been talking about Jungian psychology and the collective unconscious," said my mom.

The next day the nurse came into the dining room at nine P.M. and told me that Stan wanted a peanut butter sandwich "on wheat bread, with grape jelly," she recited. "Toasted."

Moses, who had been snoozing, snapped to. "He usually wants a simple sandwich," he said. "Two pieces of bread. Lisa, have you ever seen him want toast?"

I never had. And I'd certainly never seen him eat whole wheat bread.

Moses looked relieved. He could read Stan in ways that eluded the nurses and me completely. Bossiness was good. Especially bossiness about food. It meant that the real Stan was resurfacing, that he was coming back, that the good times would return, that it was okay to go home.

"This is definitely a sign of improvement," Moses said, smiling broadly and getting up. "I'm going to have to go and just stare at him for a while."

starting to come out of the woman's body. It felt redeeming to be a real participant in the healing that occurred in Stan's sweat lodge. Concentrating on my prayer, I felt shot through with heat and happiness.

A few days and as many sweats later, things were very quiet in Stan's kitchen. I was going home the next day. Stan was feeling better. He had parked his chair in front of the kitchen stove, which was turned on with the oven door open to keep him warm. I brought out my knitting and started working on a pink hat for my new niece.

Arilda arrived and slid in next to me on the bench.

"I had a dream that I was preparing for death," Stan told us. "I'd told the boys to go get me horses, and when they brought them around, it was the gray one that died after he was gelded."

He knew it was a death dream because it was that particular horse. In the old days, Arapahos would kill the favorite horse of a fallen warrior, so he could ride it to the next world.

"I thought I might croak in the sweat," Stan said, "but I can't think of a better place to check out."

"I felt that presence real strong, too," said Arilda. "That's why I came back over tonight. It felt like before my son Adrian died, but I didn't know who it was going to happen to."

Dammit. Stan had rearranged me with his kindness and his magic, then made me stand on the slippery slope of constant pain and unplanned death that is the Wind River Indian Reservation. I couldn't take it. Stan and his world were jewels, but dark ones, rich with the blood of people and horses and dogs that died for nothing, for carelessness or a flash of anger or too much to drink or no reason at all. I couldn't stand the thought of Stan recovering just enough from one crisis to get hit with the next one.

"I don't want you to die!" I cried, taking his arm. "Why did you do two sweat lodges in one evening? You knew two sweats were too much! What about your body?"

"It ain't my body," he said. "And I don't make the decisions."

CHAPTER 33

THE ORIGINAL POSITION

Let's review. Shortly after I first moved up here, I pulled up to Stan's house one dark, freezing night. There were maybe a dozen Chevy Cavaliers, Ford trucks, and Impalas parked outside. The sweat lodge was over, and the feast was in full swing. I hadn't participated because I was menstruating. The steam pouring from the huge aluminum pots of stew I'd helped prepare that afternoon made the kitchen window run with thin strings of water. Through the window, I could see blurred figures moving around. Someone with a plate stopped and backtracked into the food line. Somebody hugged someone else. I turned off my ignition and found I couldn't move. I couldn't move into that love. It would rearrange me in such a way that I wouldn't recognize myself. And I didn't want to become unrecognizable to myself, so I drove away.

I still didn't have enough receptors to fully receive the feeling I got around Stan, but I was developing a few of them. They certainly weren't operational when I arrived here. Dr. Wyatt's wife, Patty Outlaw, had once told me: "Physiology is at its greatest when you try to heal a wound; try to trick the body into healing." That seemed doubly true for wounds of the heart. All this time, my heart had remained as stubbornly invalid as Stan's body. It had to be tricked into healing, and my adventures here were doing that.

But wait, they weren't wounds. They weren't so much something cut as something prevented. They were like stumps. Stumps where limbs or muscle should have grown. Around Stan my insides got warm. Something reared in my blood like the quicksilver devotion of a child, devotion combined with hope and fear—a real razor's edge of fear in every cell—that this devotion would be dropped again, that it would bounce off the court while Stan was taking a water break.

But it never was. He sat there, watching. There was nothing else for him to do. He was in a wheelchair, after all. But the man did love his work.

Maybe it wasn't magic so much as it was God, the thing on the other side of the thing that is Stan Addison. Or maybe it was simply the right kind of attention. Which seems as ordinary as a baloney and mayo on Wonder bread. Stan was *made* of attention. He gave it freely. He saw me, saw what I could do. He saw everyone else, too. This seems ordinary, but it's actually extremely rare. Maybe it's even rarer than magic.

What I brought to the mix was devotion. Could it be brought out of the family icebox, defrosted, and encouraged to make its shaky offering, this time in company it took forty years to find? Company that melted my purest devotion right out of me, like modern mining techniques leach molecules of hidden gold out of heaps of gray rock? This was the upside of being Little Girl, this pure, childlike devotion that had been hidden, but which now had no choice but to come out. This time my heart unfurled not because it felt ready but because conditions were such that it was compelled to assume its original position. And that was what it felt like: my heart's original position.

I'd been warming up to this for years and years, by misfiring all over the place. I tried to get my boyfriends to help me do what needed to be done. Those poor boyfriends. At every turn I was asking for evidence that I was lovable not just to them but to my father, who happened to be dead. I wore a whole string of them into the dust, not knowing I was asking them to soothe a pain decades old, to correct a mistake that old. Since I didn't know this, my timing was less than perfect. Boyfriends tended to be unloading river rafts or flying to Massachusetts when the moments arrived loaded with the full weight of the past. And they had problems of their own. They didn't need burdens piled on their backs while they slept, burdens unknown even to the woman tightening the straps. Dear me, the pack animals I have made of people.

I think there is a love that comes before and after and above and below romantic love. It is inextricably connected to surrender. More than anyone I've ever met, Stan practiced that kind of love. Sure, his body had been reduced to only what was required to sustain life. And maybe it was easier to practice this broader love in his culture, which had been severed from victory for so long it had been freed up to explore humility in its various forms. Not expecting anything carries its own problems. But to me, coming as I do from a culture that accepts nothing less than victory, nothing less than gain, in every single situation, it felt like freedom.

The love I felt for Stan had been driving me all along. It was inside me like a mineral. The thought of losing him made me cry. But to have tears flow relaxed my heart, this same heart that was slammed shut fifteen years ago when I stood on a beach in Nova Scotia, drinking beer at my dad's wake, saying to my sister, "Do you feel anything? I don't feel anything."

CHAPTER 34

BEAU AT THE CORRAL

In June 2005, a television crew was scheduled to come and film a PBS documentary of a horse clinic Stan would run for four days. I got there a couple of days early. I liked being at Stan's before things started happening. The feeling of quiet, of slack tide, was palpable before the sweat lodges he held twice a week. But with the horse clinic and the filming due to start the next day, the lull felt that much quieter, that much more precious.

Stan was fighting off a bladder infection, but still, it was good to be back in his kitchen, talking or not talking, watching various Addisons come and go. The newly mopped floor smelled of chlorine, a smell I love. I inhaled and looked from the new pit bull pup scrabbling on the linoleum to the full coffeepot to the table laden with doughnuts, nondairy creamer, and king-size packages of hamburger.

There was going to be a sweat lodge that night. Enough phone calls started coming in inquiring when it would start that Stan started answering the phone by saying, "As soon as you get here!"

Jay-R came in from the fire that was heating the rocks for the sweat lodge. He was laughing, his stiff hair blown sideways by the wind. "This stud's still got it," he announced. "I can light a fire anywhere." He stomped back out.

Outside, Cody leaned under the hood of his Chevy truck. Every time I went out, someone new was helping him with it. Arilda shuttled them to Stan's and back out again in her huge pickup.

Beau came in. "Dad, I got a good job possibility," he said. "Seventeen-fifty an hour. A roustabout for oil and gas. I said to the guy, 'I ain't got no education or nothing.' He said, 'You got a strong back?' I said, 'Yeah.'"

Stan didn't answer.

Beau sat down on the kitchen bench. He picked up a doughnut from the pile of food and held a piece of it out to Tiny. She was back. After getting lost in the desert seven months ago, she'd hopped a ride with a truck and been found weeks later at a party on the other end of the reservation. She rotated on her delicate back legs, her olive-size paws in the air. Beau laughed and tossed the doughnut on the linoleum for her to eat. I remembered Beau doing this before, dancing backward through the corral, Tiny prancing and spinning forward toward his proffered hand, his own dancing steps. He sure loved Tiny. That was a year ago. It was the last time I'd seen him in the corral, or anywhere else around here, for that matter. His younger brother Daniel had an affectionate relationship with Stan, but Beau and Stan were usually at odds. It was obvious to me that no matter how much had gone awry over the years since his mother and Stan divorced, at this moment Beau needed Stan's approval.

Stan looked out the window at a plastic bag sailing from the dump toward the corral. I had my doubts about how much better he really felt.

"Warm and cold air mixing," he said eventually. "That's what's causing this wind."

In the sweat lodge, he seemed to get his energy back. Maria Jiron, a pretty nineteen-year-old Arapaho from Denver, assisted him. In the darkness, a regular at Stan's talked at some length about how it was time for people his age—meaning those in their forties—to look to the next generation. He said, "Beau, it's time for you to think about taking over."

I looked over at Stan, trying to search out his expression. But there was no seeing anything in the dark.

The next morning long, lean Beau and solid, round-edged Cody saddled up and rounded half a dozen horses into the corral for the clinic, which would start today. Cody was a competent rider, but Beau was dazzling on a horse. He rode a stallion called Fabian, a big, rippling bay I'd never seen before. Fabian's neck was arched even though Beau wasn't holding him back. He galloped straight forward, but he liked to do his walking and trotting in complicated sideways or diagonal gaits. Beau glided sideways, loose-hipped and straight-backed, his body always exactly over the horse, never off balance, never inclining to where it was just a moment before.

Jesus. I'd never seen Beau ride before. I remembered now that at the peyote drumming two springs ago, after he'd sung six hours in his beautiful voice, I could swear he was singing "Mockingbird." In the full light of day, I confessed to him that I thought he'd been singing that duet I knew from James Taylor and Carly Simon, and he smiled his stunning lost smile and said, "Yeah, I sang that. I ran out of peyote songs."

"Beau was such a good little boy," Arilda told me once. "Did everything his dad told him."

His father, David, appeared in old snapshots as a smiling boy-man whose closest friends were his brother George and a Catholic priest. Beau was three when his dad died. At last year's peyote ceremony, with the morning sun illuminating a yellow square on the gray linoleum of the living room floor, Beau had cried openly about how much he missed his father.

I'd heard stories of Stan getting so angered by Beau that he tried to run him down with his wheelchair; I'd heard other stories of Beau out in the sagebrush, howling with pure pain. I'd witnessed how hard he tried to get and keep construction jobs, which was difficult living this far from anywhere, and having to beg rides because he didn't have his own car.

What I'd never seen was Beau being an uncontested expert with horses. From what I'd seen of him riding, I hoped he'd stick around long enough this weekend so I could see him gentle a horse.

The film crew was delayed by flight complications, but the people who were going to participate in the clinic had arrived. They had driven up from Boulder in the requisite Subarus and Toyotas. Almost all of them had been here before, and they got right down to business. They put on huge sun hats and unfolded canvas chairs, setting them up around Stan. Licia, a fine horsewoman and college student from

South Africa wearing a dressy linen shirt and heroically inadequate sandals, immediately started working a gray mare in the mucky corral. Stan instructed her from the side.

Verlin Pitt had been waiting corralside for hours. He came from four generations of Wyomingites—military men, professional fighters, bronc busters, and oil rig workers. As wiry and lean as a Slim Jim, Verlin broke his own horses. Stan had helped him out with a troublesome roan mare a couple of years earlier. Over cups of Folgers that morning, Verlin told me that his great-uncle Harry had once wrestled a black bear for five hundred dollars, "but the bear broke his neck, and he spent about two thousand dollars on hospital care." He also mentioned he was a Lariat Laureate, which meant he was considered one of the dozen best cowboy poets on earth. He was here to read "Silent Thunder," the poem he'd written about Stan, for the video cameras.

Verlin worked as a deputy at the Lander jail. A few months earlier, he'd been on shift when a young Arapaho brought in on a warrant said, "Hi, Verlin! I'm Stan Addison's son!" It was Beau, standing there with his Fremont County–issue deodorant and shampoo, smiling his crooked-nosed Aztec poster-boy smile.

Today, as Verlin sat watching the corral from a kneeling crouch, Beau joined him, wearing baggy blue pants and a blue nylon T-shirt, "sittin' cowboy-style," he pointed out companionably.

I sat on top of the corral fence, watching the gray mare go round and round and eavesdropping on Verlin and Beau.

"I was real surprised to see you there that night," said Beau.

"You weren't the only one," said Verlin.

The young Arapaho and the middle-aged jailer discussed the warrants out for Beau's arrest not only in Fremont County but within the limits of its two towns of any size—Riverton and Lander. In terms of limiting Beau's opportunity for urban experience, this was roughly equivalent to a New Yorker having warrants out for his arrest in Manhattan, Brooklyn, Queens, and the Bronx.

"When I go to town," Beau said, "I go to Ethete."

Verlin laughed appreciatively at Beau's strategy. Being allowed to go to Ethete is like being able to go to Staten Island.

Beau's enthusiasm about seeing his very own jailer here at his dad's corral was absolutely sincere. He was sweet but he didn't know it. While his younger brother Daniel was increasingly aware of his charisma and charm and knew more and more how to maneuver himself through the world, Beau slipped around, quietly ignorant of his talent as a singer and a horseman, and, worse, unaware of his genuine ability to relate to other people.

I remembered when he was a pallbearer at Jevon's funeral last summer, leaning into the coffin for a long time, tear-swollen face to death-sunken face, crying openly. Recently, a few of us were reading the *Riverton Ranger* around the kitchen table and saw Beau's name in the blotter. He smiled slowly as he repeated the charge against him: "breaching the peace."

Oh, these boys. The arrests weren't the most worrisome thing. The most worrisome thing was this: Who shows this boy his goodness? I thought of Cody, working yesterday on his truck, with Arilda shuttling in whomever she could find who knew about fuel pumps. There needed to be more Arildas around—loving, clucking, quick-to-laugh, concerned, pain-in-the-butt moms. Cody was lucky. Any son of Arilda Chavez was.

The day wore on without the film crew. Verlin left, waving goodbye from the window of a glistening pickup truck as big and white as a beluga whale. Beau faded back to an outer fence and leaned there with nineteen-year-old Maria, Rocky, and two plump, silent, virginal Navajo sisters here for a month to study Stan's horse training methods.

Stan was suddenly gone, leaving Licia to chase the mare around the corral by herself in her impossible sandals. After a while she scanned the crowd for someone who could help. She called, "So, keep chasing him, Beau?"

"I wasn't really watching," said Beau. "But run her twice around and then say, 'Whoa.' I'll come up there and coach."

He walked to the tarp and hung on the corral fence. He'd been planning to sing peyote songs at a wake and take Maria with him, but he stayed and coached Licia for an hour. Maria waited. She was decked out in baggy jeans with an oversize basketball shirt and Sacajawea ponytails, "like a Sioux," Beau said. Maria liked to get on Chief and just sit there, talking especially to Beau.

"Once she gets to the gate," Beau said to Licia, "just stand there and say, 'Whoa.'" Licia walked slowly toward the horse, her hand extended.

"She's paying attention," said Beau. "But she's thinking you're gonna chase her. Let me show you something." He picked up the green lead rope, climbed into the corral, and snapped it at the mare, making her run. Then he barked a rough "Whoa!" that stopped her in her tracks. He backed up to her, murmuring softly, "I'm not going to hurt you." The mare looked off into the distance, but remained acutely aware of what Beau was doing. He moved steadily, slowly but not as slowly as Licia had moved. He explained that Licia had walked so slowly that the mare thought Licia was scared, which in turn scared her. When Beau touched the mare on the neck, she turned her head toward him, her black mane falling down prettily on her mottled gray hide, her dark, Oriental-looking eyes settling on his.

It was a lovely moment. But as soon as Beau achieved contact, he broke it, striding away, making me worry for other females he might connect with, like Maria. He climbed through the fence, saying, "Done."

Licia approached the horse and soon enough she'd touched the mare's neck, too.

"Stay focused on her neck," said Beau. "If you go back or up, she'll shy away."

He added that the mare was sensitive about the tops of her legs.

Stan came back, and Beau was suddenly nowhere to be seen. Stan coughed and said to Licia, "When you get close to her, you hesitate. It makes her hesitate, too." I don't think he had any idea he was simply repeating what his son had just said.

CHAPTER 35

THE FAMILY MAN

The next day the film crew arrived and aimed their cameras at Stan. My only real role was to try to get their subject to drink cranberry juice to combat his urinary tract infection. I spent the rest of my time at the trailer and in the kitchen with the nephews, or in the driveway with Cody.

Despite his efforts to fix his truck, despite his mother's efforts to bring in someone who could help him, it was still broken. Cody looked trapped, stuck out at the trailer behind Stan's with Nicole and the kids and the headache that had plagued him since his car accident the previous summer. One day he borrowed Stan's car three times. This made Stan impatient. When the cameras weren't rolling, he sat quiet and drawn in his wheelchair. His temperature had gone up to 100 the previous night; that urinary tract infection wasn't going away despite the cranberry juice.

"They're your kids," he groused on the kitchen phone to Arilda, who was at her house.

Arilda wasn't having any of it. "You're my biggest kid of all, Stan!" she shot back, audible even to me, sitting on his kitchen bench. "I've been doing for you all week!"

I could feel the approach of the inevitable. Cody wanted to use my car. He'd asked before, and I almost always said yes, even though he'd totaled his own truck. But the accident had a sobering effect on him, and while his kids littered the backseat with Cheetos and embedded hard candies in my velveteen seat covers, he always filled up the gas tank and brought the car back in reasonable time. Plus,

I couldn't resist his beleaguered, loving-dad quality. He needed some relief.

So when he asked, I was ready. "Yeah, you can borrow it," I said. "But for a price."

"What?" he said, a flicker of worry crossing his eyes.

"Riding lessons," I said, "and an interview."

"Sure," he said. Underneath all those layers of quiet, I sensed acceptance or even pleasure. I added, "A riding lesson where we don't gallop. Where we don't go over a trot. I'm an old lady, remember?"

When we set out the next day, I was glad I was riding with Cody. He was the one Stan could count on to come out and stay with him in the hospital when everyone else was off partying. He was the one I could depend on, too, because while I wished I could say that becoming an accomplished rider was among the adventures I had at Stan's, it was not. I rarely rode, and when I did, I kept to the corral like the kids did. I had a rich fantasy life involving galloping in the hills with the older boys, thundering across the desert and into the river, our pace unbroken, the water rising in great rooster tails behind us. But the truth was my favorite place to be with the horses was standing with them in the corral, smelling their noses, looking into their big eyes, my feet on the ground.

Cody and I set out, my stirrups on the shortest adjustment but still a little too long, my riding technique the opposite of Beau's: hips tight, spine crooked, body collapsed around the saddle horn. We held the horses to a trot for an hour and a half, which was a bit like trying to slow the rate of acceleration of a bowling ball dropped out of a plane. These horses were ridden for the most part by twenty-year-old Arapaho boys, a subgroup of the species very taken with accelerating through space. These were just the horses for them. They were Arabs, small bodies wrapped around oversize hearts and lungs, always thinking, always up to something.

Even Chief—the big Appaloosa the kids rode—pulled against me the whole time. ("Stubborn," Stan diagnosed. "Old. He likes to run.")

As I struggled to stay mounted and upright, Cody did something he'd never done since I'd known him. He started telling me about his life. I don't know if it was because we were alone, or because I had left my pen and notebook at home, or because he felt so comfortable on horseback. He talked about his accident the previous summer. About how nobody understood the pain he now suffered in his head and neck. About how the pain and the lack of understanding he'd gotten for that pain had almost made him want to off himself and his kids a few months back.

He described the social map of the reservation, starting on the eastern, poor, Arapaho side, and ending on the wealthier, western Shoshone side. Each tribe received the same amount from the oil and gas companies that drilled on the reservation, and most of this money was in turn disbursed to the members of the tribes. But because there were more than twice as many Northern Arapahos as there were Eastern Shoshones, the latter got about $400 per month each, while the Arapahos got about $160.

Then he described his years in high school: "I was supposed to be a nobody, but I showed them I wasn't. They thought since I hung out with the crowd from Arapaho, I'd be belligerent and nasty. I showed them I wasn't. I was a straight-A student, a good basketball player. But they wouldn't let me in. So I got obnoxious and picked fights."

"Did the Addisons have a reputation for being bad?"

He nodded.

"Who was bad?" I asked.

"Bill," he said. "David, George, Glenn, Arilda." He looked at me. "Stan."

I thought about what Stan had told me, that the crimes that sent the Addison boys to jail for a few days every now and then were no shameful thing, but a residual version of counting coup.

"Don't you take pride in your family's tough reputation?" I asked.

"When I was younger, yeah," he said. "But now it's getting harder to take."

This seemed true. In fact, I may have witnessed this very transition in him over the last three years.

The year before, Arilda and Cody had been walking when they passed a young Arapaho boy bedecked with bandanas in gang colors. Cody had said, "Hey, you! Are you a gangster?"

The kid said he wasn't.

"So Cody said, 'Then take that shit off you and take it home and throw it away!'" Arilda had recalled to me.

"I said, 'Don't say stuff like that, Cody!' And he said, 'Why not? We don't need to be acting like gangsters; we're Arapahos!'"

His conservatism seemed linked to his kids, whom he worried about constantly. The most surprising thing Cody told me while we were riding, something so out of the blue that I nearly fell right off Chief into a sage bush, was this: Cody wanted his oldest son, Quamé, to go to Brigham Young University.

Why?

"I want my son to be something when he grows up," he said. "The big basketball players here end up as winos, and pretty soon they're old and they don't have nobody or nothing. When he gets to high school, we're getting out of here. Probably to Salt Lake or Denver. Someplace close."

"Aren't you scared of racism?"

"I'm not worried," he said. "I just ignore it. They can't bring me down, as much as I've been through."

I asked him why he never came into the sweat lodge.

"I believe in the power of prayer," he said. "You can talk to him anywhere. It doesn't have to be in a meeting or a sweat. He's always listening.

"That accident kinda changed my life," he said. "I don't drink and drive no more. Never. Not even one little sip."

I remembered a few months ago, how excited he was to spend the day sledding with his kids in Lander. "God, Cody, if you had died in that car accident, it would have been just terrible."

He nodded. "I think it affected my mom, 'cause she's already lost a son . . . [The idea of] my kids growing up without a father, like I had."

"You can really feel the responsibility, huh?"

"It comes down on me like a ton of bricks."

Once when Stan was in the hospital, we teased Cody about how many kids he and Nicole were having.

"Hey, Cody, we're in a hospital," I'd said. "What a great place to get a vasectomy!" This made Stan laugh but got only a small chuckle out of Cody. He really loved being a parent.

We rode back to Stan's and tied the horses to the corral rail. On the porch, I said, "You're a present, sober dad. I think that's pretty rare around here."

"I think it's almost extinct. I'm glad I'm over the depression. It lasted five months and ended two months ago. I could think that away, but I can't think my headaches away. But now I can go on doing what I have to do. Raise my kids."

We sat for a minute, watching the corral, the people coming to and fro.

"Look," I said. "Look at your whole family. People going up to help with the horse clinic. Everyone sticking together. Do you know how hard it is for me to even get my family in one place?"

"I think that's why white families are stronger than Indian families," he said. "Because Indian families get real sick of each other."

I laughed. "You don't know how lucky you are, Cody, I swear," I said.

He thought about it. "Well, if something really bad happens, like my wreck, everyone pulls together and sticks together and gives financial support so my mom and my woman could come stay with me in the hospital for those few days. I dunno, maybe I'd give it a hair on the Native side."

CHAPTER 36

VISITING THE GRAVEYARD

The next day the six people who had come for the horse clinic and the five people from the documentary crew all left. Stan had pulled it off. In spite of his bladder infection and his 100-degree temperature and the pressure sores breaking out on both buttocks, he had done what needed to be done.

And now, while he was swimming through the hours of sleep he owed his fevered body, his house and corrals still glistened with residual energy. Stan had starred in the video, but just about everyone had participated, and everyone still felt more alert, more hopeful, than usual. Nineteen-year-old Daniel had galloped up and down the driveway on horseback for the beautiful film director Angelique Midthunder, who had crouched in the cheatgrass with her camera pointed straight at him. Then he dressed in gangsta clothing and the kind of wraparound sunglasses I always want to buy at gas stations to block out the power drill of the Wyoming sun, and he stood on a long-dead car in front of the Wind River Range, which was as effortlessly photogenic as himself, and rapped for the camera with aplomb.

> *I'm a soldier*
> *I'm a thug*
> *My name is Daniel my name is Bub*
> *Yah I'm a motherfucking rezzed-out thug*
> *I'm a different man*
> *I been killed I been shot*

I ran away I got caught
Straight-up plans straight-up plot
Calling myself things that I'm really not

The cameras had awakened a sense of possibility in the other kids, too—even the dumpy short kids, the nearly always bored kids, had looked up at some point to see a camera pointed in their general direction. What a thrill!

So even though Stan had been pulled away from us by his inflamed, exhausted body on that hot Sunday afternoon, the extended family was here anyway. There were people sitting or squatting in every square foot of shade around his house. The driveway was full of cars. Only the kids were out in the sun, in the corral with the horses, riding round and round. Different duos of them got on Chief and Niken, the feisty chestnut, and the little fat pony, whose name was Pony. The adults sat in their cars or on the porch, passing around packages of Pecan Sandies, telling stories.

The two Navajo cowgirls who were spending the month breaking horses at Stan's sat in plastic chairs on either side of the front door, as silent as bookends. They attended New Mexico State University in Las Cruces, and they were getting credit for breaking horses with Stan. Plump, chaste, and quiet as, well, Navajo cowgirls. Lacking directions from their sleeping boss, they would sit there all day.

Suddenly, someone said, "Let's go see the cave," and four of us adults and two kids climbed into Arilda's big Chevy pickup. We plowed straight off through the sagebrush to a yellow sandstone cave on a hill. It was lovely up there. Arilda told me her father used to take his kids there to search for stones for his peyote rattle. We watched Stan's stepdaughter Tisha and her little friend Quinn jump off ledges for a while.

Then we piled back into the truck and drove to the cemetery. It was the most beautiful cemetery I'd ever seen, with a wide-angle view of the Wind River Range, its early-June forests glowing with new green interspersed by the white of recent snow, the whole range grazed by the muzzles of dark gray thunderstorms. At the edge of the cemetery, a raw wooden crucifix soared thirty feet into the sky with a hubcap at its crosspiece. This was where the tribe's last chief, Sharp Nose, was buried in 1903.

Much of the rest of the graveyard was occupied by deceased members of the Addison family. Arilda's father was here, and so were her two dead younger brothers, George and David. But we weren't here to see the graves of her brothers. We were here to see the grave of her oldest son, Adrian, who had died in a car crash five years ago when he was twenty-nine, leaving a clutch of children, including Tisha. Arilda opened the metal storage box in the back of her truck; there were bags of plastic and fabric flowers she'd bought at Walmart. She cleared off the old flowers and strung garlands of new, clean white roses over the carefully made wooden cross, which was accompanied by a rack from a six-point elk killed by Marty, and a cross made of bits of colored glass pressed into the mound. Then she poked bouquets of white poppies and purple iris and bright red mallow into the dirt.

It was quiet. I looked at the sun and the mountains and searched in the dirt for pieces of wire Arilda could use to secure the flowers. Soon she was looking west, too, and then she crossed her arms over her abdomen, crying, wailing louder and louder in her big white T-shirt and baggy shorts. Her oldest remaining son—Cody's big brother Sass—wrapped his arms around her and held her. The kids went to the truck and watched her from there, and I stood a few graves away, looking into the sunset.

Arilda stopped crying, and a few minutes later, she called over to me, "You done?" as if I'd been the one crying. I said yes and we all got in the truck and went back to the house, playing oldies very loud all the way home. We sang along, especially to "Stand by Me."

Later, Arilda and I went to the casino, where I lost thirty dollars in about ten minutes. I bought us hot dogs with sauerkraut at the counter, dropped hers off where she was losing thirty dollars at a more leisurely pace, and went to stand in the parking lot, where I watched mosquitoes land on my legs and the sun setting and the Arapahos and cowboy-hatted white people walking in to gamble. Arilda eventually came out, and we went to Walmart to buy a big bottle of Clorox and other supplies for her to clean her house, where she'd barely been for two weeks because she'd been running things at Stan's. Walking down the aisle with her cleaning products, she seemed like the most resilient person on earth.

CHAPTER 37

THE TRUTH HURTS

The next day, with Stan not stirring from what would be a thirty-six-hour-long sleep, I drove back to Colorado feeling like I was carrying a load of metal in my gut. Dr. Wyatt had said before Stan left the hospital in Cheyenne seven months before: "No kidding, bro, you stay on your butt too long and you are going to *die*."

My gut was prophetic: Stan woke up so feverish that they took him to the hospital in Lander. His bedsores were acting up again and he'd need some more ischial bone shaved off. At home, I grumped around. I decided to return to Wyoming, but my body felt like it was made of lead. I liked staying in the house, preferably lying down. I could barely work. My jaw was clenched. I'd pick up a book to read and realize my elbows were smashed tight against my torso. I wanted to stay home, home, home, in Colorado, covered with sheets and comforters and Peter.

Everything about the upcoming trip back to Wyoming weighed on me. The hot wind beating through my open car windows. The endless cups of iced tea I'd have to drink to keep cool and awake. The way the point-of-interest signs in Wyoming tended to mention rattlesnakes.

Those weren't the real reasons, though. Stan had just signed his will.

"Don't you leave me," I found myself saying aloud as I sat on my porch. "I won't know what to do. I won't know what to do."

A friend I knew from the reservation called and told me that the fall she'd taken from one of Stan's horses during the horse clinic might have given her a head injury. "It took me a while to admit just how bad a fall that was," she said. I told her I felt the same way about everything up at Stan's. It was all faster, more dangerous, closer to death than you thought at the time.

After a week at home, I loaded the car and drove north. About an hour short of Lander, it turned midnight. I was tired. I had to stop. I drove off the highway to an isolated campground on a mountain above the tiny town of Jeffrey City. I got out of the car and breathed in the sharp smell of the spruce trees. A row of cottonwoods past the picnic table stood there clapping their buttery leaves at me like a row of supportive aunties. It was a perfect camping site, except for the inconvenient fact that camping alone, which had never given me pause in the past, had become a terrifying concept since Moses attacked me.

I looked at the cottonwood trees, the moon glinting off their shiny leaves. I remembered Stan had once told me: "Animals and everything used to talk—birds, deer, everything. I think that's what it was, is like a feeling—not a language but a feeling between things, because we're all connected."

What the heck, I thought. Cottonwoods had always been my favorite trees. They were common but spectacular, and I'd always felt grateful to them for the shade and beauty they provided along the banks of desert rivers. I'd always felt they were on my side. I cleared my throat.

"I'm a little nervous," I said to the trees. "Could you protect me from harm, and from my own fear? I really need a good night's sleep."

I pitched my tent, got in, and started drifting off. But I jolted back awake, got back out, and faced the cottonwoods again.

"Thank you," I said. Then I lay down and slept without waking for exactly eight hours.

The next morning at the hospital, Stan was woozy with Demerol. He looked out the window. "That meadowlark keeps stopping on the ledge and looking at me," he said. A few minutes later, he said, "Those mountains look like they're closing in."

Were these the statements of a dying man? I took my position on the metal chair with black vinyl cushions that made an embarrassing noise every time I sat down or moved, and I began the long wait for his full consciousness to return. When it did a few hours later, I launched right in.

"Stan," I said. "I want you to know how much I love you. It's not a romantic kind of love. It's purer than that. It's *love* love. I'm so grateful for having known you. I can't even tell you how much my life's changed since you came into it. I really can't tell you. Even though bad things happen, it's like every moment now is better than every moment used to be. I was always trying so hard, and now I don't have to so much. My heart gets all stretched out around you, and I'm not sure why that happens, either."

I hadn't known I was going to say this.

"If there's anything left for you to tell me, I feel like I'm ready to hear it," I continued. "Because life is so uncertain."

"Yeah," he said. "It's time to talk. Hang out for a few days, and we'll talk." He paused. "It'll change your life," he said. "It ain't like you gotta be a monk or nothing, though."

"Just tell me I won't have to live in a cave with a single candle, away from Peter and our cat, Sandy," I said.

"What are you talking about?" he said.

"Well, what are *you* talking about?" I said.

He was silent.

Okay. I would wait for a few days, and then we'd talk.

"For now can I ask you some things? About when Moses attacked me?"

"Sure."

"Did you know it was going to happen?"

"Kind of. That energy between you two needed to be released."

"Why?"

"It's hard to explain it in words. It would've come back even worse and hurt other people."

"Like who? Peter or you or who?"

"Like innocent bystanders."

"Did you protect me?"

"Yeah. In that it needed to happen then. It was safer the way it happened because that energy came out then."

"It sounds not so much like a protection as the lesser of two evils?" I ventured. "A situation we both needed to go through?"

"Yeah," Stan said. "You both needed it. To find your own strengths. You needed to learn better judgment. To be more discerning."

"I feel like I got stronger from it. But it felt terrible."

"Yeah," he said again. "The truth hurts. The truth hurts."

What truth?

"I didn't know it would be so severe," he added.

"You thought it would be just an argument?"

"Yeah," Stan said. "When you went to find Tiny, I sent you out with Moses 'cause I wanted you to know what you were dealing with. You were being too accommodating, and you needed to stick up for yourself in a way you couldn't turn back from or take back."

Accommodating didn't even cover it. I thought about how I'd stuck my finger in Moses's ear, and broke into a small, ashamed sweat.

Stan was still talking. ". . . he was really angry. What you had with Moses wasn't real; you needed to see what you really had with Peter. I could have told you, but that wouldn't have worked. People need to find things out for themselves. Things happened during that day that needed to happen. I made certain things happen around you."

I stared at him. He had played a part in what had happened that night. My heart boomed in my ears as the possibilities of rage and acceptance wheeled through me.

"It's hard to explain," he said.

More silence.

"Oh," he said from the bed. "I'm spinning."

He'd had OxyContin and Percocet. Our conversation was over for the day. I left the hospital, walked to the Lander park, and lay down in the shady grass next to my tent. What had Stan known when he sent me and Moses out to the desert together? Who would have been hurt if we hadn't gone then? What the hell was this? I would never completely understand Stan's role that night. I brought it up several times, and he would try to explain the balance he kept when he knew a situation was becoming dangerous. He guided what happened yet didn't intervene too much, because at the end of the day the energies between people have to play out naturally "or it comes back to you."

But I could have gotten raped out there. Wasn't it a violation—of my civil rights or something—to be sent out there in the first place? My fear, which hadn't had time to be expressed that night in my car in the desert, had blossomed now that I was through it. Sometimes I was unexpectedly emotional around men. During a yoga class, my instructor had us pair up to do an exercise. I lay on the floor, and the mild-mannered doctor I was paired with did what he was told and pulled my hands across the floor toward him to stretch out my chest and shoulders. I was as shocked as he was when I started sobbing. Another time, during a writing group I held at my house, a man who had just read and received feedback from the mostly female group immediately got on his cell phone and started planning the rest of his evening while the next participant—a woman—started to read.

When he hung up and stood up to leave, I stared him down. "At my house, everyone reads and everyone listens," I snapped. "Sit down. You aren't going anywhere." He sat. When the group left at the end of the evening, I stayed in the chair I'd occupied all evening, frozen with surprise at what had come out of my mouth. Peter arrived a little later. I told him what I'd said, and he roared with laughter. I did, too. I guess there was an upside to the violence that had occurred between Moses and me: I was starting to get over accommodating men.

But lying in the shade at the Lander park, I was confused. Though I figured I should be angry, my angry motor wouldn't start. I wanted to protest, to rail that it had been unsafe and unfair for Stan to send me out in the desert with Moses—whose anger he could detect so easily—but I couldn't find the rule book to define how I'd been wronged. The truth was I couldn't generate anger because, underneath it all, I knew Stan had done the right thing. He'd been right when he said the energy between Moses and me needed to be dispersed, that an innocent bystander could have gotten hurt if we hadn't released it. Before Moses and I drove out to find Tiny, my mind had been so noisy with justifications and denial that I could feel only hints of how destructive that energy could become. But I'd felt them. I was like the villager on the beach, watching the sea sliding out toward the horizon—out farther than I'd ever seen it go—and feeling apprehensive without knowing exactly why. And Stan was like a bird flying high over the bay, watching the ocean gather itself for its devastating return trip. If someone else had been hurt by what had passed between Moses and me it would have been unbearable.

Plus, right at this moment Stan was fighting for his life. My confusion would have to get in line behind all the other problems around here.

In Stan's hospital room, the next day passed in a series of visits, interruptions, television shows, trips to get burgers, and chats with Frankie, a fifteen-year-old who had been living at Stan's for a few weeks and had accompanied him to the hospital a week ago. Frankie was plump and sweet and about to enter eighth grade for the third time. He seemed glad to be away from the ups and downs of the reservation and to be safe with Stan. But he was getting restless.

"I'm all hyper, man," he said. "Like I can't stop walking around."

"Like a caged panther?" I suggested.

"Like a caged panda," corrected Stan.

Frankie, smiling ever so slightly, went over to scratch Stan's scalp with a spidery wire device made for just that purpose.

When I arrived the next day, both Stan and Frankie were asleep.

After about five minutes, I coughed.

"Who's in here?" Stan asked weakly.

"Lisa."

"Where've you been?"

"Eating breakfast."

"Oh."

He fell quiet. Twenty minutes later, he said, "Lisa, you here?"

"Yeah?"

"I was having real weird dreams."

"Weird scary or weird weird?"

"Kinda scary," he said. "Real confusing."

The phone rang. Frankie roused himself, and answered with a grunt. It was a woman. Her strong voice filled the room.

"HESLEEPIN'," replied Frankie.

The woman went on for some time.

"SLEEPIN'!" Frankie shouted, then stared, annoyed, at the phone and hung it up.

It rang again.

"Frankie," I said, "give me the phone."

It was a hyperkinetic tribal social worker of sixty-some years, a relative of Stan's.

"I get concerned," she said, "he's such a kind man, sometimes I think he needs a break. I'm the auntie that always harasses. I say, 'You're always doped up! Visiting you is such a drag!' He's God's man, though. A truly humble servant."

Next Stan had another shot of morphine and had to go have his sores photographed. As he rolled out on the gurney, he asked me to go get him a case of Diet Cherry Coke.

"No," I said. We looked at each other with mutual surprise.

"I can't do it anymore," I explained. "This buying you junk food. I'll get you bottled water and blueberries and a nice grass-fed burger from the Gannett Grill. Not from McDonald's."

"Oh," he said, looking meek. "Okay."

The next day, he was comfortable and awake when I arrived.

I said, "Can we talk?"

"Yep," he said. "Now's the time."

"What's really going on here, Stan?" I asked. "What is this bond between us? I'm trying to get to the heart of how you operate and how you're making me operate. I feel like my life is changing, and I don't know if it's because of contact with you, or the Creator through you, or what. It's so big."

He said, "It's kinda all of the above, that connection with your spirituality. It's like the Creator's trying to wake you up to more of what's ahead, to wake other people, too. Most people come into contact with the Creator, but they lose it or they run. The Creator comes to everybody different. For some people it's through the horses, or with you it's writing, but it's to help us to grow together, to where we're both feeling our end of telling people about the spiritual part of life."

"Stan, that feeling, that heart-soaring feeling, happens to me all the time with you. Just a couple of weeks after I first came up here, I told you, 'I feel like I'm in love, but not with a person.' Now I'm feeling it again. What is that?"

"It's your curiosity to learn," he said. "Your spiritual curiosity. Some of these things I can't talk about. There's a circle or cycle you're going through so you can learn your own way. There was a hole inside of you and it didn't feel like anything could fill it. It's coming, though. People have noticed you've changed. The family. They say, 'It's like she's older. Not physically, but spiritually.'"

I said, "Most of the time when I'm with you these days, I feel kind of peaceful and grounded."

Stan said, "If people would wake up to that sensation, we'd get along a lot better. We're not separate. Not from each other or the spirits."

I had felt that in the sweat lodge. I remembered when I had taken on Stan's anxiety on the night when he was beaten down physically; and I remembered how, when I'd been so emotionally trashed after the scene with Moses in the desert, I'd felt a flood of compassion for the beleaguered grandmother next to me.

Stan was tired. His voice was so soft my voice-activated tape recorder kept stopping.

"Were you chosen by the Creator?" I asked.

"I think so," he said. "In a sweat after the accident, my uncle Hiram—he was a medicine man—said that the spirits chose me.

I guess to deliver their message. Because it was like I used to talk and people would always listen to what I said."

"Some are chosen, but you were drafted?"

"We're all chosen," he said. "But we're the ones that accept it."

"But Stan, who's we? I haven't been saving my people for the last twenty-five years. I'm not like you. I'm selfish."

He looked at me. "The Creator comes to everyone, and most people run," he repeated. "But you don't run."

But I had run. I'd run from Jevon's funeral, from my attraction to Moses, and then from my fear of him. I hadn't done the fast; I'd messed up in the peyote ceremony. I'd made a quick exit when the horse I gentled got killed, and when I thought Stan was about to die. I was in flight a good part of the time, either all the way to Colorado, or to the cottonwoods of the Lander town park, or to the Gannett Grill, where I'd sit and let myself be washed over with the conversations of the fit, comfortable white patrons sitting around over their pitchers of beer, laughing about the mountain they'd climbed that day, discussing what to climb next, measuring the choices and pleasures they had in life.

"You get scared," Stan continued, his eyes on mine, dark, calm, infinite, just like they were the first time I'd met him. "But you always come back."

I didn't have time to dwell on it, though; I thought he might be slipping away—not now, I felt, but perhaps soon—and I had to go back to Colorado that evening because I'd told my four- and six-year-old nephews I would take them horseback riding and they were so excited about it I had to go. While Stan had been sleeping the day before, I'd gone out and bought them little white cowboy shirts with pearl snap buttons.

But there was more to ask Stan. "Why don't we all just go toward God?"

"I dunno," he said. "Human nature. Especially men, they don't want to be told by anybody. As soon as they get to the end, they're like"—he winced—"'Have mercy!'" He laughed softly.

The tape recorder stopped again. I switched it off.

He glanced at the television, where a woman in a tank top had her hands in a bowl of oily pasta, looking down on us like Stan's own guardian angel.

"I still don't get how you were so selfish before the accident and then you basically up and turned into something—I guess Christlike."

"One thing they made clear when I died," said Stan, "I needed to change. I needed to sincerely change. I didn't wanna go there, man. Uncle Hiram said I died four times in the Lander hospital.

"Of the things I saw when I died," he continued, "the time I was stuck in a bubble, that was the trippy one. But the scariest one was the emptiness. There was just nothing."

Suddenly, Frankie jolted to life: "Are you both-handed?" he asked Stan.

Stan explained he was right-handed but his left hand came back first after the accident, so now, yes, he was both-handed. Then he turned to me again.

"You were talking about the four times you died," I prompted. "We've got the death where you were stuck in a bubble, invisible and inaudible and watching your loved ones go on with their lives. And the death where there was just nothing. That's two. You said there were four."

"Another death was these demons, man," Stan said. "I don't know what the hell they were. Horns, tail, muscular, foul stink, they looked like dogs but they were like people, bad spirits. They hooked me in the nostril with a pool cue and asked me if I thought life was a game. They spun me around and threw me against the wall.

"I said, 'Fuck you!' I wouldn't submit. I wouldn't answer the question, man. I didn't give them the impression I was scared. It really happened. Really. My body. I was paralyzed."

I wrote this down, snorting in a you've-gotta-be-kidding way, and then looked back up at him. His face was twisted with fear and pain. He was telling the truth.

"And then there was the fourth death," he continued after a while. "A girl came in. She was standing by the door for about four days, but no one else saw her. I'd talk about her, and pretty soon the people in the room with me were accommodating me, like, pretending she was there, too. One day she took me by the hand and asked me if I was tired of the pain. I said, 'Fuck that.' I wasn't going with her. Each one was a choice."

The silence between us was as flat as a rug. His exhaustion was palpable. He'd be in the hospital for a few more days; I was glad he could rest here before he went home to all those people who needed him. I stood up, said goodbye, hugged Stan and Frankie, and walked into the midsummer sun to my car.

CHAPTER 38

DEMON DOGS

At home, I filed the demon dog part of the interview. I mean, really. Demon dogs?

Months later, I started writing about what Stan had said. Right around then Peter and I were in the lobby of a hotel we'd stopped at for coffee when I heard a low growl. There was a dog that was too big to be a pit bull and too light-haired to be a mastiff or rottweiler. His hide was vaguely mottled, his jaws looked capable of snapping my arm in two, and his eyes looked like he'd thought of nothing but murder since the day he was born. Even though he was on the end of a muzzle leash held by a dusty and angry-looking woman of Native or perhaps Mexican descent, he was the scariest dog I'd ever seen.

"That's weird," I said to Peter as we walked outside. "Those demon dogs of Stan's, that's exactly what I think they'd look like. Minus their pool cues."

That night at the pizza parlor, I told four of our friends about Stan's story and about the dog we'd seen that day. As soon as I started talking, Peter said, "Wow. Look at the TV." I looked but missed it. Peter said, "There was a shot of a rabid dog."

"Aaak," I said.

We walked home with a couple who owned a sweet, nervous border collie. This couple did a lot of their communicating in a high collie voice they attributed to their dog. Sitting in their living room, Jane pulled her collie's ears. "I'm not a demon dog," she said in her doggie voice. "Well, actually, I am, but I cover it up really well with my good looks and perfect manners."

We laughed, and the next day her neighbors' dogs ran out of their yard and almost bit her for the first time in the fifteen years she'd lived there. And two days later, a tiny white lapdog tottered over to Peter and nipped him right on the hand.

Okay, that's enough, I thought, picking up the phone and calling Stan.

"Don't act scared around 'em," he said, chuckling. "Just like the Creator comes to us in different ways, they do, too. We're like the pieces in the chess game they're playing. They're from the darker side. But they're not doing nothing. They're just letting you know they're there."

I couldn't quite chuckle along with this. I looked for and sought the counsel of a Jungian psychologist who specialized in the archetypal world, figuring it was worth ninety dollars to hear someone say, "My dear, different cultures give different names to certain energies. And what we call adrenal fatigue, they call demon dogs."

That's what I wanted him to say. What else could he say?

I drove to his office in an affluent neighborhood. Inside its diploma-lined walls, what he actually said was this: "Oh yes, demon dogs. I've been called into situations where they were quite a problem."

When our time was up, I shot out the door to a chichi coffeehouse where I nursed a four-dollar latte and watched the purebred dogs of the rich bask in the sun. Then my apprehension lifted. The truth was that one of the best things I'd developed around Stan was a place in my mind where things were neither confirmed nor denied but remained mysterious. I mean, really, do we really think we've got it all figured out? And what kind of eyes did I want to cast on the world? The eyes of someone who is okay with not knowing everything, or the eyes of a litigator, demanding a complete set of data every time the road changed direction?

I sipped my coffee and started a gazing contest with a tail-thumping dog lying at the next table. His owner announced that he was a Labradoodle—a popular dog in Colorado's urban Front Range, because it is friendly like a Labrador but smart like a poodle and doesn't shed on, say, your chocolate-brown suede couch.

"Hiya, smoochums," I said to the dog, kneeling to rub his curly poodle head and look into his faithful Labrador eyes. What a nice doggie. I laughed. Fine. Maybe there are worlds we can't see. The demon dogs could let me know they were there, as long as the dogs I met the rest of the time simply wagged their tails.

CHAPTER 39

ANIMAL MEDICINE

Moses hadn't lasted long in Wyoming after our awful night in the desert. When winter came, he tried making some money by shoveling snow for some old ladies living in Lander. But after one of them had a hard time coming up with the money to pay him, he couldn't bring himself to ask any of them for payment. Then he hitchhiked to Jackson and got some paying work, but it was full-on winter; the cold came through his duct-taped cowboy boots and turned his toes black. He got out of there, headed south and then west, and had a romance with a feisty horse trainer in California. Then he went home to Washington State, where he took care of his two grannies, both of whom were in their nineties and one of whom regularly told him to go to hell.

Back in Stan's kitchen, I joked that Moses always needed at least one woman telling him that. But my throat felt tight.

One afternoon on the porch, Stan told me, "Moses used to be real angry. Real red."

"Red, how?" I said.

"Just red," he said. "Like that hawk showed me."

"What hawk? What red?"

He sat for a moment. "That old-lady spirit and that man—those spirits all those years ago that came to me after the accident—they were showing me things to get me through that real hard time when I didn't want to be alive," he said. "They turned me into a hawk. It's real easy being a hawk. Fresh tracks are fluorescent, and old ones are hard to see. And people's moods show in different colors, too. Anger is red."

"What color's happiness?"

"It's a light blue. It gets darker if someone's trying to be that way but not really feeling it."

"Well, what color am I?"

"You're purple a lot of the time."

"What's that? Anger mixed with happiness?" That sounded about right.

"No," he said. "It's more like compassion."

That was better.

The old spirit couple also turned him into a deer. Deer see in black and white, and things that are moving or have recently been in motion are much brighter and more visible than things that have stayed still for a while. Stan took from that the ability to see the dark, unmoving parts of people, the things that were stuck; the things that hadn't been talked about or even recognized. The gift from the deer had been so precious that Three Bears told Stan he couldn't eat any more venison.

Like the demon dog story, I took this one in and and let its flavor work its way through me. Stan's story reminded me of *The Once and Future King*, when Merlin the magician turned the young man who would become King Arthur into a carp and a goose and a bunch of other creatures for his political edification.

Deer tend to be anxious, Stan said, but other creatures are nervous wrecks. Mice, for example.

"It was not very fun to be a mouse," said Stan. "I couldn't even recognize nothing. Humans sometimes let things—our problems— get bigger than they are. But problems really are big when you're a mouse."

He was also turned into a horse, which conferred speed and strength upon his efforts as a healer. And his favorite, the eagle: "They carry the prayers up; they hear and see the help that's needed; they see real clear, man, they see right almost like right through you . . . They're looking at your soul, not your body."

He used these animal gifts in the sweat lodge but also in the cor- ral with the horses. "It's dangerous in the corral," he said. "I don't want to get nobody hurt."

Okay, I said. Were there any other animals?

"Man, then they put me in a jungle or something; there were a bunch of trees and leaves, and I was a bug. It was scary being a bug. Always on the lookout. Something bigger comes along, then your life is very short.

"That was to show me to appreciate what I had . . . being a human, and the little things we take for granted. Because you never know what's gonna happen. You never know what's over the next little hill."

CHAPTER 40

HOW MUCH CAN BE SUBTRACTED?

Stan called me with news. Cody had been swimming with his cousins on the Big Wind River, escaping the August heat, when he got tumbled, swept downstream, killed. The funeral would be in a few days. I dropped to my chair. We muttered our goodbyes and hung up.

When Peter and I arrived at Stan's house, Arilda greeted me at the door with a long hug and a high, sustained wail. Over at the kitchen table, Stan and three of his brothers were sitting around his kitchen table. Four no-nonsense Addison noses. Four jackhammer jaws. Middle age doing its backhoe job on four sets of cheeks and brows. It was nice to see them all together. I never had before. Biologically reassuring, I suppose, to see the Addisons who had made it through the crux years and into their thirties and now their forties.

The only Addison brother who had left the reservation for someplace other than the graveyard was Bill. He was a talented artist who lived in Casper with Lynelle, a cheerful social worker with a round face. Bill sat at the far end of the table, hiding his eyes by offering the group his left profile, then his right. His face tacked through the evening like a sailboat on a windy lake. He waved to me and continued talking about downloading music onto CDs to Glenn, who was his older brother, but whose airy jollity made him seem the younger of the pair. Glenn's daughter had died the previous winter. He hugged me hard and caught my eye repeatedly; this was the first time I'd ever connected with him, but if not now, when?

Jay-R, the youngest brother, ate one blindingly white baloney sandwich after another. Jay-R, the teller of sideways truths. The only one Stan had wanted by his side after his own accident. He lived in a room at his mom's, with a poster of Tupac Shakur and a collection of rocks and arrowheads found on his long walks in the desert. Sitting with his back leaning on the kitchen wall, he laughed at something. His eyes shone beautifully. He looked great in a turquoise-colored cowboy shirt with pearl buttons. Perhaps his worldview accommodated a drowned nephew more easily than those of his brothers.

At the head of the table sat the only brother without a potbelly—Stan, his long black braid snaking down his back, legs propped up, speaking so quietly I couldn't hear him. I had to put my ear right next to his mouth, and even then I could hardly make out what he was saying. But I liked having my ear there, close. When I looked into Stan's eyes, it looked as if loss could physically rearrange the placement of eyes in a head. He looked out at me like a prairie dog who had gone into a deep hole to die.

Cody, Stan told me, didn't just help him but would stop his fun to help him. Him, the paralyzed uncle. The uncle who couldn't even roll himself over in bed. The uncle who needed his dressings changed, his colostomy bag emptied, his meals cut up.

I knew all this. I saw it all the time. I knew Stan just needed to say it. Two weeks before, when I had been visiting Stan in the hospital, Cody had used a plastic fork to feed Stan bites of rice from some Chinese takeout.

"Did you get your sponge bath today?" he'd asked Stan softly.

I felt scared for the Addisons, for the family's balance of weak and strong. Of restraint and outburst, of gentleness and harshness. Arilda was only fifty; how could she bear to bury her second son? What would become of Cody's cousins? Nineteen-year-old Daniel, who had been among the cousins swimming with Cody when he drowned in the rough water? Beautiful, pious, guileless Daniel, who had been seen around the house only in glimpses since Cody's death? And what about Beau, Daniel's older brother, who would sit through the wake with his head in his hands? How much can be subtracted before you hit zero, before a family is not a family, before a people is not a people?

That night at Stan's, the little kids seemed even wilder than ever.

It was almost midnight, and they were running through the house in twos and threes, holding gray kittens by one leg, screaming and laughing, needing someone to stop them. Cody would have.

CHAPTER 41

THE HEALING CENTER

When we asked what we could do for the funeral, Arilda said we could buy some things for the giveaway. At funerals, Arapahos give gifts to people who traveled any distance at all to pay their respects. So the next morning, we went to Walmart.

Stan had called Walmart the healing center ever since a woman had told him she couldn't come to the sweat lodge that evening because she was sick. Right before the sweat lodge started, Stan had to go to Walmart, and he saw the woman in the parking lot. She saw him, too, and scuttled inside.

"That's where I should set up shop," Stan had muttered to me. "It's where all the Indians are."

Peter and I went there and bought ten bath towels, three sets of dish towels, a set of bed linens, and four big square candles that smelled like pears. We also bought some white zinnias for the coffin; some Lindt chocolate balls for Stan, because I knew he'd forget to eat and his blood sugar would ricochet all over the place; and a big gourmet chocolate hazelnut bar (one dollar) for me, because my blood sugar was beginning to sag in this particular healing center. Cody had loved it here. As a child, he could tell the videos apart by their smell. He had a nose for things. I remember once, after Stan smudged a house near Walmart, Cody, Mike, Stan, and I came here. Cody ran in to buy Stan a golf game that gave them both so much pleasure.

In the housewares department, Peter and I ran into Bill and Lynelle. Bill was relaxed and friendly, inquiring about our night's sleep and laughing as he pretended to scrub his underarms with a dishwashing brush he snatched off a display. Then we saw Stan's brother Glenn poring over blank CDs, looking happy; and Cody's widow, Nicole, who was with Glenn's wife and daughter. Under the narcotic influence of acres of colorful merchandise, Nicole was just another pretty, pregnant nineteen-year-old in sweatpants, walking the aisles of Walmart, laughing and eating a candy bar.

"I'm so hungry!" she sang out to us as she waved and headed for the soft-drink department with the other women.

Then we went out to Stan's, where several girl cousins I'd never met before had left the place spotless. Stan had spent most of the day watching old westerns in his room, with Mike the Meskwaki in attendance. I walked in to say hi. Stan's response was inaudible. When he emerged at about four, he looked flustered. He rolled down the road, a nephew walking beside him, then did it again with a niece. Then he went into the teepee where Cody lay in an open casket.

"I feel better," Stan told me afterward. "He looked relaxed."

I sat in the shade on the side of the house, Tisha in my lap. I was glad I had someone to hold on to. I watched trucks pull up with teepee poles, the casket, the flowers.

Then Arilda called, "Lisa, I need your help."

I ran to her. She wanted me to fix up the teepee where Cody was lying. I helped staple up solid blue sheets and strings of white roses for the backdrop to Cody in his casket. A big patterned Indian blanket covered the floor. Another Indian blanket hung on a frame behind Cody, who lay in a brushed copper–colored coffin with a white interior. A wreath of sage lay near his feet on a table that also held a guest book. A table of flowers sat near his head. Cody's head was swathed in a white skullcap, his face a little swollen and dabbed in four places with red paint. This was applied so when his loved ones died, they would be able to recognize him on the other side. The white baseball cap his big brother Sass traveled all the way to the Foot Locker in Casper to buy lay next to his head. In his folded hands, Cody held a beaded crucifix and a spray of red fabric roses. The coffin was lined with an orange and white Pendleton blanket to keep him warm because the journey to the other side is cold. His eyes were shut but looked like they might open. Stan was right; Cody did look peaceful. It was okay to be in there. In fact, it was a relief to be in there. I always felt better when Cody was around.

As soon as she saw her son's body, Arilda started to cry. Sass held on to her. I sat next to Sass in a folding metal chair. Aaron, Cody's younger brother, sat next to Sass, looking numb.

"This is why I tell you boys not to go," said Arilda, "to stay home." She wailed quietly. Then she said, "We kept him too long." I didn't know if she meant kept him too long since his near-death in the auto accident, or kept him too long since he actually died in the river.

Flies were buzzing around Cody's face. She said, "We'll close it after the smudging." She was frantic to get a fan in there, to get a veil to put over Cody's face.

Then, standing next to the open coffin, holding her son's swollen body, she started to wail in earnest. Glenn stepped up in rubber beach sandals, nylon shorts, and a tank top that said PLAY HARD: LOSING IS NOT AN OPTION. He put his hands on Arilda's elbows and steered her back to her seat. "We've got our children to think of," he said.

Which was when my heart melted. Not that it was necessarily the right thing to say, considering the thought of her child drowning in the rushing water was exactly what could twist the knife in Arilda's heart. Plus, the grandchildren seemed fine, sitting in their folding chairs next to their uncle's body, mouthing theatrically to one another about getting Pepsis as their grandmother's wails amplified into screams and the flies descended onto Cody's coffin and walked around the gauze wrap placed over his face to keep them out.

Marty, Arilda's husband, came to me, his face collapsing, and said in a rush, "You and Peter drive safe and call us as soon as you get home, you hear me?"

Crying, I said, "You know, Marty, we'll be praying right along with you all day tomorrow." The funeral would be the next day, but we had to leave because Peter was moving to Boulder to attend graduate school in psychology. I'd join him a month later.

It was getting late. Peter and I had sworn to each other that we'd be on the road by eight. It was seven.

Then Beau, who was sitting near us with a girl outside the tent, said, "You and Peter will want to stay here until the smudging's over." We waited outside while an old white priest gave a blessing inside the teepee, and then a Native man spoke in Arapaho. After the people in the tent were smudged, Marty came out and said, "Lisa, you and Peter come in now."

After we were smudged, everyone went in to see the body. Nicole stood around the edges until a man found her a chair, put it inside the teepee, and indicated she should sit down. Nicole wore a navy blue T-shirt and jeans, her hair falling loose. She was big with her fourth child fathered by Cody, her face serious and beautiful. Her oldest daughter, Triston, a toddler, pushed a miniature stroller with a flashlight in it in lieu of a doll. She was wearing gray sweatpants with pink lettering that said DADDY'S GIRL. My throat closed around those words, around her little stroller with her little flashlight baby. She was a daddy's girl. It had always been a household joke.

Just before eight, I told Peter I was ready to go. We walked down to the corral and watched two horses gnawing on each other's hides and rubbing their necks against each other through the rough pole fence. The sun was setting behind the house. Nearly a hundred people were already there. The wake would go on all night.

Next to the teepee where Cody lay, four men pulled up chairs around a drum the size of a breakfast table and beat out a simple rhythm. Peter stopped and watched them like it was the most astounding thing he'd ever seen.

"We need to go, honey," I said.

He didn't move. "I don't want to leave," he said. "This is how people should live. In tribes. On land."

I said, "I'm so glad you know."

CHAPTER 42

DANIEL AND THE TURTLES

We were back in Colorado the next day, but if we had stayed we would have seen a long line of horses and cars inching their way up the yellow dirt track the few miles between Stan's house and Sharp Nose Cemetery. At the procession's head, Daniel kept his horse to a walk. He led Runner, Cody's chestnut gelding, on a rope. Runner was carrying some clothes and a bedroll. These belonged to Cody and would accompany him into the ground.

Behind Daniel were five other riders, including Beau, who had Cody's son Quamé in the saddle with him. Quamé cried the whole way to the cemetery. The other riders would occasionally talk and laugh among themselves, but Daniel stayed silent. When the service ended, he was the last to leave. He leaned against the painted wooden cross that served as a gravestone, shaded his eyes, and cried.

Daniel had changed. He had flirted with badness, but his essential seriousness, his inability to abandon himself, kept winning out. Daniel beat up on Luke, but Luke had picked the fight in the first place, and the next time he came around, Daniel stuck out his hand and welcomed him back. Daniel had also been arrested for drunk and disorderly conduct, but during his four days in jail he was too depressed to eat or drink, and once he got out he started riding more horses and coming to more sweat lodges.

Almost a year after Cody died, Daniel went into the desert near Stan's and prayed outside for several days. If the Creator's ears are best tuned to the prayers of those who are truly suffering, what Daniel did was akin to calling on the private line. He was out for several days, each of which was hotter than 100 degrees, not eating or drinking and rarely resting. One man who had done the same ritual several times likened it to crucifixion.

"Jesus Christ, when he gave his body on the cross, and shed his blood for redemption and everlasting life for man, you know, that's kind of the same idea," the man told me. "You sacrifice your body . . . It's really demanding. You're actually participating in a kind of re-creating the world with the Creator. It's renewal. Bringing a spiritual rejuvenation and renewal into the world."

While he was out, Daniel forced himself not to look toward home. He looked instead into the sky, its flawless, unforgiving blue. He saw faces there—women and children and, most often, a big warrior with a black-and-white-painted face, watching him. Daniel prayed for his family, Stan mostly. Then he prayed for his enemies, that they stay safe on the road, because if you make amends with your enemies, they become your friends. Later on you might need their help. Because, he'd tell me later, what you hate, you love in the end.

During his short bursts of sleep he dreamed of turtles. During the days, he tried not to think of water.

"It's the most powerful thing in the whole world," he told me later. "Water can bring you life or take life. I thought of water taking my brother. It took Cody."

Cody's spirit came to see Daniel. Cody was wearing white shoes and blue shorts and a gray tank top. He looked left and then right and then straight at Daniel, and once he knew they were in contact, he smiled and made their special joking gesture (pointing with the right hand diagonally down at nothing, but compelling the other person to look). He walked toward Daniel, smiling, then disappeared from view. But Daniel could feel him coming toward him, feel the warmth of him.

Eventually, the sun rolled out of sight over the mountains. Daniel had been out there for days, and now he was finished.

I was there. I had never seen anything like Daniel walking from the ceremonial ground back to his family. He was filthy, thin, huge-eyed, ethereal, only just able to walk. I said to his distant approaching figure: It isn't that white people don't know how to love, it's just that we aren't any good at sacrifice. We've forgotten about sacrifice, is all. Suffering is your specialty. Not suffering is ours.

Later, he ate, cramped, slept, and dreamed of more turtles. Turtles whose form was repeated in the shape of the sweat lodge in Stan's yard and thousands of others across Indian Country. Turtle, who, in the Arapaho creation story, dove to the watery depths and got the clay needed to build the land. Turtle meant family. In Daniel's dream, the turtles walked onto a man's back and started digging into his flesh, but the man didn't mind.

CHAPTER 43

SHE TALKS TO ANGELS

Two days after Daniel finished, Arilda called from Sharp Nose Cemetery and told Stan that the cows had gotten in and messed things up. The fence was down, there were tracks everywhere, and the racks of elk antlers had been knocked off the graves of her two sons.

Stan hung up by biting the phone's talk button. He barked to the boys, "Get in here!" Six boys clad almost entirely in black crowded into the kitchen and stood silently.

"Let us pray," Frenchie joked.

I laughed. Frenchie usually worked as an aide in a nursing home. But she was spending the whole summer living in a tent behind Stan's with her two youngest daughters so she could take care of her brother, cook him decent meals, and keep the boys in the house in line.

Stan said to the assembled boys: "Get some steel poles, wires, fencing pliers. About three fencing poles. It shouldn't take too long. Who wants to go?"

Three boys—each a son of one of Stan's sisters—raised their hands. Three others froze like prey that didn't want to be seen. Beau said he'd ride Wizard Jr. to the graveyard to chase the cows away.

Stan looked at the eight KOOLs in his metal cigarette box and said, "With all those boys up there, these'll be smoked up." I knew right then we were all going to the cemetery. He had someone fill the box with cigarettes, then had the boys carry him to the passenger seat of the truck. We drove the three or so miles to the cemetery. Beau galloped in the wake of our exhaust, showing off, holding the reins in his teeth and pumping his arms like a weight lifter, the gray horse drumming along in the dust and the mountains behind him.

This was the first time I'd seen Cody's grave. It was a beauty. The crosspiece of the crucifix was lying in the dirt, but the upright piece was nearly six feet tall. It said: "He walks a good path."

There was a white L.A. baseball cap on the grave, and a teddy bear from Cody's sister. There were pink, blue, yellow, and white flowers around an eighteen-inch-tall statue of Jesus Christ, and a little U.S. flag. The six-point rack, from an elk shot by his stepfather, Marty, lay in the dirt. A jar of blue beads sat on the mound, and two statuettes of a pair of galloping horses. Sprigs of white and blue flowers waved at his feet.

Stan looked happy, sitting in his truck, cuddling with Cody's daughter Triston, and looking at the far mountains through a pair of binoculars he aristocratically referred to as his field glasses. Someone began digging a hole for a fence post. Everyone else started fixing the fence and cleaning up stray plastic and fabric flowers, throwing the debris onto a rubbish pile in the corner of the cemetery.

Sass boomed from his minivan's car stereo "She Talks to Angels" by the Black Crowes. Arilda leaned on a rake. "Cody used to play this song for me," she said. "He knew I liked this song." Tears ran down her face. "I used to tell them: 'The world is yours, Cody. The world is yours, Sass. The world is yours, Aaron.'"

Then she turned back to cleaning the graves.

Stan had initially sent three boys to the graveyard to fix things up, and now nearly two dozen people were here, along with half a dozen vehicles and one green-broke horse. The Addison family was doing what it did best: being together and tending the bridge between this world and the next. At this moment it resembled an enormous sea creature sprawled on the ocean, feeling the waves surge beneath, the pleasure of its own appendages. Just the pleasure of them.

CHAPTER 44

WEDDING

We moved to Boulder, a college town built on land once central to the Arapahos' territory. The word *Arapaho* named everything from nearby high schools to ski areas and it wasn't hard to find the names of chiefs: Left Hand, Niwot, Little Raven. One evening we were walking downtown next to the bus station when a Native guy stepped toward us and asked us if we could spare any money.

"What tribe are you?" I asked.

"Northern Arapaho," he replied. "I came here to claim our land." He gestured over at a small park where homeless people slept.

"Yeah, I know it's yours," I said. "Do you know Stan Addison?"

"The guy in the wheelchair? Who does the horses? Yeah, I know Stan."

Sitting in the car at a traffic light, I said to Peter, "I don't love you as much as I love God. Is that weird? Is that unladylike? Is that okay?" It wasn't just okay; the man had almost become a monk. Not long after that, in a meadow where we'd gone for a picnic, Peter said, "Would you marry me?" I said yes, and the icy hand that had wrapped itself around my heart every time I'd been proposed to never even came close.

Stan had been involved in this. He had told me on the way home from Iowa that I'd have to wait a couple of years for Peter to really be there for me. The proposal came twenty-four months later. And I'd been practicing commitment around Stan. I had practiced not leaving him. I would sometimes leave, but as Stan had pointed out, I'd always come back.

Plus, in small ways, I was starting to separate from Stan. I enjoyed being home. I visited the reservation less frequently. And when I got there, I wasn't automatically the center of things, which was both painful and a relief. One summer I went to his place with my new friend Kim, who lived in Denver. The mercury cleared 100 every day we were there. Stan was horribly uncomfortable. Frenchie squeezed his feet, his nieces and nephews sprayed him with squirt bottles, and Kim—a cheerful presence who lit onto each passing moment like a butterfly on a flower—massaged his shoulders.

Did I mention that Kim was also extremely beautiful? Did I mention that Stan had told me time and again, "This is not a monastic tradition. The circle would be stronger if I had a companion." Or that Stan pretty much looked through me like I wasn't there and spent all his time talking to her?

"I was so jealous," I told him later.

"I know," he said. "I was observing you."

"Well, I was observing you, too," I said snarkily.

But it was clear: After close to four years, during which I spent a quarter of my time in his physical presence, I was becoming ordinary, dependable, "like family," Stan would tell me later, stinging my heart into calmness and relief. I'd wanted to be part of the scenery all my life, but I could never relax enough to stop grabbing the limelight. Until now. I liked being quiet at Stan's. I'd had his close attention for a long time. Apparently, I didn't need it for the rest of my life.

Which isn't to say that I immediately embraced my new position with an open heart and a generous smile. "Get out of my way, bitch; he's *my* portal to the divine," I'd grump to myself as I watched Stan and Kim laughing together.

"You did pretty good, though," Stan told me later.

"I know."

*   *   *

Peter and I had an unusual wedding. A few months after his proposal, we spent a March afternoon at a bar in the mountains, drinking cocoa, watching underdog George Mason University squeak past powerhouse Connecticut in a thrilling basketball upset, chatting with some of the locals sitting by the TV, and then retiring to a table by the window to quietly write our wedding vows. In the early afternoon, Peter put his arm around me and said in a voice loud enough for everyone to hear, "Let's go get married!" Everyone at the bar made noises of surprise and disbelief, and when we told them we were serious, they whooped and hollered, lifting victory fists into the air. This was even more surprising and fun than George Mason making it into the NCAA final four.

They were right. In terms of matrimony, who could have been greater underdogs than Peter and me? We were both forty-six years old. With his meditative tendencies and my jitters around commitment, our chances of getting married had appeared dim, at least to me, until very recently.

We drove to a nearby trail, skied into a thickening snowstorm, and stopped in a clearing. Peter wore a tie, and I pulled a long white ruffled skirt out of my backpack and put it on over my ski pants. Our tears froze to our faces as we read our vows: We would work to be trustworthy and forgiving; we would support each other's spiritual paths; we would practice being positive. We laughed, kissed, signed our marriage license with a pen made sluggish by its half-frozen ink (the signatures of the bride and groom are all that's required to tie the knot in Colorado), and skied off into the early dusk.

What would happen next was anyone's guess. Despite my mother's three trips down the aisle, I'd never seen her in a stable marriage, so my imagination lacked the raw materials to place myself in such a scenario. But as the months passed, our marriage didn't crumble or sink or evaporate, but grew up around us, protecting and delighting us.

Our families thanked us for the wedding snapshots Peter and I had taken of each other in the snowy forest, and delivered us a single message: "Those are nice pictures, but don't you think for one minute that we're not having a big party."

That summer they gathered in another meadow in the Colorado mountains, and we stood in front of them in our best clothes while a friend led us through our vows. We responded to each statement, "I did!"

Before we started dancing, Peter's brother made a toast to Stan. He had never met him but said he knew he'd had a major hand in all this. Stan had been invited, but his pressure sores had flared up so he hadn't been able to travel. His absence was the only shadow over the whole weekend.

CHAPTER 45

THE SUPPLICANTS

Moses returned to Wyoming later that summer. It had been nearly two years since I'd seen him. He was fixing a fence the morning I drove up a few weeks after Peter and I got married. My sweaty hands gripped the steering wheel. But I wanted to be there. In the evening's sweat lodge, the family would be praying for Stan, who had been in the hospital for over a week. I was "on my moon"—menstruating—so I wouldn't be able to enter the lodge, but I wanted to cook for those who did. Plus, I'd heard Moses had changed. These days he lived behind the house in Cody's old trailer with a bunch of the boys. Stan said he never complained. That was a change. I stopped at the fence to say hi to Moses, then drove to the house as he left the fence and met me on Stan's front porch. We went inside and made coffee, moving very quietly and deliberately so as not to wake any of the nephews sleeping on the couches. It was close to eleven, but they were still asleep.

We went back outside, and Moses said, "Sometimes I meet someone who moves me so deeply, I don't know whether to love them or hate them or fuck them or worship them or what. But I've decided to just not name it and live with the mystery instead."

He was never much for preamble.

"Yeah," I said.

We sat on the porch and looked out at things. Down in the corral, the horses tossed their heads. Pit bulls padded around my car parked in the driveway.

"I'm done with the white world," Moses said. "White women. You all really need someone to provide for you."

"Hunh," I said.

"And with my disabilities, I can't provide. I can't live in the white world or provide for its women. Even the tough ones. At first they all pretend it's going to work. But sooner or later, it don't."

"Yep," I said.

"Indian women, now, they just got less expectations."

A pit bull climbed the stairs to the porch, whining and squirming and hugely pregnant. She had a muzzle full of porcupine quills. This was not an unusual sight. Moses and I bent down and pulled them out one by one until the pain of extraction became too much for her. She squealed and labored to her feet and lumbered off.

"Time is short," I said, cupping the quills in my hand. "I have to ask you something."

He waited.

"What stopped you out in the desert? You'd had such a violent life. But right when you could have done another violent thing, you held back."

"Because I wanted to protect you more than I wanted to hurt you." He paused. "Because it would have hurt us both so much," he said. "Me especially."

My throat bunched up. "Did you know these things because of Stan?"

"Stan and all the Arapahos. For years and years. Gentling me."

"So are you Custer's ghost? I mean, here you are again, this brilliant half-crazy white guy riding around in Indian Country."

Moses delicately extracted a hand-rolled cigarette from his pocket. He stood halfway up to pat his butt pockets for a lighter and, not finding one, sat back down cupping the unlit cigarette in his palm. "This time I want to be on the right side," he said, "with the good guys."

He paused for a long time, looking out at the corral. The horses had gone quiet, standing still in the sun. "This is the home I've prayed for; the one I wanted," he said. "I regard every way I get treated here very highly. What happened with you, too. It's all part of the lesson I needed to learn."

His role at Stan's was that of a servant. He and Jay-R did the dirtiest work around the sweat lodge, pulling the cooled rocks out of the pit, sweeping the dust out. When they emerged, they were covered with ash. Moses took care of the horses even when his back was seized up, which these days was more and more often.

The following spring Moses joined three other men moving rocks from the fire into the sweat lodge with a pitchfork. Then he sat in a folding chair beside the dying fire, the pit bulls at his feet. After a lifetime of cowboying, a herniated disk, and a winter living in an often unheated trailer, Moses's back hurt too much to sit through the lodge.

"What a beautiful picture," said Kim, who was sitting next to me in the lodge, looking through its open door at Moses. A bunch of us had come up from Colorado, including Peter. He hadn't seen Moses in three years. During a break, he approached him and squatted. I couldn't hear them but I could tell from their relaxed postures that it was a peaceful conversation. Peter would say something, and then Moses would talk and talk. That made me laugh.

I nudged Kim. "There's an even better picture," I said.

Peter explained to me later that he'd told Moses how much pain Moses had caused him while he was in Asia. "I know," he recalled Moses saying. "And I'm sorry. I was learning and gaining so much from all of that stuff with Lisa, and I didn't give a single thought to how it was affecting you. I'm sorry."

"But the hardest thing to forgive is how much you hurt her in the desert."

"I know. I'm sorry for that, too."

Moses had changed. He had realized that the only posture that didn't hurt was one of supplication. Which reminded me of the greatest supplicant of all, Stan, who had been teaching us all the same thing—to bow to the unknown, to honor our mysterious interconnectedness, to see that the only way to security was through surrender. Which reminded me of the horses Stan gentled. Especially the crazy, dangerous palomino he and Moses had worked with week after week all those years ago. The one who fought so bitterly all those months and then one day just stopped fighting.

I wish I could say that this was where it all ended, and we all held these postures of gratitude and forgiveness for the rest of our lives. But that wouldn't be true. What happened is life went on. Moses got kicked out of Stan's again, and moved in with Grandma Stella and then Arilda. I got more involved in my life in Colorado, and the distance to Stan's increasingly seemed longer than one I wanted to drive alone. It was tiring having two homes. I wanted just one. More and more people from my own world—many of them my friends—were spending time with him. Although I enjoyed introducing them, I also felt jostled because I had less time alone with him. One day I realized it had been three months since I'd even spoken to him. I called him and confessed that while I'd spent years as a rapt little child in his company, now I felt like an eye-rolling teenager.

"That's good," he said. "You couldn't keep me on the pedestal forever."

Which was exactly when I found my center. Stan didn't need me to put him on a pedestal. I had needed to put him there, and the minute I stopped holding him up, he fell off. Stan had told me many times that he wasn't a god, he was a man. I'd nodded my agreement while feeling my very DNA bow down toward him like a million pilgrims at Mecca.

I thought I had taken in what he'd said, but I was working out something of my own, and I hadn't been able to really listen. Stan embodied something like Christ consciousness and I'd responded to this by being disappointed that he didn't act like Jesus Christ 100 percent of the time. But he wasn't dead, he wasn't irreproachable; he certainly wasn't virginal. He was just out here in the most broken part of America, doing his best, rising above circumstances that were very often unbearable. And sometimes he didn't rise above them, because, as he said, he was a man, not a God, and I hadn't truly accepted that yet.

But when I told him I was on the outs with him, he didn't bat an eyelash. He did what he'd always done for me: offered me a wide, smooth place to return. And because in addition to the fragile and dangerous state of adoring him there existed in me an enduring love, I did return. And so my discipleship ended and our friendship began.

ACKNOWLEDGMENTS

Stanford Addison invited me into his life in Wyoming, extending his trust to me in a way that exceeded my wildest expectations. To you, first and foremost, my thanks and love. The rest of the Addison family, unavoidably along for the ride, could have been resistant to me, but weren't. To you—all of you, including the extended and adopted members of the family—I extend my deepest gratitude. Your openness, friendliness, and humanity are not only the stuff of this book; they have changed my life.

I always knew that my mother, Kerstin Tomson, was an extraordinary woman, but writing this book made me grasp that fact more deeply than ever. As the terrific memoirist Debra Marquart said, "With every draft, my mother became more of a hero and I emerged as more of a little shit." May all daughters write memoirs that include their mothers! Thanks, Mom, for coming with me to the reservation during my early visits there, and for responding with love and enthusiasm that mirrored my own.

To my sisters, Anna Jones and Greta Jones, and to my father's widow, Chris Jones—thanks for putting up with me, having durable senses of humor and senses of self, being the best company a person could hope for, and letting me put you and our father (in Chris's case, her husband) occasionally in front of the camera.

As an extrovert consigned to the task of sitting inside and making sense for chapter after chapter, I turned to a cast of dozens for sustenance, both literary and emotional. Peter Heller and I spoke almost daily on the phone, and his time-tested affection and salty wisdom on the craft of writing were miraculous mood-lifters. When I yelled "Help!" Laurie Wagner got right on a plane from California to iron out some of the rough parts. Jay Heinrichs—trickster, master reader, angel—appeared out of the woods of New Hampshire to shine a sharp light on my mental and emotional excesses, allowing me to proceed with the requisite sense of gravity. Mary Jarrett applied grace to every word, and Alison Luterman, Maya Stein, Heather Abel, Penny Williams, and Helen Thorpe shared their enormous literary know-how at crucial moments. Then there's David Romtvedt, the Poet Laureate of Wyoming, who read an early draft of this manuscript, scrawled incisive questions and suggestions all over it, and mailed it back to me, not having any idea who I was. And Megan McFeely sprang up at the very last moment like a genie with all kinds of help.

In Boulder, Colorado, I happened on a writing group whose every last member—Julene Bair, Janis Hallowell, Elisabeth Hyde, Marilyn Krysl, Gail Storey—is a truth teller and artist. I rewrote some scenes five times for these people. Thank God there was wine.

When the manuscript landed at Scribner, my editor, Beth Wareham, greeted every doubting sound I made by laughing her big Texas laugh. Then she would talk about her confidence in this book and infect me with her belief that the next step—whatever it was—was going to be a whole lot of fun. Thanks, Beth, for your forward-driving energy, and for having a vision of completion I only recently started to share. As for my agent, Joy Harris, you may think you are just one person, but inside you dwells an entire MFA faculty, a ferocious businesswoman, a Buddhist sage, and a really good therapist. I do not know how you embody all of this, but I am its beneficiary and I blow you a kiss.

Eugene J. Ridgely Jr., who developed the Northern Arapaho Studies program at the Wind River Tribal College, helped me get a grasp on the history and current affairs of his tribe. This grasp was strengthened with the help of Margaret Coel, who, when she isn't writing best-selling mysteries based in the Wind River Indian Reservation, writes definitive histories. Her historical biography *Chief Left Hand* is a must-read for anyone who wants to learn more about the Arapaho tribe during the latter half of the 1800s. I also relied heavily on Virginia Trenholm's *The Arapahoes, Our People* and Dee Brown's classic *Bury My Heart at Wounded Knee*.

The Noble Hotel in Lander, Wyoming, embodies its name. It was a restful place to sleep and write, its staff unfailingly warmhearted despite my irregular hours and habits.

Commiseration, love, and even more literary support was provided pretty much constantly by Florence Williams, Michelle Nijhuis, Sarah Kariko, Konstanze Hacker, Laura Fasano, Nancy Carter, Merrily Talbott, Jane McGarry, Kim Yan, and Caroline Scoutt. As for Peter Williams—my husband—you are a mensch. Faced with a partner acting in some unconventional ways and taking a spiritual path you did not share, you did not get riled or try to limit me but modeled the kind of faith and respect that I am only now learning to reciprocate.

Finally, this book would never have happened without Zia Parker, who for years applied enormous energy to bringing together the red and white worlds for their mutual benefit. She contacted me almost a decade ago to drum into my mind that there was a great story up on the Wind River Indian Reservation, and in 2002 she introduced me to Stanford Addison right outside his corral. Thank you, Zia.

HAY HOUSE TITLES
OF RELATED INTEREST

Life Lessons: *Things I Wish I'd Known Earlier*, Lesley Garner

Left to Tell: *One Woman's Story of Surviving the Rwandan Holocaust*, Imaculée Ilibagiza

How My Death Saved My Life: *And Other Stories On My Journey To Wholeness*, Denise Linn

F**k It: *The Ultimate Spiritual Way*, John Parkin

Mystery of the White Lions: *Children of the Sun God*, Linda Tucker

The Power of No: *Take Back Your Life with a Two-letter Word*, Beth Wareham

The Good Retreat Guide: *Over 500 places to find peace and spiritual renewal in Britain, Ireland, France, Spain, Italy, Greece, other European Countries, Asia and Africa*, Stafford Whiteaker

Join the
HAY HOUSE
Family

As the leading self-help, mind, body and spirit publisher in the UK, we'd like to welcome you to our community so that you can keep updated with the latest news, including new releases, exclusive offers, author events and more.

Sign up at www.hayhouse.co.uk/register

Like us on Facebook at Hay House UK

Follow us on Twitter @HayHouseUK

www.hayhouse.co.uk

Hay House Publishers
Astley House, 33 Notting Hill Gate, London W11 3JQ
020 3675 2450   info@hayhouse.co.uk